# FEASTING & FASTING IN CRETE

## DELICIOUS MEDITERRANEAN RECIPES

*By*

Diana Farr Louis

KEDROS PUBLICATIONS

PHOTOS
*Diana Farr Louis*
*Poppy Alexiou*
*Panayiotis Beltzinitis*, p. 11
*Inga Sideri-Kramos*, p. 17
*From* Traditional Bread of
  Rethymnon, p. 177

THE GREEK EXPERIENCE
Books, Music, Video, Art
www.GreeceInPrint.com
262 Rivervale Rd, River Vale, N.J. 07675
Tel 201-664-3494 Email info@GreeceInPrint.com

ISBN 960-04-1953-1

© Diana Farr Louis, 2001
© Kedros Publications, S.A., 2001

www.kedros.gr
e-mail: kedros@otenet.gr

# TABLE OF CONTENTS

*In Crete the stranger is still the unknown god.*

*Before him all doors open and all hearts are opened.*

Nikos Kazantzakis, *Report to Greco*

# FOREWORD

The fabulous island of Crete has given birth to many legends, from the Minoan tales of Minos, Pasiphae and the Minotaur, Theseus, Daedalus and Ariadne to those of Kazantzakis's Zorba and his unquenchable zest for life. In recent years, the Cretan Diet and the health of its feisty inhabitants have become legendary, making headlines as we pampered lounge lizards search for the Fountain of Youth and well being.

Even before the Cretan diet began being a news item, I became fascinated with Greek regional cooking and set off to discover whether the food in Crete was good enough and different enough from typical Greek mainland fare for a book.

My quest led me all over the island, to city flats whose storerooms held buckets of snails; mountain cottages stocked with home-made tomato paste, trahana or rustic pasta, cheeses fresh and aged, sweet preserves and barrel wine; tavernas famous for a special dish; hotels catering to the rich and famous; and shops whose owners were more interested in food than in their merchandise. I found that as soon as I explained my mission, sometimes even without the assistance of an introduction from a mutual acquaintance, the typical Cretan welcome would become warmer still. Recipes would flow, accompanied by offerings of coffee, raki, or wine, and with them stories – of weeklong weddings, bride abductions, hard times and their treats, festivals and mourning, love and death. Often I'd be included in a family meal that would stretch into the afternoon or until midnight, learning again and again the lesson that sitting around a table sharing food and experiences is one of the blessings life has to bestow.

In my wanderings I was astounded by the extraordinary diversity of Crete, areas so lush on the northwest coast a broomstick would sprout if you planted it, shelves of rock on the southwest so bare even a thyme bush is a rarity. I learned that though Crete is surrounded by water, it is an inward-looking place, defined by its mountains, whose meringue-topped peaks are rarely out of sight. Its people have traditionally been farmers and shepherds, not seafaring wanderers.

The mountains have made them tough and prickly, quick to flare up and slow to forgive an insult, but they are also surprisingly sweet underneath their gruff demeanour. There is division and competition between east and west, between the milder mannered people of the plains and the fabled untamed rebels of Sfakia, who would taunt the Turks and let the lowlanders get the punishment. Nowadays they are accused of sheepstealing and they are the ones who shoot their guns into the air at weddings and baptisms and pock the roadsigns so thoroughly the names are no longer readable. The city folk too harbor resentments, the Chaniots accusing their compatriots in Heraklio of being money-minded while they in turn are called lazy and stuck up.

Some say that the Cretans are much kinder to a foreign guest than to their neighbors. That I cannot judge but I saw community kitchens manned by friends and relatives who'd joined forces for a village wedding and housewives deliberately cooking extras to take next door. As for my own reception, the Cretans gave me a whole new definition of hospitality. Their welcome could not have been warmer; in fact it was unconditional, expecting nothing in return. So this book is a way of repaying their kindness, and giving the island's cooks and their wonderful recipes the recognition they deserve.

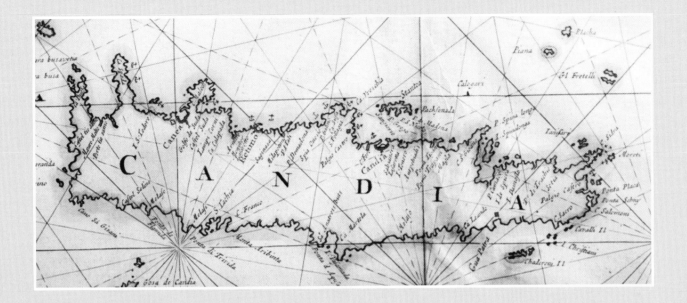

Crete, the fifth largest island in the Mediterranean (after Sicily, Sardinia, Cyprus and Corsica), lies almost equidistant from Africa, Asia and mainland Greece. Though only about 161 miles (260 km) long, 7½ miles (12 km) at its narrowest, 35 miles (60 km) at its widest, it is as diverse geographically as a minicontinent, with deep gorges, high fertile plains, its own unique flora and fauna, and several massive mountain ranges, the White Mountains, Mount Ida (Psiloritis), Lassithi and Thripte. These peaks, which rise to 8,058 feet (2,456 m) in the west and central parts of the island, have formed its people's character, dividing east from west and south from north. With the exception of Ierapetra, Crete's towns are on the gentler north coast where there are natural harbors and long stretches of beach; the south coast, wave-battered and forbidding in the past, has only recently begun to sprout resorts. And while outside influences, from Mycenaean and Roman to Arab, Byzantine, Venetian and Turkish did affect the cities of Chania, Rethymno, Heraklio, Siteia and the smaller coastal towns, they barely penetrated inland. This is why, until union with Greece in the early 20th century, Crete remained fairly isolated from a good many Greek and foreign trends, including those culinary. Crete's cooks thus developed their own specialties according to what the land produced.

# THE CRETAN DIET

Once upon a time, in fact until the mid 1960s, Cretans lived by the seasons – tomatoes and eggplant in summer, cabbage and leeks in the winter, artichokes in spring and chestnuts in autumn. Having no refrigerators, they pickled and preserved vegetables, smoked and salted fish and meat for leaner days and it never occurred to them to demand strawberries at Christmas or pumpkin in July. As if the seasons and their vagaries did not impose strict enough dietary rules, the Orthodox Church was there to ensure that they did not commit the sins of gluttony and sloth. Not only did good Christians observe three major fasting periods – forty days before Easter, forty days before Christmas and two weeks before the Dormition of the Virgin Mary on August 15th, but they also obeyed the restrictions on meat, dairy products, eggs and fish with blood every Wednesday and Friday throughout the year. To compensate, the Church Calendar was punctuated with a great number of feast days, but for the numerous poor meat was a luxury indulged in not more than five or six times a year. Even prosperous town dwellers rarely ate meat more than twice a week.

Exercise was not a matter of keep-fit classes. Besides working in the fields or following their flocks around the mountainsides, people walked everywhere they wanted to go. For one thing there were few, if any, roads between the hill villages and the market towns on the coast; there were even fewer wheeled vehicles. Men and women would routinely trudge, often barefoot, alongside their mules or donkey from Spili to Rethymno or Zakros to Siteia and back in one day to sell their cheeses, which they usually exchanged for manufactured goods not cash.

World War II and four years of Occupation put an end to feasting, and many Cretans subsisted on what must have seemed a permanent fast. There was little to eat except for a host of products made from wheat and barley grains and flour, wild greens, pulses, olive oil, a little goat's or sheep's cheese, plus wine and raki to make it endurable. In 1947, two years after Armistice, the American Rockefeller Foundation arrived in Crete to survey the condition of the war-ravaged islanders and offer any assistance they might require to rebuild their lives. Making meticulous records of the foods consumed weekly by each family in a number of villages, they were horrified at the meager amount of meat and fish on the dinner table. They were also puzzled by the degree of universal health enjoyed despite the lack of protein. Comparisons with the US population revealed that the Cretans were 90 percent healthier. Heart disease and cancer were virtually unknown on the island, nor did anyone suffer from malnutrition. Although it took the medical world some time to understand the implications of these findings, they had in fact stumbled upon the fundamental principles of the Mediterranean Diet.

Ten years later, the Seven Countries Study devised and directed by Dr. Ancel Keys, a heart specialist from Minnesota, made Crete famous. Dumbfounded by the discovery after the war that the Naples hospital he served in had no heart patients, Keys resolved to find out why. Taking sample groups of men from Italy, the Netherlands, Yugoslavia, Finland, the United States, Japan and Greece (the westernized island of Corfu and Crete), his was the first cross-cultural study to examine cardiovascular disease in terms of life style and diet; still under way, it is also the longest. During the first ten years of the study, not a single Cretan under observation succumbed to heart disease, even though the levels of fat consumed were among the highest, on a par with those of Finland. Some time after that, one of the Cretans did have a heart attack; (and this should have been a clue) he was the village butcher! The fact that the Cretans shared the same life expectancy as the Japanese, whose diet consists largely of fish and soy products and almost no fat, suggested that the type of fat must play a role. The Finns lived on red meat, cow's milk and cheese, and their arteries were clogged with cholesterol; forty percent of the Cretans' total diet came from fat – way above the US recommended allowance – but that fat was monounsaturated, derived from the olive. Forty years later, 50 percent of the Cretans are still alive and kicking, whereas not a single Finn has survived.

As early as 1959 Keys reported his findings to the US government, but his advice that Americans reduce their meat and dairy servings fell on deaf ears. The notion that diet can affect health was complete heresy, and he was laughed out of the room when he told them about the benefits of eating "leaves" – the term "greens" not being widely used yet.

Nevertheless, the findings of the Seven Countries Study continued to confirm the long-term benefits of a diet rich in olive oil and carbohydrates, low in animal fat, and other studies backed it up.

Some of the most dramatic evidence in favor of the Cretan Diet emerged from a study of heart patients conducted by French scientist Serge Renaud in the mid 1990s. He had set up a five-year comparison of the effects of diet by placing one group on the low fat regime prescribed by the American Heart Association, while the other ate like Cretans – lots of olive oil, whole grain bread, fresh fruit and vegetables, and an occasional helping of fish, meat and eggs. The results were so immediately apparent, with the latter group noticeably healthier within just a few months, that Renaud stopped the study after two years. He had proved not only that the diet could prevent disease, it could also reverse it. In addition, his temporary "Cretans" were happier, getting up from table satisfied instead of feeling hungry and deprived, because olive oil makes everything taste so much better.

By the end of the 20th century it looked as if olive oil had finally won recognition from the medical establishment and the US government. In their edition of July 19, 1999, TIME magazine published a cover-page story on "new" routes to health; olive oil was not only sanctioned, it was encouraged. Just a year and a half later, the same magazine (Jan. 8, 2001) reported that Greeks still rank high in longevity charts while keeping their wits about them ("with the EU's lowest rate of dementia in people over 65"). "The key to this comforting news may be the diet Greeks use but also abuse. Its most magic ingredient seems to be olive oil, in its virgin form… It may be coincidence, but the Greeks are by far the world's biggest per capita consumers of olive oil… Like dark clouds, Greek stomachs may have a silver lining."

In April 1997, I was lucky enough to attend a week-long symposium in Crete organized by the Boston-based Oldways Preservation & Exchange Trust to celebrate the 50th anniversary of the "discovery" of the Cretan Diet. When we were not eating superb Cretan foods and sipping wonderful Cretan wines (a symposium originally meant talk stimulated by a judicious amount of wine), we listened to experts trying to analyze the Diet. Of course, it was generally accepted that olive oil has multiple benefits (see page 31), but wasn't there something more? After all, Italians, French and Spanish also cook with olive oil. What sets the Cretans apart?

It seems to be vegetables in combination with prodigious

amounts of olive oil. While the Italians rely on pasta and the Spanish eat more fish, the Cretans eat more oil and more vegetables, home grown and wild, cooked and raw, than other Greeks, never mind other Mediterranean people. Dr. Antonia Trichopoulou, director of the Greek National Center for Nutrition, says, "If there is evidence that one particular version of the Mediterranean Diet is somewhat better than the others, the Cretan would be it. Being large and fertile, blessed by the climate, it produces vegetables, especially wild greens, in large quantities and great diversity all year round." At the symposium much discussion was given to these greens, of which there are some 80 different varieties, including some that have not yet been classified. Over the centuries travellers to the island never failed to comment on the Cretans' extraordinary passion for bowls of boiled greens dripping with oil. What is remarkable today is that this passion still endures, despite the fact that well-padded billfolds make meat and imported delicacies accessible to most households. Greens have somehow escaped the association with hard times that might make them unpalatable; instead, they sometimes command prices that are higher than the choicest steak.

As they went down the list, the scientists pointed out the possibility of the special compounds that may be present in snails (on which some families dine three times a week), or in honey; they drew attention to the fiber in the barley rusks unfailingly munched by young and old alike and to alpha-linoleic acid in the walnuts eaten by the handful and present in so many sweets. They compared the differences between Cretan full fat cheese and yogurt, made primarily from sheep's or goat's milk, and dairy products derived from cow's milk, and mentioned peculiarities in the former's fermentation process that may be beneficial. Finally, they alluded to the bonuses from quaffing a glass of wine or a shot or two of raki with meals, rather than a big mug of milk: raki spurs the metabolism, wine aids digestion and circulation, and may even have cancer-fighting properties, according to study results released in summer 1999.

After a week of feasting like Cretans (though not fasting, it must be admitted), bowled over by their open-handed generosity and hospitality, we resolved not to condemn this convivial habit of sitting round a table with friends or family, eating, drinking, talking and laughing by labelling it a "diet." It is more properly a life style. The Cretan Table represents a return to balance: companionship, in its original sense of "breaking bread together," exercise, making time for a snooze after lunch, saving rich food for special occasions rather than having a month full of Sundays. It is indeed a return to the ancient Greek ideal of the Golden Mean – "Nothing in Excess" – at least some of the time!

As a recipe for longevity, perhaps we could take to heart the answer given to Seven Countries Study researchers by an elderly but spry Cretan farmer: "I always ate simple food, I walked a lot daily, I avoided smoking, I avoided politics, courts and doctors and, as for sex, I always did my best."

Meanwhile, in Crete, Western trends and imports – fast food, buttery sweets, whiskey – continue to gain in popularity but happily not to the exclusion of local traditions. In the summer of 1999, when each news broadcast aired ever more horrific European food scandals, the Cretans were reevaluating their own bountiful resources, thinking hard about additives, hormones, fertilizers and pollution. Already, Cretan farmers account for the highest percentage of organic produce of any region in Greece. And while it is true that meat consumption is on the rise, Cretan cooks would not dream of abandoning olive oil for butter, vegetables and salads are never missing from the dinner table, and fresh fruit remains the dessert of preference. Finally, judging from the number of tavernas and restaurants that have island specialties on their menus, their patrons still crave the delicious old favorites they were raised on.

This book includes many of these old favorites, simple dishes for everyday meals, festive treats for holidays and breaking the fasts, Lenten sweets that make you think fasting could become a habit, and recipes provided by chefs in some of Crete's best tavernas and restaurants from Zakros to Chania. You will also find some modern adaptations of classic Cretan tastes, for although the cuisine of this unique island may be the oldest in Europe, it is by no means out of date.

# A SHORT CULINARY HISTORY
# OF CRETE

## The ancient Minoan kitchen

As I began reading about Cretan cooking, I was struck by the continuity between present eating habits and those of the remote past. Of course, dozens of fruits, vegetables and seasonings that were unknown to the Minoans are taken for granted today, such as eggplants, peaches, cinnamon, even lemons, not to mention New World imports like tomatoes and potatoes. Nevertheless, not only the staples but also many of their condiments, the little treats or side dishes, are still on the Cretan menu.

As long ago as the 6th millennium BC, four thousand years before there was a palace at Knossos, the area's earliest residents were cultivating barley and emmer wheat. Wheat does not grow easily in Greece, but they had found a strain of free-threshing wheat, and must have brought it along with their livestock – sheep, pigs, goats and even cows – from Asia Minor. One envisages a convoy of Noah's arks and the mind boggles at such an expedition in what must have been rather small, exposed boats. By 3500 BC this mysterious people had domesticated the vine and by the next millennium they had tamed the wild olive into a tree that would produce both oil and fruit for eating. At the time the first great palaces of Knossos, Phaistos and Mallia were being built, around 2000 BC, wine presses and olive presses had already been fashioned, taking advantage of natural declivities in the rock. There are a couple of them at sites near Archanes above Knossos, where vines still grow prolifically on the white alkaline soil and neat rows of olive trees fill the hillsides for as far as the eye can see.

The frescoes at Knossos, paintings on vases and sarcophagi and the nature of the pottery found at all the Minoan palaces tell us that olive oil and wine were essential features of both daily life and religious ritual. Storerooms lined with enormous Ali Baba jars (*pithoi*) for oil and other staples are still in place in some of the ruined pantries. At Phaistos, for example, the *pithoi* – which may have been about the same height as their makers, who were short and slight – are accompanied by a clay stool a servant would have stood on to ladle out the oil and a channel to collect spills. Molecular examination of the residues in clay cooking pots has recently proven that the Minoans were indeed cooking with olive oil, not just using it as a base for the perfumed ointments they exported all over the Eastern Mediterranean for centuries. Linear B tablets from the Late Palace Period – i.e. the Mycenaean occupation – at Knossos list many aromatic herbs and spices that were stored or imported – coriander, celery, fennel, dill, cumin, mint – all of which are still dominant flavors in Cretan cuisine.

If oil jars tend to be utilitarian, the receptacles for wine show how revered that liquid was. The Heraklio Museum's stunning libation vase in the shape of a bull's head and many other exquisitely crafted vessels were obviously intended exclusively for ceremonies. In the Middle Period to which these masterpieces belong, the Cretans still worshipped the Great Mother who controlled the seasons and the secrets of fertility in both humans and plants.

Another object found at palaces and shrines connects food with Goddess worship. This is the *kernos*, whether solid table or tray, used for offerings. Its surface was indented with round hollows, each of which would be filled with seeds, grains, nuts, beans… and dedicated to her for blessing at the time of sowing or harvesting. Many of them had a deeper well at the center for wine. The custom of seeking favorable planting conditions or giving thanks for the crop with actual offerings is still practiced in rural Orthodox communities in Crete and elsewhere in Greece (not to mention churches of all denominations round the world). But what were those crops, or first fruits? Certainly, grains, grapes and olives, pulses – lentils, chick peas, broad beans – and figs were among the earliest. Perhaps they also piled the tray with apples, melons, quinces and pomegranates – that hard-skinned fruit whose rubylike seeds twinkled brightly in the Underworld, tempting the Goddess's daughter Persephone into just one taste, a bare mouthful, which bound her to Hades for six months of the year and the rest of us to cold barren winter.

Did the Minoans thank the Goddess for the riches of the sea? For the dolphin-fish dangling from that boy's hand in the well known contemporary fresco from Akrotiri on nearby Santorini, the octopus whose tentacles twine round so many of their vases, the sea urchins whose shells have been found amidst the rubble of the tumbled palaces? Or for the snails, whose spiraled remains were discovered in the ruins of Akrotiri, and which archaeologists believe were imported from Crete? Snails are still a favorite food and the Cretans still export them – to France.

As for meat, kid, lambs and bulls were sacrificed, which we know from various paintings, and increasingly sophisticated tests are reversing earlier assumptions that meat was a rare luxury in antiquity. Since the gods ate only thighbones, at least according to Homer, there must have been a lot left over. We also know the Minoans had discovered how to make cheese, perhaps thickened with fig sap as Aristotle described, because cheese strainers not so very different from today's are among the palace finds. Greens and nuts were there for the picking, but honey was not left to chance; the Minoans had beehives.

As Andrew Dalby suggests in *Siren Feasts*, his encyclopaedic history of Greek food, it was the enlivening of the basic gruels/breads, roast meats and lentil stews with relishes such as grapes-and-raisins, olives, figs and honey that marked the beginning of gastronomy. For these condiments, though available to most people, were not just nutritious, they added interest to the diet, making eating more than just a matter of survival. It could be said that this sophisticated and creative combining of tastes is one of the distinguishing features of true civilization.

## Food in later antiquity

The Minoans were conquered by mainland Greeks from Mycenae around the 15th century BC. With them, these ancestors of Homer's heroes brought their macho gods and possibly the myths we associate with Crete arose in this final phase of Minoan civilization: the monstrous Minotaur, offspring of Queen Pasiphae's lust for the god Poseidon's handsome bull, King Minos's demands on Athens for payment in youths and maidens to slake his "son's" unspeakable appetite, Theseus's duel, and Ariadne's thread that guided him out of the labyrinth – the palace of the double-edged axe (*labrys*).

About three hundred years later (not long after the Trojan War) the Mycenaeans succumbed in turn to the Dorians, and the whole country plunged into a barbarian chaos – or perhaps a dull sleep – which left few traces. As civilization began to reemerge around the 9th century BC, Crete seems to have been close in spirit to the Dorian regime at Sparta, but we do not know whether the islanders were submitted to that community's legendary diet of black broth. Later, like the rest of Greece, the different districts of Crete grouped themselves into city-states, none of which achieved note in a world where Athens outshone all competition.

Nevertheless, because much is known about culinary trends in Classical and Hellenistic Athens as well as Rome, we can guess about some of the dishes that might have appeared on Cretan tables, at least those belonging to the wealthy. Game of all kinds supplemented the occasional lamb roast or ox sacrifice, particularly hare and the *kri kri* or wild goat, which was not then an endangered species. But in general, as Dalby says, the southern Greeks were quite puritanical in their attitude toward meat and viewed habitual carnivores as greedy and bestial. Dining on birds invited no such disapproval and the markets were full of them, from pitiful songbirds to plump pigeons, ducks, geese and quail.

By the 7th century BC, Cretan dawns were being shattered by insomniac cocks trying to impress the barnyard (the name "Persian bird" shows where Greeks thought they came from), so hen's eggs and rooster stews must have soon become standard fare. In modern Crete many of the older generation remember eggs as precious; they used them to pay for ink powder, silk thread and other luxuries that were not produced at home. Butter, still called "cow cheese" in Greek, was known but disregarded since it spoiled so rapidly, though cheese and yogurt were widespread. In fact, ancient texts contain several references to "little cheese pies with sesame seeds" that sound like very close relatives of the cheese tarts made all over Crete today.

As for fruits and vegetables, the whole onion family, lettuces and other salads, beets and asparagus were among those present; still to come – in late Roman or medieval times – were spinach, eggplant, oranges and, much later still, the artichoke and the lemon, as opposed to its larger relative, the citron or *kitrion*. Though we associate them so closely with Crete, they did not arrive in Greece until the 15th century. Bread existed in many different forms, with and without leavening: baked in the oven, in a clay pot, or on a griddle; crisp pancakes or *tiganites*, are still a children's favorite; while cracked wheat and bulgur were being made from emmer wheat. But the earliest references to the *paximadi* or rusk, which many Cretans prefer to fresh bread, do not appear until the 2nd century AD.

In 67 BC the Romans conquered Crete and united it with Cyrenaica (Libya) into a single administrative province. Under the Pax Romana the land prospered, the plain of Messara becoming one of the empire's bread baskets and the mountains its chief medicine cabinet. Even then the therapeutic properties of Crete's indigenous plants and herbs were known. While serving in Nero's armies, Dioscurides had identified and classified some 600 Mediterranean plants, 40 of which are included in modern pharmacology manuals.

Was Cretan cuisine influenced by the Roman penchant for rare tastes, the extinct silphium and garum, a pungent sauce made from fish and fish innards left to ferment for months? If so, it has left no trace.

## Byzantines and Arabs

Byzantium was another matter. As the continuation of the Eastern Roman Empire, it assumed control of Crete and the rest of the Greek world in the 4th century AD. From Constantine's new city on the Bosphorus, the emperor's authority radiated west to the Adriatic and east to the Caucasus, north into the Balkans and south to the Holy Land. Being so far from the center of this sprawling empire, however, Crete was temporarily forgotten except by the Church. After Constantine proclaimed the new religion as official, priests were dispatched to rid the empire of any vestiges of pagan worship, but when an army of Arabs vanquished the Byzantine guard in 824, many Cretans thought it judicious to convert to Islam.

The Arab occupation lasted just over one hundred and fifty years, long enough to found a new city on the north coast named Rabd al Khandaq after the moat they dug around the settlement. Khandaq was to be corrupted to Candia by the Venetians, which they used for the whole island as well as the new port, today's Heraklio. In her *History of Food*, Maguelonne Toussaint-Samat, however, suggests that the name may have originated in the sugar mill erected by the Arabs near Chania: sugar in Arabic is *candi*. It's an appealing notion. In any case, only faint Arab influences have been detected in Cretan cooking – perhaps the very un-Greek mixing of sweet and savory in the custom of offering wedding guests a piece of lamb dipped in honey or the several dishes that include green olives as in a Moroccan tajine – but they may well have their origins in later contacts, the coast of North Africa being only 155 miles to the south.

By 961 the Byzantines were back, and as the Cretans reverted to Christianity, they were introduced to a new concept: lengthy church-imposed fasting. Cretan priests cannot have been as severe as those under Charlemagne, who are said to have sentenced to death those failing to observe the Lenten fast. Although they prohibited cooking with animal blood, it took centuries before the sausages known as *aimathies* (from "aima" meaning blood) were transformed from something like a French *boudin noir* into an innocuous mixture of rice, raisins and pork and then rebaptized *omathies*, a dish still prepared on festive occasions in Eastern Crete. Another curious dish, *tzoulamas*, a layered pie containing pork liver, rice, raisins and nuts also harks back to Byzantine times, while *dolmades*, vine or other leaves wrapped around a rice filling, are another Byzantine invention, despite the Turkish name (shared with the *dolmus* or multi-passenger taxi, derived from the verb to stuff). Rice itself, native to India and the Far East, had been introduced by the Arabs but was not a staple until Venetian times.

# Four hundred years of Venetian rule

In 1204 the infamous Fourth Crusade, engineered by a vindictive Doge against Constantinople instead of Jerusalem, put Roman Catholic Latins in control of all key Byzantine possessions. Venice snapped up Crete as a base from which to monitor the shipping lanes that connected southern Italy with the ports of Aleppo and Alexandria.

The walled cities of Candia, Retimmo and La Canea (aka Heraklio, Rethymno and Chania) owe so much of their romantic atmosphere to the Venetians it is hard to remember how much they were hated. Beautiful though their buildings may be, they represented the tyrannical rule of a feudal regime, in which most Cretans were nothing better than serfs. From the start, the Venetians added insult to injury by trying to convert them to Catholicism. Later it would be said, "Better the Turkish sword than the law of the Venetians." As a 19th century visitor, Charles Edwardes wrote, "[The Venetians] had bought the island, and they deemed that the bodies and souls of the inhabitants were part of their purchase."

During the first two centuries of Venetian rule, the Cretans revolted repeatedly against their new masters, often joined by the Italian settlers who were not exempt from the exorbitant taxation. After the fall of Constantinople and the Greek mainland to the Ottoman Turks in the mid 15th century, the Cretans and Venetians warmed to each other in the face of a common enemy. The island began to prosper. Travellers in the 17th century waxed lyrical over its fertility, as in this passage from William Lithgow's *The Totall Discourse of the Rare Adventures and Painfull Peregrinations of long Nineteene Yeares Travayles from Scotland to the most famous Kingdomes in Europe, Asia and Africa*. "This Ile produceth the best Malvasy [and] Muscadine ... wines that are in the whole Universe. It yieldeth Oranges, Lemmons, Mellons, Cytrons, Grenadiers, Adams Apples, Raisins, Olives, Dates, Hony, Sugar ... and all other kindes of fruite in abundance... For beauty, pleasure and profit it [Souda plain near Chania] may easily be surnamed the garden of the whole Universe: being the goodliest plot, the Diamond sparke, and the Honny Spot of all Candy."

Despite this long association with Venice, it is difficult to detect Italian tastes in Cretan recipes. Occasional names provide clues – *lazania, kanellonia, makaronia* – but can be misleading. *Lazania*, for example, are small hand-rolled bits of pasta, more akin to the *cavatelli* of Puglia than to lasagna as we know it. And while Cretans frequently combine meat, chicken or even octopus with noodles or macaroni, they tend to like it rather softer than al dente.

## The Ottoman occupation (1669-1898)

For most of the centuries that Venice controlled the Eastern Mediterranean, she was engaged in a seesaw rivalry with the Ottoman Turks, sometimes battling, sometimes trading, but the Turks wanted the whole pie, and they were stronger. Nevertheless, it took twenty-one years, the longest siege in history, before the Venetians finally withdrew from Heraklio.

The islanders probably did not notice much difference in the shift in authority at first. They were still taxed but no longer forced to work on public works projects, galleys or state-owned fields; more important, no one questioned their religious beliefs. Despite this, about one third of the Cretans converted to Islam. Perhaps the switch was more a matter of convenience than conviction because early travellers like Robert Pashley were quick to notice that "a Cretan Mohammedan drinks his wine as unscrupulously as any Christian in the country." Unfortunately, the Pasha did not pursue the wine trade, and by the 19th century many vineyards had been replanted with olives, though households still made enough for their own consumption. The monasteries continued to produce superlative wine, much to the surprise and delight of western adventurers who found hospitality there.

Even so, in the 18th century the docks of Candia were bustling with French merchantmen loading on "oyl of olives" for Marseilles soap factories, silk, wax and honey being shipped to Aegean ports, and strong, cheap red wine bound for all parts of the Levant. More curious were the shipments of barrels of lemon juice sent to Constantinople and other places in Turkey, where G. O. Dapper (1703) reports they were in great demand for seasoning meats and stews. The French botanist Tournefort writing just fifteen years later describes Candia as the "carcass of a large city… little better than a desert, all but the market-place," but goes on to say that the island "produces more grain than the inhabitants can consume [and] abounds in wines." He then complains that though their wheat is excellent, "they do not know how to make bread. Theirs is a flabby dough, rather bruised than kneaded." Perhaps this explains the preference for rusks, also noted by all visitors.

Unfortunately, the Ottomans did little to better Crete and it gradually acquired a reputation for being the worst administered province in the empire. By the 19th century neglect combined with increasingly harsh taxes goaded the Sfakian mountaineers into at least one insurrection per decade. But they put the same passion into their celebrations. Robert Pashley, who explored the island in 1837, found the Easter revelry after the temperance at Lent extreme – "their life is passed in an alternation of extravagancies." Two hundred years earlier, Tournefort had attended a Pentecost feast. Though a Christian holiday, the Pasha had ordered "no less than 50 muttons or lambs,… nor was there any want of pullets and rice … In every house there's merry-making; some dancing, others eating and drinking: here they repeat verses, there they range the streets with musical instruments… In short, this nation, so grave, and which always seems to be on the pin, is of a sudden quite off the hinges, and run about like so many mad things." Anyone who has been to a Cretan wedding or saint's day celebration will recognize that nothing has changed. Fanatical in their pursuit of freedom, their dedication to festivity was and is equally single-minded.

Pashley and countless other writers also never failed to be astounded at Cretan hospitality. Even during Lent, when his hosts (invariably abbots of monasteries) were fasting, they always managed to procure him eggs, fowl or mutton, while they themselves sat down to a "dish of wild herbs, on which the Cretans seem chiefly to live," supplemented by bread, olives and sometimes cheese. A later compatriot, Bickford-Smith, wrote in 1898, "Another shining quality… is the open-handed hospitality. Not only do the well-to-do offer to the stranger their oldest wine and whitest cheese, but in the mountains the shepherd lays before the wanderer his little store, and bids him help himself." Hippie tourists of the 60s and 70s were to exploit this generosity shamelessly, but it is still very much alive. I, roaming kitchens in the late 90s, always returned to Athens with a car so well stocked with Cretan gifts that I could have opened a grocery.

Although the countryside was devastated by constant conflicts, travellers never failed to succumb to the beauty of the plain of Chania and its luminous olive trees (except for Edward Lear who complained of there being very little to draw) and the luxuriant vegetable garden that flourished in the moat around the city's castle. The Turks had made Chania their capital, so it was better cared for and livelier than Candia (called by the locals Megalo Kastro) or Rethymno. Charles Edwardes delighted in the oriental chaos. He discovered that the soul-piercing shrieks that startled him in the open-air market were just the hawkers' way of advertising. He inspected the "purveyors of different trifles – lemonade men, tart men, honey-water men, and others; each and all screamed to attract passers-by." Besides them were the "water-carriers, wine-carriers, oil-carriers, boot-polishers, vendors of sweet-meats, vendors of coffee with their portable fires and trays of glasses, fruit-sellers, picture-sellers, holders of pitches for gambling games, and representatives of many other itinerant trades" noted by Trevor-Battye. Every now and then a "string of donkeys" would thread its way through the crowd, laden with wine skins, building stones, firewood, pottery or oranges.

The "tumult of tongues" and mix of costumes – red fezzes, blue-smocked schoolboys, black-coated consular clerks, Sfakians in baggy britches, sashes and their legendary boots (still worn by old-timers), kilted Albanians, long-robed Egyptians, even Nubians who had their own tent city on the outskirts of town – gave Chania the appeal of an eastern bazaar. Trevor-Battye knew of "no place in Europe (not even in Constantinople herself) where a greater variety of types [could] be studied." Add to this the braying and neighing of the pack animals, the squawking, gobbling, bleating of the fowl and lambs which were often sold live, plus the probable high decibels of ordinary conversation that the foreigner notices even today and you have a very animated scene indeed. For refuge there were "picturesque little drinking places, a vine-shaded pergola or arbour in front of each."

The visitors of the late 19th century described Crete as an "agricultural Klondyke with enormous latent wealth" and "a paradise in ruins," where people "grieved more than loved and fought more ardently than either grieved or loved."

# The 20th century

In 1898 the Great Powers, England, France and Russia, sent the Pasha and his staff packing and proclaimed Crete an autonomous principality. The much-longed-for union finally occurred in 1913. World War I bypassed the island but in 1923 an event occurred which changed the island more irrevocably than any war: a misguided campaign in Asia Minor resulted in an enormous population swap. Some 30,000 "Turks" – most of them Greek Muslims – were forced to abandon Crete, while 13,000 Greeks in Turkey left lands settled since earliest antiquity to make a new life on the island. Though drachma-less and without possessions, the refugees were sophisticated and resourceful, quick to seize business opportunities and adjust to their rough and ready surroundings. Nevertheless, they were homesick, and the only thing they had to comfort them, besides their music, was their food.

As you might expect, some of their dishes show a love of spices – especially cumin – as in what has come to be perhaps the most famous Asia Minor import, *soutzoukakia* or elongated Smyrna meatballs. Pilafs accented with pine nuts and raisins, shredded carrot sweetening a chicken or lamb stew, fish wrapped in vine leaves, egg-lemon sauces, semolina puddings – *halva* – in a rainbow of flavors and studded with almonds and all the delicate oriental desserts, baklava and its relatives, made with paper-thin fyllo pastry (which may have been invented by the Turks) were some of the nostalgia foods introduced into Crete. Three generations later, many descendants of the original refugees still conjure up in their cooking the homeland most of them have never seen. It is thought that the reason why the people of Eastern Crete use so much cumin is that more refugees settled there. They are also more meticulous, striving for perfection in appearance as well as in taste, than the more spontaneous, casual natives who are specialized in the VOV school of cooking ("vale oti vreis" or put in whatever you've got).

Crete was just learning how to accommodate the newcomers, archaeologists and rich foreign travellers included, when World War II broke out. In May 1941 German parachutists fell out of the sky onto raised pitchforks and disused sabers, and the Cretans were back doing what they knew best, fighting unwanted intruders. The Occupation brought new misery, four years of resistance and retaliation, deprivation and ruin, and a collection of fascinating "poverty foods," some of which make the people who lived through it shudder and others that have them grinning with the recollection of childhood treats (see pp. 170-172). Their trusty greens, grains and olive oil kept them not merely alive but healthy, and that brings us back to the "discovery" of Cretan diet secrets.

By the 1960s, Crete was beginning to realize her latent wealth. A Dutchman saw that Europe's southernmost coast would be an ideal spot to produce early fruits and vegetables for northern markets, and now unsightly plastic greenhouses splatter the landscape from Ierapetra to Phaistos. The northern coasts of Crete also underwent a transformation, as the mania for sun, sand and sea (plus sex) spurred droves of a new breed called the package tourist to beaches hitherto scorned by the locals because they were too susceptible to pirate attack or too salty for growing anything. This seasonal invasion has wrought massive changes in Crete's kitchens. Sheer numbers (summer foreigners exceed the native population in many coastal areas) in tandem with the desire to make a fast drachma have compromised standards and originality. Because many of the visitors were too unadventurous to taste local dishes, the chefs either tried to give them something more familiar – pot roast with tinned peas and carrots – or a small selection of tried and true favorites like fried potatoes, grilled meats and fish, macaroni, moussaka, and the eternal Greek peasant salad, cut up in the morning and dressed with corn oil. Luckily, as visitors and regular customers become more savvy and demanding, this trend is reversing and many restaurants and tavernas take pride in serving traditional specialties, and inventing new ones with Crete's wonderful fresh ingredients.

# CRETAN OLIVES AND OLIVE OIL

Crete's 34 million olive trees account for 30 percent of Greece's olive oil. They grow everywhere except the mountain peaks and the high valleys like Lassithi and Omalos, everywhere below the frost line. In eastern and central Crete the groves are ordered in impeccably tended rows, often alternating with tracts of vines or wheat in a quilt for the undulating hills as far as the eye can see; in the west the trees are taller, unruly and unpruned, a tangle of dark branches and silver leaves obliterating steep slopes. At Anopoli above Sfakia, the harsh climate has made them stubby, and they are fortified with walls of stone. Many of Crete's olives are Methusalehs, thousand-year-old whorled and knotted trunks that might have watched the Arabs land or the Byzantines throw them out. The young ones are as spindly as new-born foals. It will take seven years before they start to bear fruit, many more before they are truly productive.

Olive trees are such a part of Cretan scenery that it comes as no surprise to learn that they have always been there. Along with the almond and the pear, it is one of the few plants that was not imported (by people, birds or the wind). Wild olive trees still abound in the mountains along the south coast, and traces of neolithic settlements have been found near them. By the third millennium BC the

Minoans were extracting oil from cultivated trees, a secret learned perhaps from contact with Egypt or Syria, which were the first places to domesticate the olive. Strangely, the cultivated olive does not seem to have arrived in mainland Greece until around 1500 BC. In any case, ideograms for both wild and cultivated varieties were scratched onto Linear B inventories from the roughly contemporary Late Palace period. Oil appears to have been made from both; although (or because) the wild yield was much lower, early gourmets considered it tastier. The palaces had oil for cooking, oil for lighting, oil for anointing the body, which was shipped throughout the eastern Mediterranean, and oil for treating all sorts of ailments. The Hippocratic Oath (5th century BC) describes more than sixty pharmaceutical uses for the precious liquid. In addition there were olives for eating; some preserved in jars excavated at Zakros look almost exactly like the wrinkled *throumbes* sold in Crete's markets today.

Not surprisingly, such an invaluable resource as the olive tree was given a divine origin. The legend of Athena and Poseidon arguing on the Acropolis for control of Athens is familiar; Athena's gift to humankind of the olive tree won hands down over Poseidon's horse. Oil was nourishing, healing and light-giving, at the very least; the horse could be hitched to a plow or ridden into battle. It was a rare triumph of peace over war. In the Cretan version, as Mirsini Lambraki describes in her exhaustive book, *Olive Oil*, Athena, who may be identified with the mother goddess, was herself a native of the island and bestowed the olive upon her people, the Minoans.

In every land where the olive grows, it has been held sacred. Since Noah's dove flew back to the Ark with an olive sprig in her beak, it has been a symbol of God's covenant with man and of concord. In the past temples were invariably erected near olive groves, a wick floating in olive oil provided the eternal flame that burned within them, and their priests were ordained with it in the belief that olive oil afforded divine protection. Both Messiah and Christ mean the anointed one. Christianity assimilated rather than discarded these ancient practices and today oil, along with bread and wine, still plays a central role in Greek Orthodox ritual. Newborns are rubbed with it and so are the dead, to defend them in life and in the afterlife. In baptism, after immersing the prospective Christian in holy water, the priest coats his body with holy oil. As Father Nikolaos Kontovounissios told an international olive oil symposium in Athens, "This smearing with oil functions as a shield and gives the individual about to join the ranks of the Christian Church the possibility of deflecting the darts slyly aimed at him by the devil and so of avoiding sin." He compared this shield to that of the wrestler in antiquity whose body was so slippery with oil his opponent could establish no hold over him.

Given the importance of olive oil in daily life and ecclesiastical ritual, it is not surprising that there is a special service in the Orthodox Church for blessing it. Composed by one St. Serapion of Thmouis in Egypt in about 330 AD, it hails the oil as able to banish illness and repel fever and ague, as well as bestow grace and remove sin. While modern science will never concur on the last two properties, it is increasingly convinced that as a preventive medicine olive oil may be among the best.

This is one of those frequently recurring examples of folk medicine and legend being confirmed by sophisticated contemporary techniques. And why not? If Homer could point Schliemann to Troy and Mycenae, why shouldn't ancient remedies hold valid secrets as well?

The Cretans consume the largest amounts of olive oil in the world, an estimated 23-24 kilos (52.6 - 54.8 pounds) per capita per year, according to some figures, 31 kilos (68.2 pounds) according to others. The average Greek is said to use some 20 kilos, his Italian and Spanish counterparts 11, while the average American trickles less than 400 grams – not even one pint – on selected lettuce leaves.

Coming from lands where butter reigned in the kitchen, 19th century travellers watched their hosts tuck into meals in which every single dish was served "swimming in that favorite condiment, olive oil," and were appalled. Not only did they never acquire a taste for it, they also drew some rather bizarre conclusions about the consequences of consuming so much of it. In 1834 Pashley had estimated that the average Cretan family used more than four *okes* (the *oka* was a Turkish measure equivalent to 1.3 kilos) a week in cooking (270 kilos or 604 pounds per year!). Thirty years after him, another explorer, T.A.B. Spratt, found the island suffering from earthquake damage compounded by Turkish retaliation against the continuous uprisings and was shocked by the leper colonies outside each of the big towns. "A local doctor says leprosy is due to the salt fish they eat and the quantity of olive oil they take with everything … This thus thins their blood." A Mrs. Walker, visiting the island in 1886, attributed "the existence of leprosy principally to the unwholesome food of the mass of the population … [and] immoderate quantities of olive oil. They take this oil with everything, a morsel of bread even is never eaten without it. Oil is one of the chief products of Crete, which can be procured with fatal ease."

They could never have been persuaded that the olive oil which they so scorned was responsible not for disease, and certainly not leprosy, but rather for keeping a good majority of the people both alive and remarkably healthy, considering their extreme poverty. They would have been astonished at today's appreciation of the multiple benefits of this greeny-gold liquid.

In a sense it really does "thin the blood" by lowering serum LDL, the so-called "bad cholesterol," so that arteries remain unclogged, while increasing HDL, the cholesterol which does our systems good. As Carol and Malcolm McConnell write in *The Mediterranean Diet, Wine, Pasta, Olive Oil and a Long Healthy Life*, olive oil has also been found to perform a number of functions that are "beneficial to digestion and proper metabolism, … preventing gastrointestinal disease, … [providing] the best blend of mono- and polyunsaturated fats for infants who have been recently weaned from breast feeding, … and even … definite protection from … premature aging." Having a chemical composition very similar to mother's milk, olive oil is highly recommended for children's developing brains and bones. The fact that it is a natural "fruit juice" and requires no processing other than "squeezing" also makes it much healthier than seed oils.

## From tree to market

Very few families on the island have to buy olive oil. Most have their own trees, and the harvest is so crucial that civil servants and office workers are given leave to go and pick. January and February are the busiest months, when the city populations stream out to the countryside and commit themselves to this labor-intensive task. It takes four people three weeks to bring in three tons of olives. No machine has been invented that can do this work properly without damaging the trees. Ideally olives should be picked by hand, and eating olives generally are, by children and women agile enough to climb the trees. Otherwise, the branches are struck by a long pole to send the fruit tumbling down, just as depicted in ancient vase paintings. The only difference between then and now is that plastic sheets and nets are spread underneath the trees, an innovation just a few decades old. Sometimes, people attach a rake to the pole, but this too is destructive, and many leaves and twigs are scraped off along with the olives.

Once the olives are harvested, they must be rushed to the village olive press or *fabbrica*, a word handed down from Venetian times. Sitting around in bags only increases their acidity. During the season these presses operate on a 24-hour basis. More and more of them employ impressive modern technology, designed to process the olives quickly and without exposing them to undue heat, the enemy of fine oil. The Cretans prize *agourelaio*, thick green oil from unripe olives, but most bottled oil comes from a mixture of green and black fruit. In Crete there are three main varieties of olives: the *koroneiki*, which are no larger than the tip of my little finger but enormously productive; *tsounati*, which are larger and more resistant to cold; and *throumbolia*, which provide both oil and the wrinkly, raisin-like eating olives that need no curing.

Of the 80,000 tons produced in Crete in an average year, 75 percent is extra virgin. This means that it comes from the first pressing of the olives and that its proportion of oleic acid is no higher than 1 percent. The best oil is also cold pressed, which means that the olives have simply been squeezed, temperatures (from revolving millstones, for example) have been kept to a minimum, and no water has been poured over the pulp to aid in extracting the oil. This step occurs in the second and third pressings of olive pulp, which produce so-called "pure" and plain virgin olive oil. Though olive oil producers vie nowadays to keep acidity down, there is by no means a consensus that acidity is bad for you. It is, however, stronger tasting and has a shorter shelf life.

## Cooking with olive oil

Most of the recipes in this book call for olive oil, a few for butter, and none for any kind of seed oil. You may find the amounts of olive oil suggested in some of these recipes extravagant, even though in many cases I have reduced the original amount told me by Cretan cooks. You can of course reduce the amounts still further, but your shopping bills will be lower if you keep several kinds of olive oil on hand for different uses. I encourage you to experiment with various olive oils to see what you like best. Cretan oils tend to be rich and fruity, without too much bite. Many Italian oils are much lighter, while some even have a bitter aftertaste. I am tempted to tell you to use extra virgin for all your cooking except perhaps for deep frying.

But if olive oil is terribly expensive in your area, then save your really fruity, fragrant extra virgin oil for salads, boiled greens and drizzling on fish, meat and vegetables after cooking, and for dishes that require just a few tablespoonfuls.

Ordinary virgin, which may have low acidity but is made from less superior olives, is fine for baked dishes or vegetables sauteed in oil. You can improve the taste with a tablespoon or two of your best extra virgin just before serving.

For frying, use pure or ordinary virgin olive oils with an acidity of up to 3.3 percent. It is a myth that frying with olive oil produces greasy foods; in fact, it overheats at far higher temperatures than seed oils, making it more suitable for frying. You'll be pleased with the results, especially if you follow a few simple rules. Heat the oil before adding the things to be fried but don't let it reach the smoking point. If the oil is the right temperature, it will quickly seal the foods with a light, crunchy crust that prevents them from soaking it up. Fry in small batches. If you need to top up the oil in the course of cooking, remove whatever is in the pan before you pour in more. Also, you can use this oil several times so long as you filter it after cooling to eliminate any food particles that have burned or could burn the next time you fry.

For sweets, choose an olive oil that is not too aromatic. Taste it first. Some cooks use pure, others ordinary virgin. When making sweet pies with fyllo leaves, pale refined olive oil is dandy for brushing them if you want to economize.

And finally, store your oils away from the light and heat and don't hoard them. Unlike wine, olive oil does not improve with age and is best consumed within one year, though it will last for two.

# THE WINES OF CRETE

Once upon a time Cretan wines were the best the world had to offer. So delicious were they that travellers like Tournefort, who could be quite condescending about the "state of civilization" on the island, could not praise them highly enough. "The wines of this climate have just tartness enough to qualify their lusciousness … far from being fulsome [it] is attended to with that delicious balm, which, in those who have once tasted the Candia wines, begets a contempt for all other wine whatever. Jupiter never drank any other nectar, when he reign'd king of this island."

It's hard to imagine anyone writing anything nearly as glowing today. Oz Clarke's section on the island in his *Wine Atlas* could not be more antithetical: his first line "Crete produces an awful lot of awful wine" doesn't make you want to taste a single drop. In fact, the reality lies, as it usually does, somewhere in between.

If antiquity were the key to a great vintage, Crete would win hands down. Though it may not have been the very first place to cultivate the vine or press the grape, archaeologists consider some four-thousand-year-old pips found at the Kato Zakros palace conclusive proof that specific grape types were developed there expressly for wine production. The existence of different seals and amphora types at Knossos also reveals that there was more than just one kind of wine – perhaps graded according to grape, quality or whether or not it contained additives. The vineyards at Archanes being so terribly old, it is amazing that no vintner there has yet come up with a label claiming to be "purveyors to his majesty King Minos." The quantities were also prodigious. At Myrto, a small settlement on the south coast inhabited between 2900 and 2200 BC, there were so many amphoras for wine that archaeologists have calculated an annual production equivalent to 5,000 modern bottles.

We will never know what early wine tasted like, though we know it was strong because no one would dream of drinking it straight, without a liberal amount of water added. Some writers refer to it as "cooked," which means it could have been boiled down to a kind of syrup; in that case, adding water makes eminent sense. (On occasion it was even boiled with seawater!) We also think it was probably sweet, since strong sweet wines travel better, and amphoras of Minoan wine were shipped to quite a large radius of Eastern Mediterranean destinations. Recent molecular analysis of residues found in wine jars at Myrto, indicates another divergence from modern vintages. Besides some kind of resin (not pine), there were also traces of barley, an ingredient which Homer's Circe added to wine and mixed with grated goat cheese, honey ("and her own vile pinch") served to Odysseus's men to make them lose all thought of home. A strange drink indeed, with or without Circe's sinister touch.

Wine-making flourished again in Crete during the Classical era and afterwards. *Pramniotiko* or Pramnian, one of the more famous varieties, was grown in southwest Crete, near Elafonisi, though many other localities produced it too. Well into the Roman era, Cretan wines, along with those from Lesbos and Chios, were in great demand in Italy among the nouveaux riches, much in the way Americans used to snub California wines in preference to French. *Kris tis glykis*, sweet Cretan, was a Byzantine favorite, but it was the Venetians who put Crete on the wine-lover's map of Europe, where it stayed for centuries.

Under the Venetians, Cretan wines became world famous. When the Greeks had won back Monemvasia in the eastern Peloponnese, where malvasia wines were initially produced, Venice brought thousands of cuttings to Crete and had them planted mainly in the hills behind Heraklio. Before long, barrels of malvasia (malmsey to the English) were being shipped all over Europe. As increasing raids by the Ottomans started posing threats to an unbroken supply, King Henry of Portugal ordered some Cretan vines to be transplanted in Madeira, and the rest is history.

Malvasia is no longer produced in Crete, sweet red wines having gone out of favor, but some homemade vintages may come close in strength as well as taste. In the 16th century, when island wine production was at its peak, Crete was exporting 6.6 million liters annually, the equivalent of 10 million modern bottles. Even in the 19th century, when under Ottoman influence vineyards had given way to olive groves, travellers compared the wine offered them in households and especially monasteries to anything between a light port and a full flavored burgundy.

## Cretan wines today

Today the island produces one fifth of Greece's total output. That's a lot of wine and I wonder if this statistic reflects the barrels that take pride of place in countless Cretan courtyards and storerooms. This wine is apt to have the rusty hue of old amber and it is always very strong, both in taste and in alcohol content – at least a couple of degrees above the normal 12 percent of bottled wine. It can be hair-raising in every sense, but each family invariably regards their own as sublime and almost holy. Many couples have barrels that were filled the year their children were born, which they are waiting to open on their wedding day. Others just keep adding to the same barrel year in year out, like the proverbial stew pot, without ever rinsing it. I have even seen men treading grapes in the back of a pickup lined with plastic sheets. These practices are not going to produce wine to die for.

On the other hand, these homemade wines never have preservatives and I have several friends, non-Cretans, who having acquired the taste refuse to drink anything bottled. If you approach them as *vins du pays* and accept them on their own terms, you may come to appreciate them, too. They are never resinated. If Cretan wines were ever stoppered with pine resin, the islanders long ago lost the taste for it, though now a little is produced because tourists expect it.

Most of Crete's bottled wines come from three districts: Siteia in Eastern Crete, Archanes/Peza southeast of Heraklio, and Kissamo, which also covers the region around Chania as far as Souda Bay. If it were simply a question of climate and soil, they would probably be perfect. The vineyards get the right amount of sun, the mountains shield them from the occasional Saharan blasts, melting snow waters them at the right time. And many of the wines are very good, just fine for everyday drinking, but not as amazing as the ones quaffed so pleasurably up to the turn of the 20th century. Most of them are produced by cooperatives, whose members seem to prefer the security of growing in bulk to the risk of limiting their crop in pursuit of excellence. There are signs that this may change, as more individuals join the market.

As far as whites go, the wines of Siteia, the raisin capital of Greece, are crisp and dry. Its reds are entitled to a AOC (*Appelation d'Origine Controlée*), which means they have to be made of a certain grape and to a certain standard. For these they use the *liatiko* grape, whose name as wine historian Miles Lambert-Gocs explains was originally *Iouliatiko* or July-ripening, an asset in this hot, dry part of Crete. This grape is responsible for what Lambert-Gocs calls the "utter enchantment offered the eyes" by these flame-colored vintages and the orangey hue of many homemade wines.

The rich reds of Archanes and Peza can be very dark, almost purply, while others have glints of orange in them. These areas too are entitled to an AOC. In this case, the grapes are *kotsifali*, described by Lambert-Gocs as spicy and earthy, and *mandelari*, an extremely old, possibly ancient varietal, which produces a strong, almost black wine. They are usually blended.

When experimenting with Cretan wines – though I doubt whether many are exported abroad – the thing to remember is how essential wine is to Cretan life. Drunk on a daily basis with meals, consumed in excess at milestone events and holidays, it forms one corner of the once sacred trinity (with olive oil and bread) from which Mediterranean civilization sprouted and on which it still rests. So even if the wine is not quite as wonderful as it may have been, you will always find it poured as generously. So what if it's not a *grand cru* and there's no vintage date on the label. Its function is to bring us all together. As Pashley exclaimed, "In what country of Europe should we find either a peasant or a gentleman keeping his choicest wine untouched that he might share it with the wandering stranger." That spirit of hospitality has not altered.

# Rakí

Wine is by no means the Cretans' only way of lifting their spirits. Crystal clear, potent as vodka, gin, or aquavit, raki is drunk neat from tiny glasses that hold only a couple of tablespoonsful. There is never a time when it's inappropriate to have a tipple. For breakfast to get your heart pumping, as a nightcap to slow it down, to welcome a guest, to melt the chill, banish the clouds (inside or out), cure a cold or keep one at bay, celebrate a happy event, or drown your sorrows. Winter, summer, spring, fall – little clusters of older men can always be found, at any hour of the day, in any town or village on the island, huddled round a flagon of raki engaged in earnest discussion. The only women you may see imbibing will be either foreign or eccentrics, for raki is still a man's drink.

October is the month when Crete distills its prodigious quantities of raki from the branches (*strafylla*) and pips (*tsikouda*) left over from pressing the grapes for wine. It is the tsikouda which give raki its other, equally common name *tsikoudia*. Making raki is a cottage industry, literally. It is only done by private individuals in their basements or storerooms – anywhere they have their *kazani* or cauldron – and only by those with official licenses. The state has declared a moratorium on the issuing of new licenses, so you can imagine how closely cultivated are the friendships with the households in possession of one.

The room with the raki still is invariably scruffy, walls and ceiling blackened from decades of wood fires, floors usually nothing more than tamped earth, unruly piles of uneven logs stacked inside and out. Stoking the oven and supervising the whole process seems to be a job for the elderly, perhaps because the younger men are at work. Like most tasks associated with the production of alcohol at the community level, it also generates geniality and anyone can drop in to watch, comment or sample the new liquor.

To discover when and where raki is being distilled is easy. Upon entering a village, all you have to do, if you don't smell the heady fumes, is ask "who's cauldroning today?" ("pios kazanevei simera"?) and someone will point you in the right direction. Also, because fires create coals, and it would be a shame to waste them, a raki-brewing session usually turns into a barbecue party with baked potatoes at the very least and pork or veal chops on the grill. If you smell a gathering but haven't an invitation, just stop at the butcher on the way and bring your own – a BYO party with the drinks provided for a change. Some of these parties are impromptu, simple affairs, others can be more elaborate with the womenfolk contributing dishes and singing and dancing well into the night. The amount of alcohol consumed on these occasions is nothing short of phenomenal.

This is how raki is made. First a blazing fire with many logs is set under a large black cauldron filled with the pressed branches, skins and pips that have been steeped in water for up to three weeks. This boils and as steam passes up into the kazani, an inverted, bulbous bronze cauldron with a long downward-pointing snout. The steam goes from the snout through a tube into a barrel of cold water that condenses it. From there it continues through the tube and emerges as a cool liquid which trickles into a jug, covered with a piece of muslin that acts as a filter. The resulting transparent product is 18-19 percent alcohol, but the first jug or so is almost twice as potent, up to 30 percent. Raki can also be coaxed from arbutus or mulberries. And it can vary from very harsh to exceedingly smooth and mellow. Once bottled, some people occasionally add a flavoring agent, such as walnut leaves, tangerine peel or even cinnamon.

Besides swallowing it for any reason at all, many Cretans swear by a rubdown with raki for relief from a cold and smear a few drops on their babies' gums to numb the pain of teething. A surprising but effective cure for diarrhea is 1 teaspoon of Nescafe stirred into a wine glassful of raki! And the next time you have a persistent cough, try sipping a glass of raki, a glass of water and a teaspoon of honey boiled together until the honey dissolves. Guaranteed to work whether hot or cold.

Raki/tsikoudia seems to have originated in the Middle East, despite Mohammed's proscription on intoxicating beverages, and it is drunk all over Greece, but especially in rural and mountainous areas. Perhaps the Turks brought the secret of distilling it with them, thus sweetening the conquest? In any case, it was firmly entrenched by the 17th century, though early travellers found nothing to admire in its taste or potency, in contrast to their overwhelming approval of Cretan wines. Pashley describes it as "execrable," while Tournefort found it "detestable." Whatever your own feeling about it, you would do well not to refuse a thimbleful when offered – raki has an almost ritual significance as a gesture of hospitality and good will. So have a taste to show that your heart is in the right place. You might even find it warms your cockles, tingles your nerves and sends your thoughts spinning. And accept another.

## Ouzo

Ouzo, the quintessential Greek anise-flavored aperitif, is a perennial favorite, too, but it is not typically Cretan. It is always commercially produced, and can be made from alcohol distilled from sugar beets, raisins or grape pressings. Anise is the predominant taste, but other herbs – even salt and wheat – are sometimes added in small quantities to achieve the blend desired. It can be as strong as 48 percent alcohol but is almost always diluted with water which causes it to turn milky. Ouzo and food are mutually complementary, so nibbles are invariably served with it, from a plateful of raisin-sized olives to a whole meal. Very few Cretans would ever consider having wine, tsikoudia or ouzo without something solid as an accompaniment. So despite the amounts of alcohol consumed, there are surprisingly few alcoholics.

## Extinct Turkish beverages

The Turks being Muslims and nonwinedrinkers developed a passion for a drink made from powdered carob pods, sugar and snow brought from the White Mountains. In summer, vendors would hawk it in the streets of Chania, shouting "Haroupia kria kria" – ice-cold carob-ade. *Soumáda*, made from crushed almonds, was also sold in the streets by vendors who dispensed it from a huge samovarlike container on their backs until after the Second World War. The color of watery milk and quite sweet, it was often served at weddings, too. Fruit juice essences made from lemons, bitter oranges and morello cherries were other coolers.

# CRETAN CHEESES

The cheeses of Crete have been famous since antiquity. Even during the silent years of Arab rule, Chania was shipping cheese around the Mediterranean, and cheese was a major export throughout the Venetian and Ottoman eras. Surprisingly, it was not feta, the cheese most commonly associated with Greece, but rather *myzithra*, a soft, mild whey cheese that hardens with age into a piquant ball much used for grating, and *kefalotyri*, a peppery hard cheese.

Today as in the past the best cheeses come from the White Mountains. Not only do they have the greenest pastures but they are also riddled with caves. Each shepherd clan has its own cave – called a *tripa* or hole – which the sun never penetrates and in which hard cheeses were aged until electricity became widely available for large scale refrigerators in the 1980s. The best cheeses, which hardly ever reach the market, alas, are still stored in them. Each clan also has a *mitato* or stone igloo-like shelter whose round walls are rimmed with a narrow ledge for sleeping in stormy or chilly weather. The milk used is primarily from sheep and/or goats rather than cows and is of excellent quality, thanks to the fine pasturage. To maintain this quality, most of the cheese plants – usually family-owned operations far too small to be called factories – are located in the foothills of the mountains so the pickups hauling the fresh milk don't have long to bounce about on dirt tracks. You can smell a *tyrokomio* from at least 200 meters away; the heavy sweet aroma of fresh milk seems to cling to everything. Apart from these plants, which send the finished cheeses down to the city markets, many housewives have a family goat and make their own cheese with a pinch of rennet or even lemon juice or vinegar. After boiling it twice, they store it in the refrigerator, sliced, salted and covered with its whey. Sometimes, too, they pack it in oil which gives it a pungency that is wonderful for grating or nibbling with raki.

While some of Crete's cheeses are sold in supermarkets throughout Greece, others are so local they don't even make the journey from Chania to Siteia. Here is a description of the most common Cretan cheeses.

**Myzíthra:** This is probably the cheese Odysseus watched the Cyclops make while his men held their breath in his cave. The Minoan cheese drainers collected from palace excavations could have been used to produce it, and most of the cheese pies, ancient and modern, call for this moist, fresh delicacy. Though found all over Greece, it takes its name from the conical hill of Mystra in the Peloponnese near Sparta, which it is said to resemble. To me its shape is more reminiscent of a Turkish fez. White, rindless and relatively low in fat (50%), it is similar to ricotta, and more readily found in winter and spring when milk is more plentiful. In the marketplace, you will often see white balls of salted myzithra hung up to dry; wrapped in cloth and tied with red or yellow ribbon, they look like oversize Christmas baubles.

Nowadays, the Cretans do make feta and the whey left over is heated and strained again into wicker baskets to produce myzithra. The baskets have a cross on the bottom; they'll turn out better with God's blessing. In the old days before running water, people would wash both clothes and themselves in the whey.

**Xinomyzíthra:** Literally sour myzithra, this cheese is made only in Crete. It too is a whey cheese but is crumbly, shapeless, less moist and with a lower fat content (23% fat). Whereas myzithra spoils very quickly, this cheese is salted, hung in bags for a week and then packed into airtight barrels and stored in a cool place for two months. Its characteristic dry, tangy taste goes well with ouzo and raki and becomes sweeter when baked into a pie. Ilias Mamalakis, an authority on Greek cheese, thinks it must be as old as Cretan cheesemaking. Although it was exported to Europe in the 18th century, it is very difficult to find anywhere but Chania, though some top Athens supermarkets have recently begun stocking it.

**Anthótyro:** This is another white, soft whey cheese, which is confusingly similar to myzithra. But because it is made with the addition of whole milk or cream, its fat content is higher and therefore tastes sweeter and more buttery. It is also a bit moister than myzithra and slightly salted. "Anthos" in Greek means flower but also the top of the milk, ie the cream. In this book, anthotyro may be used interchangeably with myzithra in almost any recipe. Anthotyro is more readily available in Greek supermarkets, but you could also use ricotta mixed with mascarpone or a mild French goat cheese. Anthotyro is much lighter in consistency than Philadelphia cream cheese.

**Graviéra:** Graviera takes its name from gruyère and was not made in Greece until 1914. When I came across this information in Mamalakis's book on Greek cheese, I was flabbergasted since I assumed this delicious cheese had been an institution in this country for far longer. Many regions – from Epirus to Tinos and Naxos – produce a graviera, but the Cretan variety is the most renowned and the most requested in supermarkets. Made of unpasteurized ewes' milk, sometimes combined with goats', the cheeses are smaller and lighter in color than the Swiss prototype, and may contain a few tiny holes and a horizontal crack or two. They are left three months to ripen and would be even better if left to age longer, as they were in the past. In the 1980s a Cretan shepherd gave us a whole head that must have been stored in his tripa for at least six months. It tasted like the best old parmesan. I have been looking in vain for more like it ever since. Cheese-mongers toss out various excuses: customers prefer the blander less aged cheese; the rind gets moldy and unappetizing; demand is too great, etc. It's a pity, but even so the gravieras we have to settle for are still excellent, pleasant, light cheeses that go well with wine and have been awarded a DOC (Dénomination d'Origine Controlée) by the European Union. This is the equivalent of the guarantee standard used in recognizing the wines of certain localities.

**Maláka:** This awkwardly named cheese (which is the same as Greece's most frequently used cussword) is simply very fresh graviera. White, mild and elastic, it resembles mozzarella and melts in the same way. This is another cheese peculiar to Crete.

**Kefalotýri:** This hard cheese made from sheep or goats' milk or both can be found all over Greece. It is salty and sharp, good for grating and nibbling with wine. A satisfactory substitute is pecorino but try to avoid pecorino romano, which is sour rather than peppery.

**Pichtógala from Chania and Xinógala from Siteia:** These creamy fresh cheeses are the consistency of thick Greek yogurt. They do not travel.

**Feta:** Though this is not a traditional Cretan cheese, it is still widely used. In fact, 40 percent of the cheese consumed by Greeks on a daily basis is feta, that white, sometimes chalky, sometimes creamy, usually quite salty cheese which has become the country's best known product. Its name, which means slice, comes from the slices made in the block of cheese while it's still in the cauldron.

**Stáka:** This is such a rich substance your cholesterol level might soar just by thinking about it. This is how staka is made. For several days the housewife or dairy owner will skim off the fresh cream from the top of the milk (preferably ewes' or goats' or both) and store it, with a little salt added, in a refrigerated container until there is at least 500 grams worth. At this point, she cooks it, sprinkling in a little flour, in a pan over a low flame until the fat separates from the solids in the cream. These unite with the flour to form a thick pale yellow mixture, which looks a bit like a curdled mayonnaise and tastes like a slightly sour crème fraiche. The liquid, clarified butter essentially, is used to cook with. Both will keep in the refrigerator for some time.

Another product not found outside Crete, and only occasionally as far east as Heraklio, staka is added to wedding pilaf, eggs are sometimes fried in it and the people of Anogeia are known to pour it over their makaronia. Some fearless souls even spread it on their bread. If you'd like to create the same effect, you can try substituting mascarpone, crème fraiche, Devonshire clotted cream or even strained Greek yogurt. A simpler solution to achieve that extra richness is just to add a little extra olive oil with a tablespoon or two of butter to your dish.

**Yogurt:** Yogurt is good almost everywhere in Greece, but I had never seen yogurt so thick it could be cut in slabs until I went to Crete. It was as rich and delicious as it looked. Some places are renowned for their yogurt. Vrysses, a large village by a stream between Rethymno and Chania, has several cafes luxuriating in the perpetual shade of some giant plane trees. You have to be really pressed for time to drive through without stopping for a dish of the lightest, sweetest, most soothing yogurt imaginable. When asked what makes it so outstanding, the waiters knot their brows and answer, "it's fresh."

The recipes in this book call for strained yogurt (*yiaourti strangisto* or *sakkoulas*). If you cannot find it, strain commercial plain yogurt through several thicknesses of cheesecloth or a clean dish towel placed in a colander for a few hours until most of the liquid drips out. It should be creamy and scoopable, far softer than cheese.

# CRETAN HERBS

Without any question, the most popular herb in the Cretan kitchen is mint. It is essential in pies of all kinds, vegetable stuffings, fritters and any dish that calls for myzithra. Litsa Anagnostaki of Chania's Rififi Cafe speaks for many Cretan cooks when she says, "If you don't have mint, you have nothing." Although it is almost always used in its fresh form, if you only have dried, add that; it's better than none at all.

Other popular flavorings are dill (always fresh), oregano (almost always dried), thyme (gathered from the mountainside but also dried), and parsley, the flat-leafed Italian variety, not the curly decorative leaf. Wild fennel is a great favorite. It has a much stronger taste than bulb fennel but in the absence of it, just add more bulb fennel as well as the stalks and feathery tips if you can find them. The only dishes that call for rosemary are roast pork and snails, fish or pumpkin with a vinegar sauce. Sage is almost exclusively reserved for tisanes.

## Herbs in peasant remedies

Cretan herbs are legendary. During the Roman era, Crete could almost have been considered the medicine chest of the empire; it was the single most important supplier of medicinal herbs. The knowledge lingered on and until a few decades ago every community had its naturopath or healer – a woman or man with an intuitive gift who had been indoctrinated by an older person and who would pass on their secrets to a successor. They knew how to treat illnesses, even major ones, by administering the right herbs, in ointments, tisanes and infusions and could also set bones and deliver babies. Because they usually had a sound acquaintance with their patients, they could treat the whole person rather than just the symptoms. Even today, many Cretans have a good idea of what conditions the most common herbs can alleviate. I've listed here what they told me, but I do not pretend to be a herbalist. I was also told some stories that are difficult to take seriously. For example, can the dried, powdered skin of a chicken's stomach really be made into a drink that will ease renal colic?

The following remedies are more reliable:

**Mint tea** - *dyosmos* lowers blood pressure, and so does sage tea, *faskomilo*, which is a wonderful antidote to the common cold. Inhaling the steam from fresh boiled eucalyptus leaves clears the sinuses, and an infusion made from bay leaves is another remedy for colds.

**Fliskouni:** A tea made from *fliskouni*, known to us as penny royal, is taken for stomach pain, diabetes, gout and also minimizes the effect of cholesterol.

**Dittany** (*erontas* or *diktamo* locally), a plant with small, round, velvety grey leaves, is endemic to Crete and prefers the mountains to the lowlands. It could almost be called the miracle herb, because it is used to soothe gall bladder problems, menstrual cramps and is even said to retard the ageing process! It is not used in cooking, only in tisanes.

**Camomile** boiled in water and then cooled soothes the eyes and also calms down the gall bladder.

**Balsam:** Tea made from either *balsam* (another kind of mint) or *marjoram* is a remedy for heartburn.

**Mastic:** If you have a bad burn, an ointment made by boiling together a little *mastic, olive oil, bee's wax, wine* and *lamb fat* will heal it in no time.

Sitting on a *hot brick* was prescribed as a cure for diarrhea.

**Dried figs:** Another remedy for coughs is *dried figs* boiled with grape must syrup (*petimezi*).

**Bee's wax:** Hand lotion with *bee's wax, olive oil* and a little *wine* is said to be more effective than any storebought brand.

**Oregano:** One grandmother in Rethymno told me: "*Oregano* (*rigani*) in too large a dose can make you swell up, but *tea made from oregano* is good for coughs. And if you leave a handful of oregano in a jar of olive oil in the sun for a few weeks, you'll have an ointment that soothes cuts and wounds." (Do the same with St. John's wort and you'll have your own lotion for muscular aches and pains.)

More than two millennia ago, Archestratos, the great-grandfather of gastronomy, travelled to some fifty towns and cities around the eastern Mediterranean just to taste their local delicacies. He found these foods so enthralling that he wrote an epic poem about them, the *Life of Luxury*, which we know only from excerpts quoted in Athenaeus's *Deipnosophists*. Over and over, as Andrew Dalby makes clear in *The Classical Cookbook*, he repeats his chief concern: the true flavor of fresh produce, chosen in the right place at the right time of year, should always be allowed to come through, should never be masked by layers of spices and strong seasonings.

To me this is still the essence of Cretan cooking. To be sure herbs and spices are added to enhance, but the fundamental goodness of the ingredients themselves is what makes it linger in your memory. Don't forget that when you use these recipes. Only if you pick the freshest produce from the farmers' markets and grocers and stick to fruity Greek extra virgin olive oil, will you be able to really eat like a Cretan.

# SNACKS, STARTERS & SALADS

## Mezédes

All over Crete, morning, noon and night, winter and summer, you will see small groups of men huddled around a plain metal table on a narrow sidewalk, under a shady tree, or next to a gas heater, sipping raki from squat shot glasses and nibbling something to fuel their conversation. The accompaniments to this fiery liquid are likely to be simple and impromptu. They might consist of a plateful of tiny black Cretan olives or a few sticks of local graviera cheese, dipped, surprisingly, in honey. Finely sliced, raw baby artichokes sprinkled with lemon juice, delicate young broad beans in the pod, chick peas still attached to their stalks are spring-time favorites. Summer fare is often a few wedges of red tomato and long spears of cucumber glistening with sea salt, pale green romaine lettuce leaves also with salt and lemon juice, and chunks of ruby watermelon. In the autumn, when the raki is being distilled from the vine stalks and grape skins and pips left over from wine making, potatoes baked in the coals that fire the still are the rule. In colder weather, roasted chestnuts, broad beans mashed with olive oil and garnished with slivered onions, and even a wedge of halva, dusted with cinnamon and pepper, wrapped in foil and heated in the fireplace, are all mezedes (appetizers) considered to go best with raki.

Mezedes are also an inseparable element of Cretan hospitality. No matter how sophisticated or humble a Cretan household, its hostess will offer you a glass of raki and try to feed you something almost as soon as you cross the doorstep. We westerners are sometimes slow to offer, we also take the first "no, thank you" as carved in stone, whereas further east to accept with too great alacrity may be considered rude. Cretans therefore are inclined to take one, even two refusals as mere politeness and there is no escaping their generosity. Having a guest in their home without providing refreshment violates all their notions of normal, civilized behavior. Even workmen are catered to if they stay longer than half an hour.

But there are no rules as to what constitutes a meze, which Greeks are likely to refer to in the diminutive plural as mezedakia, almost as an endearment. Some are nothing more than what's on hand, produced spontaneously to balance the drink of the moment, whether raki, ouzo or wine. Others are more elaborate, requiring as much preparation as a main dish. They may even be smaller helpings of such dishes.

If it's morning, the lady of the house will think nothing of popping a few miniature cheese pies out of the freezer and into the frying pan. Before you can say, "I can't possibly eat that many," you're sitting at the kitchen table before a plateful of light as a feather, melt in the mouth pies drizzled with thyme honey. Around noontime, from a capacious pot bubbling on the stovetop she might extract a trio of stuffed vine leaves no thicker than your little finger and not even as long. Or she will uncover a bowl and lift out a couple of slices of pumpkin, fried and doused with vinegar and rosemary. In the evening, for friends who are invited or who might drop in, there'll be a table spread with little bowls of olives, nuts and miscellaneous dips, like the well known taramosalata, which the Greeks group under the generic term, salad. Scooped up with a knob of Cretan rusk, creamy puréed eggplant or potatoes mashed with capers seem to have been invented to bring people together. There could also be plates piled with fish-roe balls, vegetable croquettes or octopus stewed with fennel. Speared with a toothpick, they seem to spur the conversation, inspire fellowship. As you leave, much later than planned, you sense that regardless of the state of the world or the economy, all's right with this particular piece of creation.

Quite apart from all their associations with hospitality, as items on a menu mezedes are for many people the most appealing aspect of the Greek way of eating. Meze is actually a Turkish word meaning table and ordering up a tableful of little dishes, hot and cold, provides an opportunity to sample several different tastes without the limitations imposed by the one person-one dish formal traditions of the west. Often they are so satisfying that the main course never gets ordered.

The recipes in this chapter are for only some of the little dishes served in Crete with raki, wine or ouzo. You'll find others under the headings Savory Pies, Fish, Meat and Vegetables, all preceded by an asterisk.

# Roasted walnuts
*Karýdia psitá*

From the thickly forested mountain village of Elos, these walnuts are traditionally served with raki, but they would be a popular snack with just about any drink, alcoholic or not. To make them, all you need is a heavy, nonstick frying pan, 2 cups of shelled walnuts, a teaspoon of salt and 3 tablespoons of sugar.

Heat the walnuts and the salt over a low fire, stirring from time to time, for about 15 minutes. Then sprinkle the sugar over them, while continuing to stir, until the sugar caramelizes and partly coats the walnuts. (If you don't cook them with the salt first, the sugar doesn't stick to them properly.)

Not too sweet, not too salty, these were around long before honey-roasted peanuts and are quite irresistible.

*With thanks to Marika Daskalogianni for sharing this recipe.*

# Fresh almonds
*Fréska amýgdala*

(CHANIA)

Up until about thirty years ago, you would often see peddlers carrying baskets of fresh almonds strewn on mulberry leaves around a small block of ice. Just pried from their soft, pale yellow shells still covered with their green velvet coats, the nuts are milk-white and have the delicate taste of an exotic sweetmeat rather than the roasted or dried almonds that we're used to.

But you can almost capture their cool sweetness if you soak 500 grams / 1 pound of the dried variety overnight (up to 24 hours) in a bowl of water with a tablespoonful of salt. The peel slips off easily, but they have to be eaten quickly or their "freshness" ages.

You can see almonds soaking in large tubs in the Heraklio market, next to tubs filled with lupin seeds, capers and at least ten varieties of green and black olives.

# Mashed broad beans and olive oil

*Koukiá pouré*

(RETHYMNO)

This is very simple but extremely tasty, depending on the quality of the olive oil. The only thing you have to do is soak the dried beans overnight and slip off their tough outer skins and black tip before boiling; otherwise you'll be left with a very recalcitrant heap of vegetables that will resist any attempt to mash them.

Boil the beans until soft, drain and crush them with a fork. Stir in as much oil as you see fit, salt and pepper, a big pinch of dried mint flakes, a squeeze of lemon juice and you've got an original dip.

In Puglia, the heel of the Italian boot, this purée (called fava there) is served warm with boiled wild greens, but in Crete it is usually just one of many little dishes to help the raki go down. It is normally eaten at room temperature.

# Purslane yogurt dip

*Tzatzíki me glistrída*

This variation on the familiar yogurt dip substitutes purslane for the cucumber. Purslane, a summer weed with fleshy leaves and stalks which may be found at your farmers' market if not in your flower pots, is a key ingredient in the Mediterranean Diet. Like soy beans and walnuts, it contains alpha-linoleic acid, a compound said to reduce the possibility of cardiovascular disease. This dish, a common meze on the Aegean coast of Turkey, must have been one of those recreated to ease the nostalgia of the Asia Minor Greeks who moved to Crete after 1922.

*1 packed cup purslane leaves and tender stalks, washed and trimmed*
*360 ml (1 1/2 cups) strained yogurt*
*1-2 tablespoons olive oil*
*2-3 tablespoons fresh lemon juice*
*1 clove garlic, crushed*
*salt to taste*

Pull the leaves from the stalks and leave whole, reserving a few of the leaves for decoration. Coarsely chop the stalks. Whip together all the ingredients except the purslane in the bowl you're going to serve the dip in, mix in the purslane, decorate the surface and refrigerate for an hour or two to let the flavors mingle before serving. Serves 6 to 8.

# Caper salad
## *Kaparosaláta*

*4 medium potatoes, washed but not peeled*

*1 medium onion*

*3 heaping tablespoons capers*

*3-4 small gherkins*

*1 tablespoon vinegar*

*1 egg yolk*

*1 tablespoon mustard (or more if desired)*

*120 ml (1/2 cup) olive oil, approximately*

*juice of 1 large lemon, or to taste*

*salt and freshly ground pepper, to taste*

In Greece it is customary on the two Saturdays before and after the start of Lent (*Psychosavvata*) to visit the family grave and share an ancient dish called *kollyva* – hulled wheat with almonds, sesame seeds, pomegranate seeds – with any friends and neighbors who may be in need. In some parts of Crete, they distribute portions of this salad instead, along with a helping of black eyed peas and rice (Fasoulorizo, see page 85). The custom cannot be very venerable, however, for potatoes were not known in Crete until the second half of the 19th century. This New World tuber arrived in Greece along with Independence, and though viewed with misgivings at first, it soon became indispensable, after a certain amount of trial and error – some farmers' families cooking and eating the leaves before discovering that the goodness lay underground. Initially called earth apple (from the French *pomme de terre*), the potato was ideally suited to the Lassithi plateau, for the soil there gives them a unique flavor. So good are they in fact that visiting mainlanders have been known to load up their cars with sackfuls, in preference to more conventional souvenirs such as model windmills or hand-carved spoons.

Like many other Greek "salads" – taramosalata, melitzanosalata – this is actually more of a dip, something between *skordalia* (garlic-potato purée) and mayonnaise.

Boil the potatoes in plenty of water with the onion. Drain and peel when cool enough to handle, and push through a ricer. Chop the capers and the gherkins in a food processor. Then before they have a chance to cool off, add the potatoes, the onion and all the other ingredients and process until you have a thick, smooth purée.

**CAUTION:** The potatoes can get gummy if processed for too long. Ricing them first reduces this danger, but if it should occur, add more oil and lemon juice. Adjust seasonings and serve. Makes 1 medium-sized bowlful.

# Chick pea salad
*R e v i t h o s a l á t a*

For a simple refreshing salad, take a cup or two of cooked (or canned) chick peas, sprinkle a handful of chopped spring onions and a tablespoonful of chopped fresh mint on top, and mix with olive oil, lemon juice and salt and pepper.

# Amaranth Rethymno style
*V l í t a   s a l á t a*

**Vlita, which you sometimes see on taverna menus translated as blite, is the Greeks' favorite summer green for boiled salad. It deserves a wider following for its tender leaves are as flavorful as spinach. It can be boiled or steamed with a few zucchini and served with olive oil and lemon juice, but in Rethymno it is dressed with cooked tomato purée and vinegar. At the Araxovoli taverna near the Venetian castle, chef Vassilis Morakis turned this humble salad into a vegetable extravaganza with a minimum of effort.**

**If you cannot find amaranth, I suggest you substitute green leafy Swiss chard, which has a similarly mild taste though its texture is smoother.**

*1 kg (2 lbs) amaranth*
*8 very small zucchini*
*1/4 kg (8 oz) young runner beans or*
    *string beans*
*4 ripe tomatoes, grated, skins*
    *discarded*
*1 onion, thinly sliced*
*olive oil*
*garlic vinegar (skordostoumbi)*
*salt and freshly ground pepper*

Trim the greens of all thick stalks and any weather-beaten leaves. Bring a large pot of water to the boil and cook them for about 15 minutes or until they are tender but not mushy. Drain well. In a separate pot boil the zucchini and beans and drain. Place the vegetables in a bowl with the zucchini and beans surrounding the greens, add the tomato purée and sliced onion, and dress with as much olive oil, vinegar and seasonings as you like. Serves 4.

---

*Skordostoúmbi* **can be made easily by filling a bottle with your favorite white wine vinegar and adding several peeled garlic cloves to it. Within a few days, it will have a heavenly garlicky taste.**

# Mediterranean "salsa"

*Mesogeiakí sáltsa*

FOR 1 CUP

*1 large ripe tomato*
*1/2 onion*
*1 leek, green part only, finely
    chopped*
*1 red and 1 green pepper, seeded and
    finely chopped*
*1 tablespoon black olive paste*
*salt and freshly ground pepper to
    taste*
*2 tablespoons olive oil*
*1 tablespoon chopped parsley*

**This salsa can be used to accompany roast meat or grilled fish as well
as a spread for bruschetta or rusks. It was given to me by Panayiotis
Delvenakiotis, chef at the Istron Bay Hotel's two prize-winning
restaurants, where all the vegetables are of the utmost freshness and
organically grown.**

Peel and seed the tomato and then dice it. Finely chop the onion
and mix it with the diced tomato. Add the leek and peppers, olive
paste, pepper and seasonings and toss gently with olive oil. Just before
serving sprinkle with finely chopped parsley.

Another of Panayiotis's touches, which reflects his passion for
making food lively and as beguiling to the eye as to the palate, is adding
thin slices of raw beetroot to a salad of lettuce and arugula. The sweetness of the beet is a wonderful counterpoint to the pungent arugula.

# Garlic bread

*Skordópitta*

FOR UP TO 6

*6 pieces of Arab pitta bread (8 cm,
    4 inch size)*
*3 tomatoes, grated (skins discarded)*
*3 (or more) garlic cloves, crushed*
*1 tablespoon olive oil*
*60 grams (1/2 cup) kefalotyri cheese,
    grated*

**This appetizer is served at the Anaplous taverna in Chania's
medieval district. Fabulously simple, it will satisfy your craving for
pizza with a minimum of bother.**

Mix the grated tomato, garlic and olive oil together in a small
bowl. Place some of the mixture on each piece of bread, top with a
little grated cheese, and place under the grill for a few minutes to
bring out the flavors.

# Cretan bruschetta

### *Dákos, Koukouváyia*

**In Kato Zakros, tavernas on the beach serve these round barley rusks (paximadia) topped with chopped tomato, olive oil and oregano to foreigners under the name dog biscuits. The rusks are hard and crunchy, but there the resemblance stops. In fact, the word "koukouvayia" used around Rethymno means owls; perhaps their roundness reminds people of owl eyes. In any case, once you acquire the taste for this appetizer, it's hard to start a meal without it. Found on taverna menus all over the island, this is one of a number of instances of a traditional peasant snack being elevated to a delicacy.**

**If you have no access to rusks, thickly slice a loaf of your favorite whole grain bread and bake it for an hour or more in a very low oven until hard on both sides and you'll have a reasonable alternative.**

Sprinkle the rusk on both sides with water from the tap to soften it a bit. Pour 1 tablespoon of the oil over it, then add the chopped tomato and the other tablespoon of oil, the cheese crumbled on top, the herbs and some salt and pepper.

If you like garlic, mix it in with the tomato (though most Cretans would not do this). This is a wonderful snack, filling and satisfying, crunchy, piquant and creamy at the same time.

You can also crumble a rusk into your "Greek" salad: small chunks of ripe but firm tomatoes, thinly sliced green pepper, a little cubed cucumber, plenty of sliced onion, a sprinkling of capers, a few black olives, a few sprigs of lemony purslane if you have it, shredded arugula or basil for bite, some parsley perhaps and either mild creamy feta or myzithra cheese. Douse with as much olive oil as you choose with some vinegar if you like it and sprinkle with a little oregano if you're not using basil. This combination is very similar to Andalucian gazpacho and the bread salads of Puglia and Tuscany.

When the ingredients are garden fresh it's impossible to tire of this salad, but if you encounter the ordinary run-of-the-mill taverna variety where the vegetables have been sliced in the morning and all the little extras are missing, you might as well forget it.

FOR 1-2 PEOPLE
*1 large barley or whole wheat rusk*
*2 tablespoons olive oil*
*1 large tomato (or 2 smaller ones), chopped*
*1 tablespoon myzithra, anthotyro or soft, mild feta*
*1 teaspoon oregano or marjoram*
*1 clove garlic, crushed (optional)*

When faced with a recipe that calls for juicy ripe tomatoes and your supermarket only has some pale imitations, while the farmer's stand has closed for the season, by all means use canned tomatoes. Adding a few chopped sun-dried tomatoes may intensify their flavor, though some are heavily salted and should be soaked in a cup of water first.

# Mary's zucchini fritters
## *Kolokithokeftédes*

FOR ABOUT 32
SMALLISH FRITTERS

*1 kg (2 lbs) zucchini*

*1-2 eggs, beaten*

*2 tablespoons chopped mint*

*1 tablespoon oregano*

*1 tablespoon marjoram*

*1 tablespoon cumin*

*1 cup dried breadcrumbs*

*salt and freshly ground pepper, to
    taste*

*1-2 tablespoons olive oil plus more
    for frying*

*2-3 tablespoons flour, plus extra for
    dredging*

**Zucchini fritters are among the most delectable of summer treats and every cook seems to have a different recipe for them. I think these, which Mary Daskalaki perfected during her years running "Maria's Taverna" in Kato Zakros, are about the best I've had so far. She parboils the grated squash to make them manageable, and coats the balls with flour "so that the zucchini mixture will dance inside when you fry them and get a nice crust."**

Wash and trim the zucchini, grate them and parboil them for about 3 minutes from the time the water returns to a rollicking boil. Drain and when cool enough to handle squeeze all the water out of them. Thoroughly mix the zucchini with the eggs, seasonings, breadcrumbs, 2-3 tablespoons of flour and the olive oil. Refrigerate for at least an hour before cooking.

When you're ready to eat, shape the fritters into slightly flattened little balls by rolling a tablespoonful of the mixture between your palms, and then dredge them in flour – either on a plate or by shaking them gently, a few at a time, in a paper bag with a few tablespoons of flour in it. Heat a few centimeters (an inch) of oil in a wide frying pan until it is hot but not smoking and fry the balls – don't overcrowd – until they are browned on both sides and drain them on paper towels.

These zucchini fritters are very versatile. If you keep them small, made with about a teaspoonful of the mixture each, they can be an elegant meze for an ouzo party. Medium-sized ones are fine for family dinners (children love them), either as a side dish or as a main course with a light tomato sauce.

If you add 120 grams (1 cup) of grated kefalotyri (or the cheese of your choice), 2 more beaten eggs and 1 tablespoon of baking powder to the grated zucchini mixture, turn it into a lightly oiled pyrex dish and bake it for 30-35 minutes at 190°C (375°F), the result is a delicious, easy zucchini flan.

# Eggplant patties
*Melitzanokeftédes*

(CHANIA)

You can make keftedes or "meatballs" out of almost any vegetable – spinach, tomato, zucchini – but I had never seen eggplant-balls until I was taken to the Rififi Cafe in Chania. These deserve to be on more menus.

Despite its echoes of the old French thriller, there is no hint of mystery or danger about this undistinguished collection of white plastic chairs and tables set out under the mulberry trees in a minute square off Daskalogianni Street. Though it looks a pleasant enough spot to sip a coffee frappe or a soda in the shade, you'd never dream that anything but the most rudimentary of mezedes would come out of its kitchen. Nevertheless, thanks to Litsa Anagnostaki, the owner's wife, a feisty grandmother with the vitality of a teen-age disco dancer, you can eat better at Rififi than at many of the larger, more famous restaurants in town.

This is just one of her inventions.

*3 large eggplants*
*1 large onion, grated*
*1/2 bunch wild fennel sprigs or*
*1 small fennel bulb, finely chopped*
*1/2 bunch parsley*
*1/2 bunch mint*
*2 tablespoons kefalotyri or pecorino*
*cheese, grated*
*2 tablespoons flour*
*1 tablespoon olive oil*
*1/4 teaspoon baking soda*
*1 egg white*
*salt and freshly ground pepper*
*to taste*
*flour for dredging*
*olive oil for frying*

Cut the tops off the eggplants and cut in half, but do not peel. Parboil them for 5 minutes and then drain. When cool enough to handle, squeeze as much excess water out of them as you can and chop in a food processor. (Litsa calls her mini Moulinex chopper, "to diavolaki" or little devil.) Put in a colander and squeeze small handfuls of the mixture between your palms as hard as you can again. Eggplants seem to be mostly water.

Chop together the various herbs and add them, along with the grated onion, cheese, flour, olive oil, baking soda, egg white and seasonings to the chopped eggplant in a bowl. Mix thoroughly and refrigerate for an hour or two.

When you're ready to eat, form the mixture into little balls or patties, dredge in flour and fry in hot oil on both sides until crisp. Drain on paper towels before serving. Makes about 30.

# Sea urchin salad
## *Ahinosaláta*

*"A Spartan was invited to a banquet at which sea urchins were served at table, and took one. He did not know how this food is eaten and did not notice how his fellow diners handled it: he put the urchin in his mouth, shell and all, and cracked it with his teeth. He was getting on badly with his helping, having not come to terms with its surface resistance, and said, 'Pestiferous dish! I'm not going to weaken and let you go now – but I'll take no more of your kind!'"*

**From *The Deipnosophists* by Athenaeus**
**(as quoted in Andrew Dalby's *Siren Feasts*)**

If the Spartan had been sitting in a taverna on the waterfront in Chania and had just been served a bowlful of sea urchin salad, he would have had no such difficulties.

To make this delicacy yourself, besides proximity to a source of supply, you will need considerable patience and will power to detach the five coral/ocher colored egg segments from each prickly shell* and put them into a bowl untasted. (For sea-urchin lovers this involves almost superhuman willpower.) After you've cleaned at least 40 or 50 of them (enough for 4 people), then simply pour a little virgin olive oil over them followed by the juice of one lemon. Words cannot describe the sheer pleasure that comes with eating this dish accompanied by chunks of fresh bread to mop up the juices and a frosted glass of white wine.

*The French, who adore sea urchins and buy them for 7 francs apiece in Paris, have invented a special tool, *le coupe-oursins*, which resembles the device for cutting the tops off soft-boiled eggs. It slices the creatures in half and greatly speeds up the preparation time.

# Fish roe balls

*Taramokeftédes*

**Taramosalata is one of Greece's best loved mezedes. Mixed with potatoes and seasonings and then fried, the salmon-pink fish roe paste makes light and unusual patties that go beautifully with ouzo or chilled white wine. They are good even lukewarm, which simplifies kitchen logistics.**

100 grams (3 1/2 oz) tarama paste
3 large potatoes
1 medium onion, grated
1 tablespoon chopped parsley
1 egg, beaten (optional)
freshly ground pepper, to taste

Boil the potatoes and then put them through a ricer to purée them. Mix the purée with the other ingredients when still hot. Make little balls, the size you prefer, between your palms, roll them in flour and fry in hot oil. The mixture can also be made the night before and kept in the refrigerator. Some people add a beaten egg as a binder but it isn't really necessary. Serves 8 as an appetizer.

# Shrimp-filled crepes

*Krépes me garídes*

**This is another recipe from the Rififi Cafe in Chania. Litsa, though a native of Messolonghi, exemplifies the eclecticism of Cretan cooking at its best. Not only has she mastered the intricacies of the local cuisine, but she also incorporates ideas from Asia Minor as in these crepes, and then adds her own inimitable touch.**

FOR THE BATTER
240 ml (1 cup) soda water
240 ml (1 cup) milk
210 grams (1 1/2 cup) flour
1 tablespoon melted butter
1/4 teaspoon salt

FOR THE SHRIMP FILLING
1/2 kilo (1 lb) shrimp, cleaned
juice of 1 lemon
4-5 spring onions, very finely
    chopped or processed
1 tablespoon finely chopped parsley
1 tablespoon olive oil
90 grams (3/4 cup) feta cheese, crumbled
cayenne pepper to taste
1 tablespoon flour
milk, breadcrumbs

Combine the first set of ingredients in a bowl to make a thin, smooth batter. Set aside.

Bring a cup of water mixed with the juice of one lemon to a boil. Add the shrimp and cook them until they turn pink. Drain and when they are cool enough, chop them into small pieces. Combine the shrimp with the other ingredients in a bowl and mix thoroughly.

Make the crepes in a hot non-stick or crepe pan. (Actually you can freeze crepes nicely, so you can have made these at any time.) Place a couple of tablespoons of filling in the center of each one. Litsa doesn't roll them like cannelloni, she folds the sides over towards the middle, paints the crepes with a little milk and rolls them in dried breadcrumbs before placing them in an oiled baking pan. Preheat the oven to 220°C (425°F) and bake until golden brown (about 10 minutes). Makes 12 crepes with a little filling left over.

# Marika's baked omelette
## Omelétta sto foúrno tis Maríkas

(EASTERN CRETE)

*2 medium zucchini*
*2 medium potatoes, peeled*
*2 small tomatoes, grated, skins discarded*
*6 tablespoons or more olive oil for frying*
*5 eggs, beaten*
*salt and freshly ground pepper*

**Marika Petraki has a taverna by the sea in the hamlet of Mochlos, opposite an islet where a Minoan cemetery has yielded many valuable artifacts. This is a dish she created for the team of archaeologists who used to dig there in the summers. The original recipe called for 25 eggs and a kilo of vegetables. Baked rather than fried, it resembles the *fritadas* of the Sephardic Jews rather than a French or even a Spanish omelette.**

**The Cretans also make thin stove-top omelettes with all kinds of vegetables, including wild asparagus, artichokes and mustard greens, often with the addition of tomato, onion and herbs. A typical Cretan omelette will have the vegetables sautéed first in olive oil and the beaten eggs poured over them. The dish is cooked over low heat with the pan covered. If you wish a lighter dish, beat the egg whites separately and fold them into the vegetable-yolk mixture just before you put the dish in the oven.**

Slice the zucchini and potatoes in thin rounds and fry them separately, browning them to your taste, in some olive oil. Drain them on paper towels. Pour off most of the oil, add the grated tomatoes and simmer for 5-10 minutes. Transfer all the vegetables to a lightly oiled pyrex souffle dish.

Preheat the oven to 190°C (375°F). Beat the eggs well, add them to the vegetable mixture, mix well and bake for 20 minutes. Serves 2.

# CRETAN PIES

## Píttes & Kallitsoúnia

I cannot begin to calculate the number of pies I must have eaten in the course of researching this book. At least half of the housewives I visited from Chania to Zakros, and especially in the villages, offered me a few little fried pies the moment I stepped into their kitchen. Whereas in other parts of the country a guest is routinely given a spoonful of sweet preserves with a glass of cold water, in Crete *kallitsounakia* seem to play the main role in this welcoming ritual and quantities of them are kept in the freezer. The word has its origins in the Italian "calzone" (or shoe), a pastry envelope folded over a filling, but while the concept is the same the Cretan version is much smaller and more delicate.

In what to some extent has become a blurry sequence of delicious but similar welcomes, one pie fest stands out. I was in Eastern Crete and having heard rumors about Georgia Vasilaki's prowess as a cook, I had told her over the phone that I wanted to learn how to make Cretan pastry. She obliged on condition that I eat a large square of honey-drenched walnut cake while she demonstrated five different techniques – yeast-leavened piroski, *sarikopittes* coiled like a sultan's turban, pancake-like *nerates*, baked cheese crescents and a fyllo-layered classic with greens. But what I will never forget was her and her husband's complete acceptance of me the unknown foreign stranger, their unconditional hospitality and their stories.

At first I sat alone in Georgia's small kitchen in Piskokefalo, a large village south of Siteia, while her husband Iosif watched the news on television. As she rolled out the pastry, shaped it into half moons or coils, baked and fried, she told me a bit about her life. "I grew up in Ziros. We had food but no money, and I didn't have a pair of shoes until I was fifteen. My father had a thousand sheep, though when he started he had only five. He slept outdoors with them for forty years and died at 100 without having ever seen a doctor. My mother was even busier. She made the cheese, took care of the pigs, did the laundry and cooked for us children. There were four of us but my sister had had osteomyelitis and she never recovered. Mother would walk the three hours from Ziros to Zakros carrying cheese to trade for her medicine. She died a little while ago at 98."

Even now Georgia and Iosif are virtually self-sufficient. Their one thousand olive trees in Ziros produce five tons of oil, their vines produce 250,000 drachmas worth of raisins. They raise all their own vegetables and rent pasture to a shepherd who pays them in cheese. When the news and baking were over, Iosif joined us in the kitchen. He brought out the wine (home-made, of course) and we sat until midnight nibbling the pies, sipping the wine and telling story after story. I finally left, carrying a doggie bag filled with pies, cake, raisins and a bottle of raki "for my husband." Ordinarily I wouldn't recommend basing a dinner party on five different pies preceded by walnut cake, but that evening the combination was magic.

Iosif told me a proverb as we parted. "As long as there is oil in the lamp it will light, so it is with the life of a person."

Although any of the pie recipes in the chapter can be considered meze material, the large baked ones are also suitable for a main course.

# * Foolproof kallitsounia pastry and basic filling

With this recipe you are guaranteed success, even if pie-making is a feat that has so far eluded you. My friend and colleague June Marinos learned it from a relative in Chania and has kindly passed it on. You can use it for any of the savory pie recipes described in this book. On the other hand, once you've gained confidence with this pastry, you'll probably be tempted to experiment with the others. The filling used is encountered from one end of Crete to the other, in towns and in villages. Cheese and mint seems to be a favorite Cretan marriage of tastes, the tangy mint giving the mild cheese a refreshing zip. But if you'd rather a hot than a cool effect, do as the Jews of Chania once did, add 1 or 2 finely chopped chili peppers to the cheese instead of mint.

FOR THE PASTRY
*350 grams (2 1/2 cups) (bread) flour*
*3 tablespoons olive oil*
*1/2 teaspoon salt*
*about 180 ml (3/4 cup) warm water*

FOR THE FILLING
*1/4 kg (2 cups) myzithra or*
  *a combination of cream cheese*
  *and ricotta*
*1 1/2 tablespoons chopped mint*

Make a well in the flour and add the olive oil and salt. Then swirl in the water, little by little, mixing with your fingers until you have a medium soft dough. Knead it with the heel of your hand for about 5 minutes, punching, rotating and pushing in the sides until it is smooth and malleable. Cover with cellophane wrap and set aside to rest in a cool place for at least 30 minutes. It will keep in the refrigerator for up to 3 days.

Drain the cheese on paper towels spread over layered newspapers if it is very loose and watery. Then with a fork, mash the cheese and mint together in a bowl until the cheese is smooth and well blended.

Separate the dough into 2-3 balls and roll out on a lightly floured surface until it is no more than a centimeter (1/3 of an inch) thick. Using a teacup or cookie cutter, cut the pastry into circles. Put a teaspoonful of filling in the center of each circle and fold one side over into a half moon. Press edges together to seal (a tiny bit of water on your finger will help). Repeat until you have used up all the pastry.

Fry in hot oil on both sides until very lightly browned, drain on paper towels and serve immediately.

This pastry freezes well. Makes about 18 half moon pielets.

By adding 1/2 kg (1 lb) spinach, washed and dried the previous evening, and increasing the chopped mint to 1/3 cup, to the cheese along with some salt and pepper, you can make another classic Cretan filling. Chop the spinach fairly finely along with the mint and then mix it with the cheese until thoroughly blended. Proceed as above.

# * Marika's miniature spinach pies
*Spanakopittákia tis Maríkas*

FOR THE PASTRY

*140 grams (1 cup) flour, sifted with*

*1/4 teaspoon salt*

*2 tablespoons olive oil*

*1 tablespoon fresh lemon juice*

*80 to 120 ml (1/3-1/2 cup) tepid water*

FOR THE FILLING

*1/2 kg (1 lb) spinach, washed and trimmed*

*250 grams (8 oz) Swiss chard, washed and trimmed*

*3 spring onions, finely chopped*

*1/2 cup finely chopped wild fennel leaves or bulb fennel tips (or if unavailable, dill)*

*2 tablespoons olive oil*

*1 teaspoon cumin*

*salt and freshly ground black pepper to taste*

**Marika Petraki has a taverna in Mochlos, a tiny fishing hamlet between Agios Nikolaos and Siteia that has somehow been overlooked by tourists. Marika's main customers are the archaeologists digging at the little island within swimming distance, where there was a Minoan settlement, shrine and cemetery. The miniature cheese and spinach pies that she serves at her taverna at Mochlos are among the lightest and most delicately flavored that I have tasted. Square in shape, they resemble big ravioli but they are fried, not boiled or baked. These pies keep well in the freezer and you can pull them out a few at a time. The recipe is easily doubled, the dough very manageable.**

Make a well in the flour, fill it with the olive oil and lemon juice and some of the water. Stir with your hands, adding water gradually, and knead until you have a tough dough. Cover with cellophane wrap and set aside for 30 minutes or more.

Boil the spinach and chard together in lots of water until tender. Drain thoroughly and when cool enough to handle, squeeze out as much water as you can. Chop finely (do not process), stalks included. In the meantime sauté the chopped onion and fennel leaves in the olive oil until the onions are soft and the fennel wilted. Then mix all the vegetables together in a bowl and season to taste with salt, pepper and cumin.

Roll out the dough as thin as you can. Cut into rectangles about 5 x 10 cm / 2 x 4 inches to a side. Put a tablespoonful of filling onto one half, fold over and pinch the sides to seal (moistening your index finger with water and running it around the edge will help) or press with a fork. When you have finished, you can either freeze the pies or fry them in hot oil and serve immediately. Makes about 30 pies.

# * Baked spinach "crepes"

*Krépes sto foúrno me spanáki*

(CHANIA)

**This is another recipe from the Rififi cafe in Chania. Though Litsa Anagnostaki calls these crepes, they are actually little pies with a yogurt-based crust. Like so many of her creations they have a touch of mint, her favorite seasoning. This pastry, made with olive oil and yogurt, may appeal to the health freak in you.**

**Litsa's kneading of the spinach before cooking is the method used in Western Crete; it produces a "crisper" taste and consistency than the Eastern Crete habit of boiling the spinach or other greens, squeezing out the liquid and then sauteing them with olive oil and onions, before putting them in pies. Either way works, you do what's best for you.**

Sift the flour, baking powder and salt together in a bowl and make a well in the middle of it. Pour in the yogurt and olive oil and swirl in the flour with your hands, a little at a time. The dough is ready when it no longer sticks to them. Wrap the dough in cellophane wrap and refrigerate for an hour or two. The dough will be smooth and soft and extremely easy to work with.

Meanwhile cut the spinach into fairly fine strips and knead it, pressing all the liquid out with your hands, as if you were wringing a raggedy sweater, over and over again until it is substantially reduced in size. As Litsa says, "This has to be hands-on work. Otherwise it can't be done." Then mix the spinach with the other ingredients in a large bowl. If you blend the cheese, mint and oil first, they combine more easily with the spinach.

To make the crepes, divide the dough into 12 "golf" balls and roll out each ball into a circle about 12 cm (5 inches) in diameter. Put a couple of tablespoons of filling in the center and fold over to make a half moon, pressing the edges together to seal. Preheat the oven to 190°C (375°F). Place all the crepes on an oiled rack over a baking tin, paint with a little milk and bake for about 30 minutes until golden. Makes 12 pies. Serve at once; equally good the next day warmed up.

FOR THE CREPES
*200 grams (1 cup) strained yogurt*
*60 ml (1/4 cup) olive oil*
*210 grams (1 1/2 cups) flour*
*1 scant teaspoon baking powder*
*1/2 teaspoon salt*

FOR THE FILLING
*250 grams (8 oz) spinach, washed and trimmed, tough stalks removed*
*2 spring onions, finely chopped*
*3 tablespoons finely chopped mint*
*2 tablespoons olive oil*
*100 grams (3/4 cup) myzithra or ricotta cheese*
*salt and freshly ground pepper to taste*

# * Cheese pies from Sfakia
## *Sfakianés píttes*

FOR 10 PIES
*210 grams (1 1/2 cups) flour*
*2 tablespoons olive oil*
*a pinch of salt*
*about 120 ml (1/2 cup) tepid water*
*450 grams (1 lb) myzithra or ricotta
    cheese*
*honey*

In the travel books of past centuries, adventurers were always remarking on the delicious little pies served up to them in the wilds. Robert Pashley, who visited Crete in the 1830s, had this to say about them after celebrating Easter at Askyfou: "Our fourth or fifth breakfast consisted of lamb, and fried cakes filled with a kind of cream cheese, and which are a very general article of feast-day food in Sfakia. They are about three times as thick as a common English pancake, of nearly the same superficial size. The Sfakians call them misethroftes."

Today they are still a popular snack anywhere near Sfakia, resembling crepes rather than pies. While they used to be cooked on a tile over a wood fire, they are now fried but on no account should any oil be added to the pan.

I had my first "genuine" Sfakian pie in Askyfou on the road between Vrysses and Hora Sfakion, watching the coaches rumble by filled with dozing passengers returning from their trek down the Samaria Gorge. It was prepared and served by Sifis Karkanis (photo), a not merely genuine but quintessential Sfakian. Mountain man turned cafe owner/cook, Sifis was dressed in the local "uniform" – black shirt, black trousers, knee-high black boots and mustache. Instead of the black tasseled head kerchief, he had trained his naturally wavy salt-and-pepper hair into a fetching ringlet that fell just so in the center of his forehead. Ruddy cheeked, blue eyed like so many Sfakians, he was a bit distant at first, perhaps thinking us ordinary foreign tourists or casual patrons. But when he realized it was stories we wanted, he sat down and obliged. We had the pies as a snack at 6 and then ordered all his specialties for dinner at 9. In between he talked.

Born and bred a shepherd, Sifis told us about trips up to the mountain pastures, where he learned to cook meat by making a fire between two stones, sweeping away the ashes and then simply placing the piece of meat like a sandwich filler on top of one and below the other; it roasted in 15 minutes. He talked about *Kouzina Ananghis* (the cuisine of necessity) when potatoes fried with rice and topped with a little cream (something shepherds always seem to have on hand!) was a meal fit for a king. Halva wrapped in foil, sprinkled with pepper and cinnamon and roasted on the coals; hyacinth bulbs cooked in the ashes like a baked potato; a stew simmered in a German soldier's helmet for want of a pot – Sifis made everything sound delicious. As for his pies and the rest of the meal, they were superb.

Make a softish dough with the flour, olive oil, salt and water. Let it rest for 30 minutes or so. If the cheese seems to contain some liquid, drain it on paper towels placed on several thicknesses of newspaper for an hour and squeeze out any remaining liquid. Divide the cheese into 10 chunks and roll them into balls between the palms of your hands.

Divide the dough into 10 portions, and, with your hands again, flatten each one into a round, flat "pancake" about the size of a salad plate. Cup the pancake in one hand, put one cheese ball in the center of it, close the sides over it and start working the cheese towards the edges, until you have a flat pancake once again. Fry in a crepe or nonstick frying pan for about 2 minutes on each side and serve with honey.

These pies freeze well but are rather tricky to execute.

# * Savory Easter cheese pies
## *Kallitsoúnia paschaliná*

FOR THE FILLING

*1/2 cup fresh mint leaves*

*200 grams (1 1/2 cup) myzithra or ricotta*

*200 grams (1 1/2 cup) anthotyro, curd cheese or soft goat's cheese*

*100 grams (3/4 cup) malaka or mozzarella, diced*

*1 egg*

*salt to taste*

FOR THE PASTRY

*250-300 grams (2 1/2-3 cups) sifted (cake) flour*

*180 ml (3/4 cup) warm water*

*2 tablespoons raki or vinegar*

*2 tablespoons olive oil*

*3 teaspoons lemon juice*

*1/2 teaspoon salt*

*beaten egg or a little milk for glaze*

*sesame seeds*

**These delicious little pies are a specialty of Chania and call for the three fresh cheeses the city is famous for – myzithra, anthotyro and malaka (see Cheeses, page 41). They will not be easy to find outside the island but you can achieve a similar result by using your local farmer's cheese, ricotta and mozzarella. It is also important to use a lot of fresh mint. Cretans seem to binge on cheese before and after Lent; I'm sure we would, too, if we'd fasted for 40 days.**

Prepare the pastry in the usual way by making a well in the flour, pouring the liquids in the well and swirling in the flour with your fingertips until you have a ball of dough. Knead well for about 5-7 minutes, cover and set aside to rest for at least 1 hour.

Wash and dry the mint leaves on a paper towel before chopping them finely. Put them in a bowl with the cheeses, egg and salt and beat together until smooth and creamy – the malaka/mozzarella should be the only lumps.

Preheat the oven to 200°C (400°F). Roll out the dough until it is about 1 cm (1/3 inch) thick and cut out circles about 9 cm (4 inches) in diameter with a teacup or cookie cutter. Place a tablespoon of filling near the center of each circle and fold over the other half to make a half moon. Press down on the rim to seal. Place the pies on a large, well-oiled baking pan, paint with beaten egg or a little milk and sprinkle with sesame seeds. Bake for 15 to 20 minutes or until the crust is golden. Makes about 40 pies.

# * Onion pies

## *Kremmydopittákia*

**Onions and herbs encased in pastry are yet another variation in the Cretan pie repertoire. These are sweet and aromatic.**

Prepare the pastry as usual, making a well in the flour and mixing in the liquids little by little until you have a soft dough. Knead well, cover and let rest for about 1 hour.

Toss the onions in a bowl with a little salt, mixing well with your fingers. Then sauté the onions in half the olive oil for about 10 minutes. Let cool and mix in the mint and fennel, flour and pepper.

Preheat the oven to 200°C (400°F). Roll out the dough until it is of medium thickness and cut out rounds with a glass or teacup. Place a tablespoon or 2 of filling on one side of each circle and fold over into a half-moon shape. Press the sides down, a little water on your fingertips will help them stick. Place the pies in an oiled baking tin and bake for about 20 minutes or until they are golden brown. Makes about 35 pies.

FOR THE PASTRY
*350-420 grams (2 1/2-3 cups) (bread) flour*
*1/4 teaspoon salt*
*2 tablespoons olive oil*
*2 tablespoons raki or vinegar*
*approximately 180 ml (3/4 cup) tepid water*

FOR THE FILLING
*4 big red (Bermuda) onions, coarsely grated*
*salt and freshly ground black pepper to taste*
*3 tablespoons olive oil*
*1-2 tablespoons flour*
*1/2 cup fresh finely chopped mint*
*1/2 cup finely chopped wild fennel or fennel bulb tips*

# * Spinach pie with wild greens
## *Hortópitta*

FOR A LARGE PIE

1 kg (2 lbs) assorted wild greens,
    washed and picked over
1/2 kg (1 lb) spinach, washed
    thoroughly and chopped
3 tablespoons finely chopped parsley
3 tablespoons finely chopped mint
3 tablespoons finely chopped fennel
    tips or dill
1 bunch spring onions, including 2-3
    inches of green, finely chopped
1 medium onion, finely chopped
200 grams (1 3/4 cups) feta,
    crumbled (optional)
120 ml (1/2 cup) olive oil
1 teaspoon sugar
salt, 1 teaspoon freshly ground pepper

FOR THE PASTRY

1 packet fyllo or
450 grams (1 lb) (bread) flour
4 tablespoons olive oil
1/2 teaspoon salt
120 ml (1/2 cup) red wine
approximately 240 ml (1 cup) warm
    water
olive oil for oiling the pan and
    painting the fyllo, if using

This is another of Marika Daskalogianni's recipes. She finds the little touch of sugar makes all the difference, bringing out the flavor of all the greens. Her other signature "trick" is to put red wine in her savory pastries, which gives them a special taste and turns them darker than conventional crusts.

In Crete, you don't have to live on a mountainside to take advantage of the island's prodigious number of greens. The mountainside can be found in every city market; some women put as many as fifteen different herbs/greens in their filling. And for those in a hurry, small bunches of wild greens called *yiachnera* can be bought in the Heraklio and Chania farmers' markets. *Yiachni* is a Turkish word that means meat, vegetables or pulses cooked with sautéed onions and tomatoes; thus *yiachnera* are to be simmered along with whatever else you have in the pot, or in this case the pie, to give it extra flavor. The mixture varies with the time of year. I have seen it include wild carrot, leek, wild fennel, spinach beet, while Paula Wolfert in her encyclopaedic compendium of *Mediterranean Grains and Greens* describes it as also containing salsify tops, corn poppy leaves, edible chrysanthemum and a furry thistle called eryngo, among other tender shoots.

For those of us who don't have access to this verdant wealth, we can experiment with such vegetables as collard or turnip greens, chicory (*radikia*), dandelion, broccoli rabe, curly endive, beet greens, Swiss chard, arugula. Try to have a mixture of sweet and bitter, but be careful, bitter greens are not to everyone's taste.

Before you chop the vegetables, try to squeeze all the water out of them with your hands. Then chop them all finely and mix the greens and spinach in a bowl with the herbs and the two kinds of onions. Lightly sauté them in a large pan with the olive oil (adding more oil if you wish or need to) and the other seasonings. When the greens have withered and lost their bulk, take off the heat and set aside. If you wish, mix in the crumbled feta at this point; it will make the greens a little less dense.

Preheat the oven to 190°C (375°F). Make a well in the flour and add the salt, liquid ingredients and a third of the water, swirling the flour into the well with your hand. Add the rest of the water slowly until you have a soft dough and knead it well to make it pliable. Separate the dough into two balls, one slightly larger than the other, and roll out a thin pastry with the larger one on a lightly floured surface.

Have ready a large (25 x 35 cm / 9 x 13 inches) buttered baking pan, line it with the pastry and place the sautéed greens on top of it. Roll out the second piece of dough and place it on top, folding over the edges to seal. With a sharp knife score the top into serving portions, and if desired paint with a little beaten egg yolk or milk. Bake for about 1 hour. Serves 8-10.

If you're using store-bought fyllo, oil a large baking tin (25 x 35 cm / 9 x 13 inches) and line it with 4 or 5 sheets of fyllo, painting each one with a little oil as you place it. Spread the greens on top and cover with 4 or 5 more sheets. Preheat the oven to 190°C (375°F). Cut the pie into serving portions, paint the top sheet with oil and bake for about 1 hour, or until the crust is golden brown.

# Sweetened liver and rice pie
## *Tzoulamás*

FOR THE FILLING

*450 grams (1/2 kg) pork liver or
    chicken livers*
*125 grams (1/4 lb) butter*
*300 grams (1 1/2 cups) long grain
    rice*
*1 liter (4 cups) chicken broth or a bit
    more*
*150 grams (1 cup) seedless raisins*
*150 grams (1 cup) almonds or
    walnuts, finely chopped*
*2-3 tablespoons sugar*
*salt and freshly ground black pepper*
*1/2 teaspoon cinnamon*

FOR THE PASTRY

*1 packet fyllo or homemade pastry
    made from*
*350 grams (2 1/2 cups) (bread) flour*
*2 tablespoons olive oil*
*1/2 teaspoon salt*
*about 180 ml (3/4 cup) warm water*

**This is one of the island's most unusual recipes and no one knows its origin. The combination of meat and rice with raisins, nuts and sugar sounds medieval – Arab or Byzantine. The sugar and cinnamon combined with liver and baked in oriental pastry echoes the famous Moroccan pigeon pie, *bisteeya*; raisins and pine nuts are often found in anatolian pilafs, but this is just a bit different. Nevertheless, despite its Turkish sounding name, there is no doubt that it is Cretan. It was eaten during the Carnival season. It also bears some resemblance to the Byzantine sausages, *omathies*, of page 134, which were a Christmas specialty.**

Cut the liver(s) into small pieces and sauté them in 2 tablespoons of the butter. Pour in the rice and stir until it becomes opaque before pouring in 850 ml (3 1/2 cups) of chicken broth. Cover the saucepan and simmer the rice, until the broth is absorbed. When there is still a little liquid in the pan, add the raisins and nuts and salt and pepper. Mix well.

Preheat the oven to 190°C (375°F). Prepare the pastry in the usual way to make a soft, pliable dough. Divide it in 3 parts and roll out the first until it is of normal thickness. Lay it in an oiled baking pan and sprinkle it with one third of the sugar and a little cinnamon. Spread half the filling, roll out and place the second sheet of pastry on top of it, dot with butter and sprinkle with sugar and cinnamon. Add the remaining filling and top with the final sheet of pastry. Pour the rest of the broth over the pastry, dot with the remaining butter, sprinkle on the remaining sugar and cinnamon and bake for about 30 minutes or until the crust turns a golden brown.

If using fyllo instead of home-made pastry, place 5 buttered sheets in the bottom, 3 in the middle and 4 on the top layer. Sprinkle with sugar and cinnamon in the same way and bake for 30 minutes. Serves 8 -10.

# PASTAS & PULSES

## Makarónia & 'Ospria

The Cretans are fond of pasta. In fact, in Eastern Crete macaroni boiled in lamb broth is the preferred dish at virtually all major celebrations the way pilaf is in the west of the island. Orzo and "kofto" (macaroni "cut" into fingertip size pieces) are very popular additions to meat and octopus stews, while braised cockerel with noodles and tomato sauce is a panhellenic favorite. After tasting home-made pasta in many Cretan homes, I also discovered that it can be every bit as good as that produced in Italy. Delicious though it may be, however, there are few recipes for pasta sauce, and it is usually eaten plain with a sprinkling of grated dry myzithra cheese.

Besides pasta from flour and water dough, the Cretans make another sort from cracked wheat and sour milk. Found all over Greece, Turkey and other parts of the Balkans, it is called *trahana* or *xinohondros* and has a sourish, earthy taste. It can be eaten on its own like porridge but is more often added to soups and stewed vegetables, not to mention snails.

As for pulses (legumes), they are eaten at least once a week in most Cretan households either in thick luscious soups, salads dressed with a vinaigrette and chopped herbs and onion, baked with other vegetables or molded into croquettes and fried.

Perhaps you wouldn't mind making pasta at home if you knew where to put the strands to dry. After looping them over the back of every chair in the kitchen, we came up with a space-saving solution. Rest a broom handle on the tops of two chairs, hang some coat hangers from it and drape your fresh noodles over them.

# Egg noodles
## *Hilopíttes*

1 kg (2 lbs) flour
5 eggs, beaten
240 ml (1 cup) milk, approximately
1 teaspoon salt

**In Greece, these egg noodles are usually cut into tiny squares for some reason, but if you prefer simply leave them long. They dry nicely and will keep in an airtight container indefinitely.**

Sift the flour and salt into a large bowl. Make a well in the center and pour in the milk, salt and eggs. Mix in the flour gradually (add a little milk or flour if you have to) until you have a fairly tough dough. Knead on a lightly floured surface for about 10 minutes until it is smooth but firm (don't worry if it seems stiff and unelastic, it just needs to rest). Set aside, wrapped in cling film, for an hour.

Separate the dough into 10 balls and flatten them with your hands. Roll out each ball into the thinnest possible strip with a rolling pin. Or if you're using a pasta machine, insert the first piece into the largest opening 2 or 3 times before proceeding to the next settings up to no. 5, until you have a long thin strip. Do the same with the other balls. Cover the rest of the dough with a damp cloth while you work. Spread the strips out on a floured table or board and cut the pasta into squares about the size of a paper napkin. Then cut these into tiny (1 cm / 1/3 inch) squares, if you want to be traditional. Lay the pasta on a cloth to dry, but don't let the squares touch each other or they'll stick together. If you don't boil the noodles right away, store them in a metal tin. Serve with stews, plain with butter and grated cheese or with your favorite sauce.

# Fresh pasta, half boiled, half fried
## *Mangíri*

For conventional long thin noodles, simply cut each strip into ribbons about 1 cm (1/3 inch) wide, and dry on hangers as on previous page.

**This is nostalgia food. Everyone who talked about this dish described this treat from their childhood as if it were the greatest delicacy. It**

would certainly appeal to anyone who, like my husband, finds fried left-over spaghetti the best of snacks. This combination is also a favorite in the southern Italian region of Apulia, where it is served with chick peas.

Using the above recipe for egg noodles, boil two-thirds of the noodles in a little salted water. Note the difference here from cooking Italian pasta which requires a large amount of water. For mangiri, the noodles should absorb almost all the water. Meanwhile, fry the rest of the noodles in a pan with two or three tablespoons of olive oil, stirring, until the pasta is crunchy. Put the boiled noodles into a bowl, pour the fried noodles and their oil on top of them, and serve with grated cheese. If you're a garlic lover, sauté a tablespoon of chopped garlic along with the noodles.

Other cooks maintain that mangiri should be made without eggs, so here is another version:

## Eggless noodles

Sift the flour into a large bowl and make a well in it. Put the salt, lemon juice, olive oil and vinegar in a jar, screw it tight and shake vigorously for a minute. Pour the contents into the well. With your hands, slowly mix in the flour until you have a well-blended dough. Knead for about 15 minutes, cover and let rest in a cool place for about 1 hour.

Separate the dough into 10 more or less equal parts and roll out one by one into long, thin rectangles. Cut each piece into narrow strips 2 cm (2/3 inch) wide and then (if you have the patience) into 3 cm (1 inch) squares. Divide the pasta into two.

Fry one half in hot olive oil until crisp and set aside to drain on paper towels. Then boil the other half in 1 1/2 - 2 liters (6-8 cups) of salted water (this takes only a couple of minutes). Place the boiled pasta in a bowl with a little of its water, top with the fried noodles and some of the frying oil, if desired. Serve with freshly ground pepper and grated cheese. Serves 6.

You can of course make these using the pasta machine. I find they are better if a little thicker than fettucine, so you could stop with the no. 4 setting.

*1/2 kg (1 lb) (cake) flour*
*1 teaspoon salt*
*1 tablespoon lemon juice*
*2 tablespoons white wine vinegar*
*60 ml (1/4 cup) olive oil plus olive*
*    oil for frying*
*grated cheese*

# Cretan lazania, as made in Eastern Crete

The name's the same but there's no similarity with lasagna as we know it – either as flat sheets of pasta or noodles. Being about 2 inches long, these macaroni curls most resemble the cavatelli of Puglia. And like cavatelli, they require enormous patience and team work plus a knack with the knitting needle. Maria Pangalou (photo) made them for me one brisk October evening in her home in Krousta, a village about 30 minutes drive and at least fifty years away from the luxury hotel at Elounda where her daughter Popi works.

Like most Cretan cooks, she dispensed with wooden spoons and mixers in favor of her fingers and quickly stirred the simplest of doughs, just water and flour (ground from the family's wheat) – the same that she would use for her cheese pies – and then to my surprise unveiled her Italian pasta machine. I was to discover that this is standard equipment in most Cretan kitchens, not as an aid to making spaghetti but rather for the ultra thin wrappings for kallitsounia and the other pies in every cook's repertoire. She then fed the machine hamburger-size patties of dough until she had a droopy sash about 1 1/2 meters (4 1/2 feet) long. These she placed on her floured pasta board, which looked like an heirloom, and Popi cut them into 5 cm (2 inch) squares. Then, one by one, we all set to winding these squares, starting at one corner, around a souvlaki stick (knitting needles being strung with sweater wool), placing them on a pink and white striped tablecloth (woven by Maria), until we'd finished the dough and the table was full. I have to admit that my few labored twirls were not nearly as neat and precise as theirs.

In the old days, Maria told me, they would have rolled long snakes of dough between their hands, cut it into 7-9 cm (3-4 inch) pieces and then pressed down with three fingers to make a kind of thick but hollow tube.

Maria cooked a handful for me in a small saucepan with a little water and sprinkled the plate with grated hard myzithra before she ladled them out, still dripping. They were delicious and for the umpteenth time I wondered why, given four hundred years of Venetian occupation, pasta does not have a stronger grip on Cretan appetites and why they have not invented a host of gorgeous sauces to go with it rather than eating it plain.

A straight-forward woman with wide-set, intelligent brown eyes, Maria has the erect bearing and high cheekbones of a Sioux. And while she is only just past the half century mark, she clearly believes the old ways are good ways. Although she has an electric stove, she does all her cooking (when she's not using the wood-burning oven in the courtyard) perched on a low stool in front of the fireplace, where she's placed a basic two-burner gas cooker. Tucked around it are all the necessaries – jam jars with salt, olive oil, rigani.

Maria's kitchen was literally the family living room. It had an upholstered sofa, where her elderly mother sat swathed in several layers of sweaters, a glass-doored cabinet where the best china and glasses were kept along with tulle-wrapped sugared almonds from her daughter's wedding, reproductions of bucolic scenes on the walls and her grandson's red teddy bear atop the TV. The kitchen had wonderful workspaces – a large table, a special board for drying and cutting pasta, a smaller table where I propped my notebook. Bunches of drying herbs hung from the shelves, below jars of olives and a row of large plastic Coke bottles stuffed with vacuum-packed vine leaves. There was home-made cheese in the fridge, home-made wine in the barrel, home-made bread in the bin, and then she told me she'd woven all the contents of her daughter's dower chest.

"When I was young, we used to gather our almonds and olives and with the money from selling them, we'd buy silkworms, gorge them on mulberry leaves and months later unwind their silk thread. We would embroider like mad in those days. Popi's sheets, curtains and tablecloths are woven with a blend of wool and silk. I made her rugs and blankets, too. But they're all sitting in a trunk. Her husband wanted store-bought curtains."

# Spaghetti with sun-dried tomatoes and feta

*Makaronáda me iliópastes domátes kai féta*

*4-5 spring onions, cut in thin strips*
*4-5 garlic cloves, thinly sliced*
*10 sun-dried tomatoes, cut in thin strips*
*100 grams (3/4 cup) feta, cubed*
*200-300 grams (half a packet) thin spaghetti*

**This recipe is from Chrysanna Karelli, who owns one of Heraklio's most upmarket restaurants. The Pagopoieon (Old Ice House) near St. Titus's Square is glamorous and exotic, the wine cellar is excellent and the food imaginative, decorative and delicious. Chrysanna believes that "whatever you eat should make you feel sexy, not leaden and weighted down." This dish definitely meets that criterion.**

Sauté the onions and garlic in a few tablespoons of the oil from the sun-dried tomatoes. When they are soft, add the tomatoes, cook for a few minutes and then add the feta. Cook over a low heat stirring for another 5 minutes. Pour over freshly boiled, al dente pasta. Delicious, quick and easy. Serves 2.

Many of the Pagopoieon's patrons like to sit at the bar after the theater or the movies. Both for their benefit and hers, Chrysanna offers anyone still drinking when the restaurant closes at 1 am, something that will stick to the ribs and "anchor" the alcohol. Usually this freebie is pilaf or spaghetti cooked in the broth made from a year-old goat, trimmed of all fat.

# Trahaná or xinóhondros

*Hondros* means coarsely ground wheat. When it is parboiled, it becomes bulgur, which became famous in the west as the main ingredient in the Lebanese salad tabbouleh. But *xinohondros*, sour cracked wheat, is the Cretan name for a food that is a staple all over the Balkans. Known in Turkey as *tarhana*, in the Middle East as *kishk* and in the rest of Greece as trahana, it is cracked wheat that has been boiled with soured milk until all the liquid is absorbed and then left out in the sun to dry. Properly stored, this ingenious way of preserving both wheat and milk has an almost infinite shelf-life.

While I find the slightly sour, earthy flavor of Cretan trahana irresistible, there are those, like the English explorer T.A.B. Spratt, who have turned their nose up at it. In 1865 he wrote this after sampling it for the first time: *"His [the abbot's] kind hospitality ... soon provides me with a supply of milk and a porridge of new wheat and sour curds, which is called Xino Vari (heavy acid – a name truly characteristic of its nature), which I am obliged to take and pronounce excellent. No doubt in early times, as now, this was a Cretan dish, though one which only Spartan palates could relish or Spartan stomachs digest."*

In fact, although some food historians think the porridge made from it cannot be very different from the gruel that formed the basis of the daily diet in ancient Greece and Rome, it may be an invention of Turkic nomadic tribes who needed portable nourishment. You can find it in Greek and Middle Eastern groceries, but look for brands that appear homemade. The factory-produced variety resembling tiny white wampum beads is bland and tasteless. Turkish *tarhana* is often blended with tomatoes, onions, celery and wild carrot and even fruit, cherries for example.

# Homemade cracked wheat pasta

*Trahaná or xinóhondros*

*400 grams (2 cups) cracked wheat*
*960 ml (4 cups) fresh milk (goat's milk is best, but cow's will do)*
*coarse sea salt*

**I developed a passion for this "primitive" pasta while I was researching this book. Many country women still grind the wheat themselves in the heavy stone handmill which was once standard equipment in every Cretan house. They boil it together with soured milk and spread it out in the sun to dry for a week or two before storing it in large sacks in their capacious larders. Invariably they would press me to take a little bag of it with me – I never left a Cretan home empty handed, in any case. Sometimes the grains would look no different than coarse bulgur, sometimes they would be stuck together in small clumps, but sometimes they would resemble little nests the size of the woman's palms and the imprint of her fingers would be embedded in them.**

**Trahana is rock hard but loosens up when added to liquid. It heightens the flavor of vegetable and meat soups, giving them a piquant earthy quality. It can also be a substitute for meat as in the next couple of stew recipes.**

**If you can't find it locally, you can try making it yourself according to the following instructions given to me by Eftyhia Mavrokosta, an archetypal little old lady in black who lives in a mountain hamlet named Kalohori or Good Village south of Heraklio. She makes it in July when the sun is hottest.**

Boil the milk, add a little salt, and set covered with a clean cloth in a warm place. Give it a good stir every 2 days – it can stay as long as 10 days – or until bubbles start to form. (It should smell sour but not nasty.) Most people think 3 to 4 days are enough for the milk to sour.

Put the sour milk in a large saucepan and when it starts to boil add the wheat slowly and stir constantly, until tender and thick. Eftyhia, who makes it with 20 kilos (44 lbs) of milk and 4 kilos (almost 9 lbs) of wheat, stirs it with a thin rolling pin and when the stick stands up by itself, she stops adding wheat (anywhere from 15 to 30 minutes). Cover the saucepan and let stand overnight. The next day break it into clumps with your hands, place them on a tray or cloth and leave them in the sun, turning from time to time, until completely dry.

Make sure to keep it away from cats; in their *Traditional Cretan Cooking*, M. and N. Psilakis warn that felines are the greatest hazard since they love it almost as much as catnip.

# Trahana stew
*Xinóhondros stifádo me kremmydákia*

(ELOS, WESTERN CRETE)

**This recipe uses the tiny onions preferred for the rich stews in which hare or veal are usually the main feature. This is an invention of the "kitchen of necessity" referred to by many cooks from the Cretan mountains, who did all they could to make their meager ingredients as tasty as possible. Anyone who has come to crave the earthy, "ancient" taste of trahana will love this combination. The women of western Crete also used to dry tomatoes, a special egg-shaped variety known locally as *amouschlodomates*, for winter cooking. This is a stick-to-your-ribs stew for a frosty evening by the fireplace.**

*1 kg (2 lbs) stewing onions*
*120 ml (1/2 cup) olive oil*
*10 whole black peppercorns*
*1 medium tomato, grated, skin discarded and 1 teaspoon tomato paste or*
*4 sun-dried tomatoes, chopped*
*250 grams (2 cups) "sour" trahana*
*1 bay leaf*
*1 piece dried orange peel (optional)*
*360 ml (1 1/2 cups) warm water or half water/half red wine*
*cayenne pepper to taste*
*salt and freshly ground pepper, to taste*

Peel the onions and make a little cross at their base to help them cook more quickly. Heat the olive oil in a deep nonstick pan and brown the onions with the peppercorns for at least 20 minutes or until they start to soften. Then stir in the grated tomato and tomato paste or sun-dried tomatoes and the trahana, coating it with the oil. Add the bay leaf, orange peel, seasonings and the warm water/wine and simmer until the trahana is soft – like rice or bulgur – and the water absorbed. Add more water if necessary. Serves 6 as a main dish or 8 as a side dish for roast meat or chicken.

If your trahana consists of large chunks, you may want to soak it in a little warm water first and separate the clumps of grain; sometimes they stick together and do not cook evenly.

# Eggplant with trahana or bulgur
## *Melitzánes me xinóhondro i bligoúri*

*1 kg (2 lbs) long, skinny eggplant, washed*

*120 ml (1/2 cup) olive oil*

*2 large onions, chopped*

*2 cloves garlic, chopped*

*2 tomatoes, grated, skins discarded or 1 tablespoon tomato paste diluted in 240 ml (a cup) of water*

*1/2 cup chopped parsley*

*2 bay leaves*

*360 ml (1 1/2 cups) or more of water or chicken or meat stock*

*250 grams (1 1/2 cups) trahana or bulgur*

*freshly ground black pepper*

**This is another dish left over from the days when cracked wheat was far more common than rice. Although it is the essence of simplicity, the sweetness of the onions and eggplant and the slightly sour grain give it a wonderfully complex flavor.**

Remove the stems and cut the eggplant in thick slices about 2.5 cm (1 inch) thick. Soak them for 30 to 60 minutes in a large bowl with salted water to leach out any bitterness. With your hands squeeze out as much liquid as possible.

Heat the olive oil in a large nonstick frying pan and sauté the onions and garlic until they begin to soften. Add the eggplant and continue to sauté, stirring to color them on both sides. Mix in the tomatoes or tomato paste, parsley and bay leaves. Cover the pan to coax the liquid out of the tomatoes for five minutes, reduce heat to a simmer and if necessary add a little water or broth if the eggplants start to stick.

When the eggplants are half done, stir in the trahana or bulgur, add 240 ml (1 cup) of water or broth, cover and simmer until the liquid has been absorbed and the grains are tender. Check the pan from time to time to make sure they are not sticking and add more liquid as necessary. Season with freshly ground black pepper. Serves 6.

# Lentils and rice
## *Fakórizo*

This is a recipe for leftover lentil soup or stew. For 480-720 ml (2-3 cups) of lentil soup use 50 grams (1/4 cup) of rice. Wash the rice and sauté it in 2 tablespoons of olive oil until the grains become opaque. Stir in 1 teaspoon of tomato paste and then add the lentil soup, pouring in a little water if necessary, from time to time. When the rice is tender, season with cumin and freshly ground pepper and you have supper for two or three. Lentil soup is even more delicious with a handful of trahana stirred into it about 15 minutes before it's ready.

In some parts of Crete you will see strips of orange peel hanging to dry from window handles, door knobs, plate racks, almost anywhere in fact. Cretan cooks like to add orange peel to lentil soup, bean soup, black-eyed peas, fava beans and meat stews.

# Black-eyed peas with rice
## *Fasoulórizo*

**More often than not, this would be a way to use up leftover beans or rice, but it is a typical example of Cretan nutritional good sense. In Eastern Crete this dish was eaten on November 21, a day commemorating the Presentation (dedication) of the young Virgin Mary to Solomon's temple in Jerusalem, where she remained for twelve years before her betrothal to Joseph.**

*150 grams (1 cup) black-eyed peas*
*60 ml (1/4 cup) olive oil*
*1 large onion, finely chopped*
*150 grams (3/4 cup) long grain rice*
*salt and freshly ground pepper*
*3 tablespoons finely chopped parsley*

Boil the beans in plenty of water until just tender, and drain in a colander. Pour cold water over them to keep them from splitting, drain again and set aside. Sauté the onions in the olive oil until translucent. Then add the rice, stirring for about 5 minutes until the grains become opaque (as if you were making a pilaf). Add 360 ml (1 1/2 cups) of water, cover and simmer until the rice is almost cooked, about 15 minutes.

Stir in the beans, season and cook gently for another 5 minutes or until the rice is tender and the beans heated through. Sprinkle with the chopped parsley and serve. Serves 4.

As a variation on this, you could mix left-over lentils with rice, warming them up in a saucepan with a little olive oil, tomato paste and water and seasoning the dish with pepper and cumin.

# Maro's chick pea fritters

*Revithokeftédes tis Máros*

**FOR THE FRITTERS**

*250 grams (1/2 lb) chick peas
(garbanzos), soaked overnight*

*3 onions, finely chopped*

*1 handful finely chopped mint leaves*

*2 big tablespoons finely chopped
parsley*

*salt and freshly ground pepper, to
taste*

*1 tablespoon cumin (optional)*

*2 big pinches oregano*

*2 1/2-3 heaping tablespoons flour*

**FOR THE GARNISH**

*red, green and yellow peppers
(1 each), sliced in thin rounds*

*2 cloves garlic, crushed (optional)*

*4 tomatoes, cubed*

*olive oil for frying*

**I met Maro Manolidou on one of those days that are so clear and vibrant the Greeks call them "the joy of God." So instead of chatting in a portside coffee shop, she took me up into the hills to a place appropriately named Doxa or "Glory," half way between Heraklio and heaven. Condors were whirling overhead, swathes of bright yellow and new green shone on the slopes, and on closer inspection I saw that the earth by the road was speckled with white cyclamen, small lapis-blue irises and pink orchids with velvety black bodies that look like bumblebees. We pulled into a simple cafe whose name should have been Panorama and ate *tiganites* (Cretan pancakes) with honey and tiny pies filled with wild greens while we talked about food and life and I gaped at the view.**

**Maro has never opened a cookbook, but she loves to cook and would not dream of "having people over to sit around a pizza rather than giving them something special." With her touch, chick pea patties become indeed something special.**

Grind the chick peas in a meat grinder or food processor. Place them in a bowl with the chopped onion, mint, parsley, salt, pepper, cumin and oregano. Slowly add the flour, kneading the mixture with your hands until you can form balls with it.

Make the mixture into flat patties, about 1 1/2 cm (1/2 inch) thick and 8 cm (3 inches) in diameter. You can either fry the patties right away or let them rest for several hours for the flavors to blend.

Have ready two large frying pans, one for the patties, the other for the vegetable sauce. First fry the patties in a few tablespoons of hot olive oil, browning them on both sides. Drain them on paper towels and set aside.

Heat a few tablespoons of olive oil in the other pan and sauté the peppers for 5 minutes, then add the tomatoes and crushed garlic (if using) together with 1/4 cup of water and cook quickly – they should not disintegrate. While there is still a little liquid in the pan, add the patties and cook a further 2 minutes on each side. Arrange them on a platter with the colorful vegetables and serve. Makes about 30 patties.

# A harvest dish of mixed beans, hulled wheat and corn

*Papoudiá*

(ALL CRETE)

It is said that this dish goes back thousands of years and may even have been made by the Minoans. Psilakis compares it to the *panspermia* (all seeds) offered by both the Minoans and ancient Greeks to their gods in thanks for a successful harvest. One of the many names for this living artifact is *Photopapouda*, because it is traditionally eaten on the eve of Epiphany, the Day of Light, January 6th, when Jesus was baptized. Up until recently not only was it fed to all the family members but also to the farm animals, particularly those that plowed the fields and even the wild birds. In Eastern Crete it is also called *Pallikaria*, which means gallant youths, but the connection is obscure. For this dish you need all the pulses you can get your hands on. The amounts can vary depending on how many mouths are to be fed, domestic and otherwise.

*200 grams (1 cup) hulled wheat*
*200 grams (1 cup) chick peas*
*200 grams (1 cup) borlotti beans*
*200 grams (1 cup) fava beans*
*200 grams (1 cup) lentils*
*200 grams (1 cup) dried sweet corn,*
*    called kechri in Greek*
*1 large onion, chopped*
*60 ml (1/4 cup) olive oil*
*lemon juice, to taste*
*salt and freshly ground pepper*
*3 tablespoons chopped dill*

Soak all the pulses except the lentils separately overnight in water to cover. The next day drain, rinse and boil them together in plenty of water for about 2 hours until they begin to soften. Before you add the fava beans to the pot, peel off the little black "tail" and the outer skin. When all the legumes are tender, drain, saving a little of the cooking water, and toss them with chopped onion, olive oil, lemon juice and seasonings. Can be eaten warm or the next day at room temperature.

# Bean soup
## *Fasoláda*

500 grams (1 lb) haricot beans,
    soaked overnight
2-3 carrots, cubed
2-3 celery sticks, sliced thinly
1 large or 2 medium onions, chopped
2 tablespoons chopped parsley
120 ml (1/2 cup) olive oil
1 (450-gram / 16-oz) tin chopped
    tomatoes
1 tablespoon cumin
salt and freshly ground pepper

**Some people think of bean soup as the Greek national dish, it is so ubiquitous and such a universal favorite. Mary Daskalaki of Zakros has the secret to making perfect fasolada. She discards the water from the first boiling, puts the beans back to boil with the carrots, onions and celery but does not add the olive oil and chopped tomatoes until the skins on a spoonful of beans puff up when she blows on them. Olive oil, tomatoes and salt slow down the cooking, making it practically impossible for the beans to soften.**

Place the beans in a large saucepan and cover with cold water. Bring to the boil and then drain. Rinse the saucepan, replace the beans and add the carrots, celery, onions, parsley and fresh water to cover. Bring to the boil and simmer until the beans are just tender (you can try blowing on them to see whether they are ready). Then add the olive oil, chopped tomatoes and seasonings, and boil vigorously for 10-15 minutes. Serves 6.

Other cooks believe that a sliced potato added to the other vegetables will reduce the beans' "tooting potential", that a strip of dried orange peel improves the flavor, and that a chili pepper makes it even better.

The Cretan kitchen is not noted for any soups besides those containing fish or pulses. Strangely, other soups – based on chicken, meat or vegetable broth – are considered by most to be only fit for the sick and old.

# FISH & SEAFOOD

## Psária kai Thalassiná

"*C anea is ill provided with fishermen. There are six boats owned by Italians or Maltese. When it is fine their red sails, all in a line, against the blue sea are a pretty sight; but they are excessively prudent and never go out far enough to catch anything big.*" (Charles Edwardes, 1890)

Though surrounded by water, the Cretans are not first and foremost seafarers but people of the land – farmers and shepherds preoccupied with their olives, vines, fields and flocks. Historically, the coasts have been dangerous places, open to pirate raids and subject to volatile, sudden storms. Nowadays with better weather reports and more modern equipment, fishermen are less cautious about hugging the shore and the markets have an ample supply of "big" pelagic fish, but the preference still seems to be for rockfish like groupers, scorpion fish, bream, parrotfish and the miscellaneous smaller fry – sardines, anchovies and the like – that hover on the surface. Other favorites are the frightening gape-mouthed monkfish, whose tail is firm and absolutely delicious, and the red mullet whose endearing whiskers give it its Greek name *barbouni*.

Apart from these fish, there is an abundance of seafood, especially that of the cephalopod family – octopus, squid and cuttlefish. These too do not require braving the open sea, and one very common sight is a row boat with a man leaning over the prow, head invisible inside a cylindrical can, searching for the tell-tale signs of an octopus, while his mate dips heavy oars gently into the glassy waters. If he spies the beast itself down plunges his trident into its leathery head, but if he only sees the white stones lined up neatly around a hole in the sand or an opening in a rock wall, he may try to lure it out with a line tied around a stone from which flutters a white hanky. Octopuses are so fond of white that they will cling to the hanky and stone all the way to the surface. Shrimp, lobster and mussels are relatively recent additions to the Cretan table; in the old days, people were content with limpets, tiny snails and sea urchins, plucked gingerly from the rocks.

Whereas in other coastal areas around Greece, people are hard put to give you recipes for fish other than the most straightforward "boiled, fried or grilled" – the natural response to freshness – the Cretans add to those a wealth of dishes involving fish or seafood and vegetables. At times, the catch from the sea seems almost an afterthought, something to accompany the bounty from the garden. But the combinations, though unfamiliar, endow both vegetables and fish with new dimensions of taste.

# Parrotfish with tomatoes and onion

*Skáros me domátes kai kremmýdi*

(SITEIA)

The parrotfish, so-called because of its beakish mouth and flamboyant coloring – the male being a deep reddish-purple with yellow trim – is plentiful in the warm waters around Crete. Highly prized for its white, delicate flesh, it is usually cooked intact, with only the gall bladder removed. For this dish, however, it is probably preferable to get rid of its large, carp-like scales.

When G.O. Dapper visited the island in 1703, he recorded a curious custom. It seems that parrotfish love to dine on stringbean leaves, so the monasteries and peasants grew vast quantities, eating the beans themselves and using the leaves as bait. They would entwine the leaves in their nets, attracting the fish, which were otherwise very difficult to catch. Even today, parrotfish are trapped with zucchini leaves. One wonders who discovered this bizarre craving.

Marika Petraki often cooks parrotfish at her taverna under the tamarisk trees at Mochlos. She told me that the parrotfish is indeed a vegetarian but that the squash leaves used to tempt it also act as a purge, which is why it is unnecessary to remove any innards except for the gall bladder.

If your fishmonger doesn't stock parrotfish, substitute a large bream, red snapper or monkfish tail in this recipe.

1 whole parrotfish, about 1 kg (2 lbs), gall bladder removed
3-4 tablespoons olive oil
1 large onion, finely chopped
1-2 cloves garlic, sliced
half a bunch parsley, finely chopped
4 medium tomatoes, grated, skins discarded or 1 tablespoon tomato paste diluted in 240 ml (1 cup) hot water
salt and freshly ground pepper, to taste
1 tablespoon cumin

In a nonstick saucepan large enough to hold the fish, heat the olive oil and fry the fish whole, 5 minutes on each side. Remove the fish and drain on paper towels. In the same oil sauté the onion, garlic and parsley, until the onion is soft but not browned. Add the tomatoes or tomato paste, salt and pepper and boil gently, covered, for 15 to 20 minutes. Stir in the cumin.

Preheat the oven to 200°C (400°F). Place the fish in a nonstick roasting pan, cover it with the sauce, bring it to the boil on top of the stove and put it in the oven to bake for another 20 minutes or so or until the flesh flakes easily when tested with a fork. Serves 3-4.

# Grouper with okra

*Rofós me bámyes*

1 kg (2 lbs) okra, washed
240 ml (1 cup) strained lemon juice
    for the fish and the okra
1 whole fish, preferably grouper
    (1 1/2 kg / 3 lbs), scaled and
    cleaned
salt and freshly ground pepper
1 large onion, sliced
3 cloves garlic, chopped
6 tablespoons olive oil
3/4 kg (1 1/2 lbs) tomatoes, grated,
    skins discarded
3 tablespoons chopped parsley

**This recipe comes from Agapi Hourdaki who has a taverna by the sea at Petres about 20 kilometers west of Rethymno. Besides cooking, she also spearfishes, harvests sea urchins for sea urchin salad and collects limpets, clams, winkles and small crabs for a delicious sauce for pilaf or spaghetti. In this dish, the firm, tangy okra are an admirable counterbalance to the sweet, soft flesh of the grouper. The Duke of Kent is among the many notables who have dined at her taverna.**

Trim the tips of the okra, if desired (see introductory note p. 136) and toss them in a bowl with 1-2 tablespoons salt and 120 ml (1/2 cup) of lemon juice. Set them aside (in the sun, if possible, or in a very low oven) for 1-2 hours.

Marinate the fish in another bowl with the rest of the lemon juice, salt and pepper and refrigerate until 30 minutes before you're ready to cook.

Sauté the onions and garlic in the oil until soft and translucent, then add the okra, tomatoes and pepper and simmer, covered, for 10 minutes, stirring in the chopped parsley at the very end.

Meanwhile, preheat the oven to 190°C (375°F) and lightly oil a baking pan large enough to hold the fish. When the vegetables have given up some of their liquid, line the pan with half of them, place the fish on top, and cover the fish with the rest. Bake for about 1 hour or until the fish flakes easily even close to the backbone. Serves 4-6.

# * Danae's spicy sardines

*Vrastí sardélla*

**Though Danae Malinaki calls these boiled, in this non-typical dish they are in fact steamed in their own juices. Flavored with bay leaf, lemon and hot red pepper, they are more succulent than you ever thought a sardine could be. The addition of crushed chilis is unusual for Crete, but is not unheard of in the districts west of Chania.**

**I won't give exact amounts for this dish, since the proportions depend on how big your saucepan is and how many fish you feel like preparing.**

*large sardines*
*bay leaves (optional)*
*lemon slices and the juice of 2 or 3 lemons*
*2-3 tablespoons olive oil*
*chili pepper flakes or freshly cracked black pepper*

Try to get hold of large sardines for this dish. Danae prefers to make this in the summer when these fish have no scales. Clean and gut the fish. If you cut off their heads, the innards come too. Wash them well, two or three times.

Line a heavy bottomed large saucepan with bay leaves or with lemon slices. Pack the sardines into the saucepan tightly, but don't put more than one layer of the fish. Add the juice of 2 or 3 lemons, red pepper flakes or cracked black peppercorns, and a little olive oil. Cover the pan and bring to the boil. When you hear the sound of boiling, turn down the heat to the lowest possible and simmer for 15 minutes. Smaller fish will be ready in 10.

You can also cook this dish in the oven (200°C or 400°F) in a pyrex covered with aluminum foil. The fish are delicious hot or cold.

# Fish with artichokes
*Psári me anginánes*

*fish, 4-6 slices*
*lemon juice*
*salt and freshly ground pepper to*
*    taste*
*8 medium artichokes*
*1 bunch (7-8) spring onions,*
*    chopped*
*80 ml (1/3 cup) olive oil*
*4 medium potatoes, sliced (optional)*
*1/4 cup chopped parsley*
*1/4 cup chopped dill or fennel leaves*
*salt and freshly ground pepper*

FOR THE SAUCE
*juice of 1-2 lemons*
*1 heaping tablespoon flour*

**The villages on the high corniche between Agios Nikolaos and Siteia are among the prettiest in Crete. They have a magnificent view of the expansive Mirabello Bay and each of them has at least one superb church. I remember the church in Myrsini best: walls as white as icing sugar, with soft honey-colored stone windows and doorways sculpted with garlands of flowers wreathing a round-faced St. George on rearing horse or Madonna and child, half-moon cupolas the dark red of sun-dried tomatoes, and above them twin gables topped with double scrolls from which a small cross rises. The people I met there and the food they cooked were as delightful as their architecture.**

**This dish is an example. Its invention can probably be attributed to the prodigious amounts of artichokes produced in Crete each spring. While artichokes and lamb or kid are stewed together all over Greece, this is a rather unconventional marriage. But in fact I find the delicate flavors of the herbs and artichokes even better suited to fish than to meat. Use thick slices of white fish with few bones or, if you prefer, a whole fish. The potatoes are added for the sake of economy, to make the dish go further. Any of the grouper family or large bream would be appropriate here.**

*As told by both Despina Makrynaki in Myrsini,*
*and Marika Petraki in Mochlos.*

Marinate the fish in lemon juice, salt and pepper until you're ready to cook. Keep, covered, in the fridge.

Clean the artichokes by removing the tough outer leaves and tips. Halve them, scrape out the chokes and cut them into slices about 1.5 cm (1/2 inch) thick. Drop them into a bowl of water acidulated with some lemon juice to prevent them from darkening while you prepare the rest of the vegetables.

Wilt the onions in the olive oil in a large saucepan and add the artichokes and potatoes, if using. Sauté the vegetables gently for another 5 minutes, add 360 ml (1 1/2 cup) of water and salt and pepper and bring to the boil. Cover and simmer for about 15 minutes (until the artichokes are approaching doneness). Stir in the chopped parsley and dill, and add a little water if necessary. Place the fish slices on top of the vegetables, baste them with the juices in the pan, cover and boil for another 10 minutes, or until the fish is white even close to the bone. Remove from the heat. Carefully lift the fish out and place the slices on a platter and keep them warm in a low oven.

For the sauce, whisk together the lemon juice with the flour in a small bowl with the flour until smooth. Slowly add 4-5 tablespoons of the saucepan liquid and return the mixture to the saucepan, shaking rather than stirring it into the contents. Adjust seasonings, adding more lemon juice if desired. Simmer briefly until the sauce thickens. Place the vegetables on the platter around the fish. Serves 4-6.

# * Oven-baked anchovies

*Gávros sto foúrno*

(RETHYMNO, WESTERN CRETE)

**Stamatis Manos, the Grecotel chef who provided this recipe, emphasizes that the garlic must be "heard" – "prepi na akougetai" – an unusual culinary direction meaning "don't stint." This dish is equally good with sardines, small tuna and mackerel. The addition of chopped basil and chili pepper flakes is a variation from the district of Elos, southwest of Chania, and Kissamo.**

*1 kg (2 lbs) fresh anchovies*
*5-6 ripe tomatoes, grated, skins discarded*
*6-8 cloves garlic, finely chopped*
*1/2 cup finely chopped parsley*
*salt and freshly ground pepper or chili pepper flakes, to taste*
*120 ml (1/2 cup) olive oil*
*2 tablespoons shredded basil leaves*

Wash the anchovies and cut off their heads, removing their innards at the same time. If using larger fish, you can leave the heads, just eviscerate them.

Preheat the oven to 190°C (375°F). After you have grated the tomatoes, pour off half of the juice, otherwise the sauce will be too runny. Mix the vegetables and seasonings, except for the basil, in a bowl with the olive oil. Arrange the fish side by side in a large baking pan. Pour the sauce over them and bake for about 30 minutes (time depends on the size of the fish). A few minutes before the fish are done, sprinkle the basil on top. Serves 6-8.

## Cod

The cod referred to in this book is invariably the salted variety. It always comes as a surprise that this Atlantic import should be such a staple in the Mediterranean where fresh fish are assumed to be as plentiful as olives. Instead, it owed its popularity even on islands to the fact that it kept indefinitely and satisfied the craving for fish when the seas were too rough for caiques to leave port. In Crete, where so many islanders worked the land or tended herds and the fishing grounds were far less productive, it was doubly prized.

Salt cod may have been introduced to Greece as early as the 15th century, when the Portuguese first started mining the seas, but it became all the rage in the mid 19th century. In her book on the subject, Mirsini Lambraki relates that, despite its availability, in the years just preceding World War II the smart set of Heraklio was holding cod parties, serving the fish prepared in all sorts of ways, with fried cod as the pièce de resistance. Nevertheless, before overfishing in the Grand Banks depleted the stocks and raised prices, cod was something almost anyone could afford, and it became a traditional Lenten food. As entrenched an institution as Easter lamb, fried cod with garlic sauce is almost required eating on March 25th (the Annunciation of the Virgin), Palm Sunday, August 6th (St. Sotiros, the Savior) and the pre-Christmas fast. And because it can be combined with virtually any vegetable and cooking treatment, the Cretans have invented dozens of ways of serving it, first and foremost with their stewed wild greens. No one outdoes the Portuguese, however, who have more than a thousand recipes for cod.

# Salt cod fried in zucchini batter

*Ftohoyiánnis me kolokýtha*

(EASTERN CRETE)

**Ftohoyiannis literally means "poor John" and was the nickname Cretans gave to the lowly salt cod, being something even cash-poor shepherds could occasionally afford and which would keep for weeks without a fridge. Fried cod with garlic sauce is traditionally eaten on special days during fasting periods, when even fish is forbidden, but an exception is made for salt cod, which arrives on the market both scaleless and bloodless. This is no mere fried cod, however; the batter is good enough to be eaten on its own, being made with either wine or beer, orange juice and grated zucchini.**

*1 salted cod or 1/2 kg (1 lb) cod fillets*
*1/2 lemon*
*2 medium-sized zucchini, scrubbed and grated*
*120 ml (1/2 cup) beer or red wine*
*120 ml (1/2 cup) strained fresh orange juice*
*2 tablespoons olive oil*
*250 grams (1 3/4 cups) flour, approximately*
*3 tablespoons chopped parsley (optional)*
*freshly ground black pepper (don't add salt without tasting first)*
*olive oil for frying*

If you are using the whole fish, shake off the loose salt, cut in large pieces and soak in a large bowl with several changes of cold water for a minimum of 24 hours (see p. 99). Soak the fillets in the same way if they are not presoaked.

When you are ready to cook the fish, peel off the skin and remove the bones. For 8 people, you'll only need about 3/4 of the fish, so if you are unable to find fillets, put the rest in a covered bowl or container and reserve for a future use. Cut the flesh into smaller pieces (about 2.5 cm or 1 inch square) or with your fingers separate it into chunks; it will flake naturally. Sprinkle the fish with fresh lemon juice and set aside while you prepare the batter. With your hands, squeeze all the liquid out of the grated zucchini. Put them in a bowl with the beer/wine, juice and olive oil and slowly mix in the flour until you have a fairly thick batter. Fold in the fish flakes and chopped parsley and season to taste, adding a little water if necessary.

Heat a couple of inches of frying oil in a large saucepan (or in your deep fryer). When it's piping hot, dip a few pieces of cod in the batter, and fry quickly on both sides. Do not overcrowd the frying pan and drain the fish on paper towels. Makes about 24 fish fritters.

Serve with garlic sauce (**Skordalia**, p. 99) and a salad of boiled beets or amaranth, tossed in oil and vinegar.

# Salt cod with spinach and leeks

*Bakaliáros me spanáki kai prássa*

*1 salt cod, cut into serving portions and soaked (see p. 99)*
*1/2 kg (1 lb) leeks, thickly sliced*
*1 kg (2 lbs) fresh spinach, washed and trimmed*
*120 ml (1/2 cup) olive oil*
*2-3 medium onions, chopped*
*1 bunch spring onions, chopped*
*3-4 medium potatoes in slices of about 2 cm/less than 1 inch*
*2 tomatoes, grated, skins discarded or 1/2 can (200 g / 8 oz)*
*1/2 cup chopped parsley*
*1/2 cup chopped dill*
*2 tablespoons flour*
*60 ml (1/4 cup) fresh strained lemon juice or more, to taste*
*freshly ground black pepper (taste before adding salt)*

**This is another of those dishes where the vegetables and fish exchange flavors to the benefit of both. It should appeal even to people who feel dubious about salt cod. The flour and lemon sauce, *derbiye* (see p. 117), imparts a light, intensely lemony flavor with no floury undertones.**

Bring 240 ml (1 cup) of water to a boil and parboil the leeks 4-5 minutes. Lift out the leeks and place them in a colander. Add the spinach gradually to the same pot and cook for a couple of minutes until the leaves are limp. Drain in the colander, reserving 240 ml (1 cup) of the broth.

Heat the oil in a large stew pot and sauté the onions gently until they are wilted (about 10 minutes). Add the leeks and spinach, together with the sliced potatoes, stirring to coat with oil. Pour in the grated tomato and the broth, cover and simmer on top of the stove for about 10 minutes. Add the chopped parsley and dill, place the fish on top of the vegetables, cover and cook for another 20 minutes.

Meanwhile, in a small bowl mix the flour with the lemon juice, a little at first, to get rid of any lumps and when the fish is flaky and the potatoes tender, add to this sauce 5 or 6 tablespoonsful of the cooking liquid. Stir briskly with a fork and return the contents of the bowl to the saucepan. Mix in gently and simmer for another few minutes and your dish is ready. It is also good at room temperature. Serves 8.

For another recipe for salt codfish, see page 161, **Sautéed spinach and winter greens**, to which you can add the cod fillets, when the greens are almost tender. Just place the fish on top, moisten with the vegetable juices, cover and boil gently for another 15-20 minutes. Make the lemon-flour sauce as described and serve at once.

# Garlic sauce

*Skordaliá*

Peel the potatoes and put them through a ricer while they are still warm. Pound the garlic with the salt in a mortar and pestle or, mash the cloves with a garlic press and add them to the potatoes. Using an electric beater, mix in the oil, lemon and vinegar and beat until the liquids are absorbed and the purée smooth. This is the traditional accompaniment to fried salt cod, but it also goes well with boiled beets, boiled amaranth (vlita), or fried zucchini or eggplant slices. It will be gummier than conventional mashed potatoes and is eaten at room temperature.

FOR 2 CUPS
*3 medium-sized or 2 large potatoes,*
  *boiled in their skins*
*6 garlic cloves or more*
*salt to taste*
*120 ml (1/2 cup) olive oil*
*juice of 1 lemon*
*2 tablespoons vinegar*

The secret to de-salting salt cod is much like a Japanese bath: you must rinse as much of the salt off as you can before you put it to soak, and you must change the water frequently. So, first hold it under the cold water tap to get rid of the surface salt. Then fill a large bowl with cold water. If you have a piece of plastic or wire netting or a steamer rack, place that in the bowl and let the fish rest on it. The salt that permeates its flesh will sink to the bottom of the bowl, so unless the fish is "suspended" above it, it will reabsorb it. If you want a relatively salt-free fish, soak for 24 hours, if you have a salt tooth, it can do with a bit less. But do change the water at least four times. Once soaked, the fish will keep in a closed container in the refrigerator for up to 6 weeks.

# \* Octopus with lemon sauce
## *Ktapódi lemonáto*

**Octopus with an oil and vinegar dressing is very common all over Greece. Cooking it with oil and lemon makes for a delightful change.**

Cook the whole octopus slowly in a covered, nonstick saucepan in its own juices and just 2-3 tablespoonsful of olive oil. When its liquid has evaporated, lift out the octopus and cut it into bite-sized pieces. Return it to the pot along with the juice of 2 or 3 lemons and simmer until tender. Serve at room temperature, sprinkled with oregano.

If you happen upon a fresh octopus that has not been tenderized – ie beaten against the rocks by the fisherman – you might want to freeze it for a couple of days rather than cooking it right away. Freezing for a short time breaks down the cells, softening the flesh, and does not detract from the taste.

# * Octopus with tomatoes and red wine

*Ktapódi me domátes kai kókkino krasí*

**Danae Malinaki, one of Chania's best home cooks, always serves this at her lunch party on Clean Monday, the start of the Orthodox Lent. When you see the way Greeks feast on fasting food on this day, it's easy to understand the appeal of self-denial. Fish is forbidden, because it has scales and blood; seafood – lobsters, crawfish, shrimp, clams, octopus – is not. Need I say more?**

*1 kg (2 lbs) octopus, 1 big one or 2 or 3 small ones*
*4-5 tablespoons olive oil*
*2 onions, chopped*
*3-4 tomatoes, chopped*
*240 ml (1 cup) red wine*
*2 bay leaves*
*1 cup green olives (tsakistes), soaked for 30 minutes in water if very salty*
*3 tablespoons chopped parsley*
*freshly ground black pepper*
*200 grams (1 cup) orzo (optional)*

Simmer the octopus whole in a covered nonstick saucepan without adding any water. It will cook in its own juice. If it stops exuding liquid before becoming tender, add a little of the wine. A frozen octopus will produce more liquid and is likely to require less cooking. If you have too much juice, pour it away unless you intend to make the "pasta pilaf" described below. When the octopus is fork tender, remove it from the saucepan and cut the tentacles into bite-sized pieces, discarding the head.

Heat the oil in the same saucepan and wither the onions in it. When they are soft, return the octopus to the pan along with the tomatoes, wine and bay leaves and cook over moderate heat, covered at first, until you have a thick sauce. Add the olives, parsley and a few grindings of black pepper, simmer another 10 minutes, and serve.

This dish can also be made a day ahead and eaten at room temperature; the flavors will only improve. Serves 10 as an appetizer, 8 as a main course (with rice or pasta).

If you want a more filling, substantial dish, make a "pasta pilaf." Cook the orzo separately in 720 ml (3 cups) of boiling salted water. When it is al dente, drain it and toss it with the octopus in a large bowl.

# * Octopus with fennel and green olives

*Ktapódi me máratho kai prásines eliés*

*1 octopus weighing about 1 kg
    (2 lbs), or 2-3 smaller ones*
*240 ml (1 cup) dry red wine*
*3-4 tablespoons olive oil*
*1 bunch wild fennel, leaves and
    stalks, coarsely chopped or*
*2 fennel bulbs, finely sliced*
*1/2 cup flat-leaved chopped parsley*
*1/2 cup cracked green olives
    (tsakistes)*

**It seems to me that octopus, fennel and green olives is one of the great marriages, even if it is a ménage à trois. It is also another of those dishes that should be made a day ahead to give these three strong tastes a chance to harmonize. When I was testing it in our Andros kitchen, our guests approached it dubiously, for being dark in appearance it is not instantly mouth-watering. But they kept coming back for more – "to find out what made it so good" – until the bowl was wiped clean. You could serve it as an hors d'oeuvre scooped up with slices of country bread, as a first course or even as an exotic spaghetti sauce. And don't be deterred if you can't find wild fennel, bulb fennel makes a very delicious substitute.**

If you buy a frozen octopus, simply defrost it, wash it and then boil it in a covered, nonstick saucepan over medium-low heat without adding any water. If it's fresh, have the fishmonger clean it. Fresh or frozen, it will cook in its own juice, but if it stops exuding liquid before becoming tender, pour in a little of the wine. As it starts to reabsorb its liquid, you have to watch the pot closely or risk the beast sticking, so add the wine before this can happen.

When the octopus is tender, remove it from the saucepan and cut into bite-sized pieces, removing the eyes and beak. Adding the oil to the saucepan, gently sauté the fennel and parsley for a few minutes before you return the octopus pieces with the rest of the wine. Simmer until you have a thick sauce. Stir in the olives and cook another 10 minutes. Serves 10 as an appetizer.

Cuttlefish can be substituted for octopus in this dish; just prepare them as described on page 107. And you can use squid or even baby octopus instead of cuttlefish in the recipes that follow, although they may need a little more cooking.

**Do not add salt when you cook octopus and check the olives for saltiness. You might want to soak them in lemon juice diluted with a little water while you're preparing the octopus to make them tastier and less salty.**

# Cuttlefish with wine

*Soupiés krassátes*

**Please don't be put off by the fuss of cleaning these critters. It is not as great an ordeal as it sounds and their exquisite taste and tender (definitely not rubbery) texture more than justifies any inconvenience. They also marry well with the ingredients they are cooked with, imparting a wonderful flavor to all. If you can only find frozen cuttlefish, which thanks to modern freezing techniques are excellent, buy the ones that still have their ink sacs, which give an extra "little something" to the sauce. They also make it (and your lips) very black indeed, so don't serve this dish when you're aiming for elegance. Of course, you can choose not to use the ink sacs or add only one or two.**

**The addition of vinegar here is a particularly Cretan way of giving naturally sweet flavors a little tang.**

*With thanks to Akrivi Mouzouraki for this recipe.*

*1 kg (2 lbs) cuttlefish, fresh or frozen*
*120 ml (1/2 cup) olive oil*
*2 onions, chopped, or*
*1 bunch spring onions, chopped*
*2 cloves garlic, finely chopped*
*240 ml (1 cup) red or white wine*
*120 ml (1/2 cup) good vinegar*
*freshly ground pepper, to taste*
*1 cup chopped parsley*

Clean the cuttlefish in a basin over the sink. First grab hold of the head/tentacles and pull it away from the sac/body, pressing your thumb into the sac to detach the connective tissue. Make a tiny slit in the top of the sac and push down so that the cuttlebone pops out. Slice down the middle of the soft side of the sac and open, scraping out gills, etc. but taking care not to puncture the ink sac at the bottom. Remove it and set aside. Pull off the mottled membrane that covers the body and discard. Now attack the head, cut or push out the beak and eyes and any little yellow fat globules. Rinse the tentacles carefully to get rid of any sand. Cut the cuttlefish into bite-sized pieces.

Sauté the onions and garlic in the oil until translucent. Add the cuttlefish and brown gently for about 20 minutes. Pour in the wine, vinegar, ink sacs (puncture them with a knife), pepper and parsley, cover, and simmer for another 30 minutes or until the cuttlefish are tender. Taste before you salt. Serve with rice. Serves 6-8.

# Cuttlefish with greens, beans and olives

*Soupiés me hórta, fasolákia kai eliés*

1 kg (2 lbs) cuttlefish, cleaned and
    cut into bite-sized pieces (see
    previous cuttlefish recipe)
1 large onion, coarsely chopped
120 ml (1/2 cup) olive oil
120 ml (1/2 cup) white wine
freshly ground pepper, to taste
1 kg (2 lbs) sweet greens, washed and
    trimmed
1/2 kg (1 lb) fresh string beans,
    trimmed and halved
2-3 medium potatoes, cut in chunks
1 whole tomato
1 cup green olives (tsakistes), soaked
    in lemon juice

**In this recipe, like so many others where seafood and vegetables are combined, one feels it must have been invented one day when the fisherman came home with a tiny catch. His wife threw the few cuttlefish, which wouldn't have been enough for a dish on their own, into the pot with the vegetables she was stewing. And discovered that they became utterly succulent when cooked with these humble cephalopods. For this, sweet greens are preferable to sour or bitter, so failing anything wild, you could use Swiss chard or amaranth.**

Sauté the onion in the oil for about 5 minutes and then add the cuttlefish and their ink sacs (optional). Brown very lightly, pour in the wine and pepper (fresh cuttlefish need no salt), cover and simmer for 30 minutes.

Add the greens, beans and potato, along with the tomato and olives (with their lemon juice). Pour in 240 ml (1 cup) of water, cover and simmer over very low heat until both the vegetables and cuttlefish are meltingly tender (at least an hour). Give the pot a good stir from time to time to make sure the vegetables cook evenly, and keep it simmering longer than you think you should to reduce the sauce to a flavored oil without excess liquid. Discard the tomato. Serves 6-8.

# Stuffed squid

*Kalamarákia yemistá*

In Crete where wild greens are so highly prized cuttlefish are also simmered with ferns (*fteres*) and bryony (*avronies*), which resembles a slightly bitter wild asparagus and is as much a spring favorite as strawberries are in England.

**To get in the mood for this dish, picture yourself eating it in a taverna with nothing between you and the sea slapping against the quay. It's an evening in late September, still warm but nippy enough for a light shawl or cotton sweater. Red, blue and green fishing caiques are getting ready to set out to sea, decks heaped with bright**

yellow nets. **Somewhere a cassette-recorder is wailing a Cretan lament, the evening star and the new moon can just be glimpsed above the vermilion streaked horizon. The heady aromas of garlic and onions being tossed in thick green olive oil waft out to your table as you sip a crisp white Siteian wine and nibble on crunchy barley rusks spread with creamy sheep's cheese fresh from the farm.**

**When choosing squid for this recipe, bear in mind that small ones are tastier, large ones less fiddly to handle.**

First, scald the squid (if fresh) by pouring boiling water over them. This softens them and makes them easier to clean and to stuff. To clean the squid first detach the head and tentacles from the rest of the body. Cut out the eyes and beak and discard. Chop the head and tentacles, and put somewhere convenient for these will go in the stuffing. Pull the innards out of the body sac and slip out the "plastic" cartilege and discard. Scrape off the purple membrane lining the outside of the tail. Rinse the sacs and drain in a colander.

Heat 60 ml (1/4 cup) of the olive oil in a large frying pan and sauté the onions until softish. Add the rice, garlic, tentacles and almonds and sauté, stirring, over medium heat, until the rice turns opaque. Pour in half the white wine and 60 ml (1/4 cup) of water, season with salt and pepper, cover, lower heat and simmer for about 10 minutes, until the rice has absorbed almost all the liquid. Just before you remove the pan from the stove, stir in the parsley and dill and cook for a minute or two.

Let the mixture cool a bit before you start stuffing the squid sacs with it, using a small spoon. Handle them gently and don't overpack the stuffing because the rice will expand. Fold over the ends and skewer with a toothpick to close. Place the squid side by side in a large saucepan, pour in the remaining wine and 120 ml (1/2 cup) water, bring to a boil, cover, lower heat and simmer until the squid is fork tender (about 30 minutes). Then pour in the lemon juice – shake don't stir – and cook another 5 minutes. Serve immediately or eat at room temperature the next day. Serves 8.

*1 1/2 kg (3 lbs) fresh or frozen squid*
*120 ml (1/2 cup) olive oil*
*1 cup chopped onion*
*70 grams (1/3 cup) long grain rice*
*2-3 garlic cloves, chopped*
*75 grams (1/2 cup) blanched*
    *almonds, finely chopped*
*120 ml (1/2 cup) white wine*
*salt and freshly ground pepper, to*
    *taste*
*1 cup finely chopped parsley*
*1/4 cup finely chopped dill*
*60 ml (1/4 cup) lemon juice*

# FISH SOUPS

## Chrysanna Karelli's kakkavia

*Kakkaviá tis Chrysánnas Karélli*

*1 grouper or other "boiling" fish,*
*    1 kg (2 lbs) or more*
*240 ml (1 cup) olive oil*
*3-4 onions, sliced*
*2-3 potatoes, cubed*
*salt and freshly ground pepper*
*juice of 3-4 lemons*

**The difference between a kakkavia and a fish soup (*psarosoupa*) is that the latter contains vegetables and herbs, while the former – named after the pot (*kakkavi*) fishermen used to cook it – has only onion and potatoes. The recipes for soups given here call for large quantities of olive oil, which make the soup extremely rich and smooth, but if you wish to reduce the amount, do so and it will still be good. Fast boiling is another prerequisite for blending the oil and water into a veloute.**

**Chrysanna Karelli, a politician's daughter, is a 30-something divorced mother of two who studied history of art and photography in France, before changing careers. In 1995 she dared to turn an old ice factory on Agios Titos square in Heraklio into one of the city's most adventurous restaurants. In it she has cultivated the stark look, ultramodern black leather chairs, bare brick walls, wild contemporary art and an African-inspired bar covered by the hide of a large black and white animal. Moreover, her oxblood-tiled bathroom looks like something out of Satyricon with a marble fountain in the center where water spouts from several gilded faucets. You would not think people would go to the Pagopoieon for a serious meal. And yet Chrysanna gets all her ingredients from the countryside, she uses no tinned or frozen products, her menu follows the seasons, and her spoon sweets are all homemade by village women. She likes to take traditional ingredients and mix them in unorthodox ways to arrive at new flavors. She also knows when a recipe is just right and needs no further fussing, as in this simple soup.**

Heat the oil in a large soup kettle and wilt the onions in it. Add 2 liters (8 cups) of water and boil rapidly for 10 minutes (Chrysanna follows the fishermen's advice that "it should boil and bubble like the froth on a Greek coffee three times"). Add the potatoes, cook another 10 minutes and then add the fish. Boil rapidly for another 10 or 15 minutes, partially covered. Pour in the lemon juice, cover, turn off the heat and let stand for 10 minutes. If you decide to eat the fish and leave the broth for another day, it will turn to jelly within an hour. Serves 6.

# Michali's fish soup
## Psarósoupa tou Micháli

(CHANIA)

Michalis Makrakis, who gave me this recipe, is the chef at the Amphora restaurant in the middle of the waterfront in Chania's old Venetian harbor. The food there is so good that even locals patronize it, while ignoring most of the establishments on the water as for tourists only. The *pescatritsa* or monkfish called for here is so ugly you might never have seen it intact. It has an outsized triangular head with bulging eyes and a gaping maw that tapers into a disproportionately narrow body, rather like a weight-lifter who has neglected his legs. But the flesh in its tail makes gourmets swoon it is so firm and delicate in flavor. Cretan fishmongers display it belly up, slit open to display a plump liver, which is also prized. And they call it "kotta" or hen, "chicken of the sea" perhaps?

If you feel squeamish about cooking such a monster, get your fishmonger to give you the fillets from the monkfish and the head from a more ordinary looking fish. But do include a head in your soup because it is that which produces the gelatin and the extra taste. As for the olive oil, Michalis would have added a whole cupful, so do add more if you wish.

*1 kg (2 lbs) grouper or monkfish (pescatritsa), cleaned and scaled*
*1/2 kg (1 lb) potatoes, peeled and quartered*
*2 medium onions, quartered*
*2 medium carrots, sliced*
*3-4 stalks celery, sliced*
*2 bay leaves*
*80 ml (1/3 cup) olive oil*
*3-4 tablespoons lemon juice*
*salt and freshly ground pepper to taste*

Put the vegetables in a large saucepan with the olive oil and some salt and pour in water to cover and then some. Boil furiously until the vegetables are barely tender. Strain, reserving the liquid, and set the potatoes and carrots aside. When cool enough to handle, cut the vegetables in small pieces.

Pour the liquid back in the saucepan, add the fish, including the head, and add a little more water if necessary. The fish should be about 3/4 covered. Boil rapidly until the flesh near the bone is no longer pink (about 15 minutes). Lift out the fish, remove the bones and fins, and cut into chunks. Strain the broth and return it to the pot along with the fish, vegetables and lemon juice. Reheat if necessary and adjust seasonings. Serves 6.

# Fish soup from Andoni's taverna in Rethymno

*Psarósoupa tou Andóni*

1 1/2 kg (3 lbs) small or medium-
   sized rock fish
3 stalks celery
1 onion, thickly sliced
1 large carrot, thickly sliced
salt and freshly ground pepper
240 ml (1 cup) olive oil
as many slices of grouper (sfirida),
   as you are diners
60 ml (1/4 cup) lemon juice

**Andoni's taverna has only five tables inside and three outside on a narrow sidewalk not far from the Arimondi fountain in the old section of town. If you didn't know it was there, you would never find it. But his fish are caught by his brother every day and they are impeccably cooked. All the waiters from the tourist traps on the port come here to eat when they have a moment free. Here is Andoni's recipe for fish soup. It is perhaps the richest of the three.**

Boil the rockfish in a large pot with 2 liters (8 cups) of water until the flesh is falling off the bones. Strain the broth into another large pot, pressing the fish to extract all the juices, and discard or give them to your favorite cat.

Add the vegetables, salt and pepper and olive oil to the broth and boil until half cooked. Lower the fish slices into the pot and boil until just tender (there should be no pink flesh near the bone). Off the heat pour in the lemon juice and serve immediately.

Marika Petraki in Mochlos solves the problem of how to cope with the bones by boiling all the small fish in a muslin bag and placing that in the colander to drain. She presses all the liquid out and then just tosses the whole thing in the garbage bin.

# MEAT, GAME, POULTRY & RABBIT

## Kréas, Kynígi, Kotópoulo kai Kounéli

As a general rule it is said that Western Crete is the land of the meat-eaters and Eastern Cretans tend more to a diet of vegetables, but I find such generalizations misleading, especially nowadays. True to type, Sifis Karkanis, a Sfakian shepherd turned taverna owner and cook, turns up his nose at all vegetables and eats meat every day with no damage to his cholesterol level, or so he maintains. Yet Evrydiki Katsouloudaki, also a native of Sfakia, says, "we used to eat meat only with our eyes," though she does wax lyrical when remembering the family pig. Nevertheless, even pastoral families with huge flocks of sheep and goats, whether in Lassithi, Psiloriti or the White Mountains, rarely ate meat more than 5-6 times a year since they sold their animals rather than slaughtering them for home consumption.

In the old days (before the mid 60s – not so very long ago) meat was festive fare, lamb or kid boiled for a wedding or christening, pork at Christmas, something special for a nameday celebration or to commemorate an anniversary. Except in the case of the boiled kid/lamb with pilaf, which is simple to the extreme, most of the meat dishes were stews combining one or two vegetables and potatoes to make the meat go further. Beef was never as popular or as common and, in any case, beef in Greece is rarely from a full grown steer but rather *moschari* or veal from a yearling. Its tender red meat is used in stews of course but more often ground to be molded into bread-padded meatballs or stuffings for virtually every vegetable that can be hollowed out or used as a wrapper – dishes where a little bit of meat can go a long long way. You will not find many recipes here for the various kinds of veal stews eaten in Crete – with tomato sauce, onions and wine, or lemon – because they differ very little from those found in the rest of Greece.

In some of the recipes, especially those for lamb with yogurt, a common thread can often be found linking them to the traditions of other pastoral societies, and every now and then there's a touch of honey that surprises, as in the bits of lamb dipped in honey served at weddings in Sfakia, which has echoes of North Africa.

Not surprisingly, game was an important source of protein particularly in mountain areas, where dove, quail, thrush, partridge and woodcock were hardly a luxury. These wild birds were stewed with potatoes or rice for a pilaf. Hare, on the other hand, would be made into *stifado* – a rich dark stew gleaming with onions and seasoned with many spices and wine – or *tsitsiristos* – browned then braised in wine. Sadly, the long hunting season and the universal Greek passion for shooting everything that flies has made feathered game a rarity, and hares too are scarce, so I have included only two recipes in this category. But there are several wonderful dishes for rabbit, which lends itself to so many different herbs and spices.

The universal favorite, chicken, may seem under-represented, but that is only because I did not want to duplicate the roasts, stews and pilafs found in other parts of Greece. Nineteenth century travellers commented frequently on the poultry served them when their hosts were fasting. Charles Edwardes feasted on "an entire boiled fowl of very large size" plus rice soup, hard-boiled eggs and myzithra while the monks had "nothing but a plate of snails and some vegetable snippings." And Pashley describes a turkey which he could not "but think tenderer and more delicious than was ever tasted in civilized Europe." Even so, poultry was saved for special occasions until fairly recently since a hen was never sacrificed to the pot before her laying days were over; eggs were as good as money in a cash-free society.

# Lamb with yogurt
*Arnáki me yiaoúrti*

(HERAKLIO)

This is one recipe that surely does not exemplify what we normally think of as the Mediterranean diet. The original version called for a leg of lamb, 1 1/2 kilos (3 lbs) of thick strained yogurt and no less than 10 eggs. The family who provided it told me that they eat it on Meat Sunday (*tis Kreatinis*) before Lent. They feel entitled to go overboard since they will not be tasting meat or eggs or dairy products until Easter. I have reduced the amount of yogurt and eggs without any reduction in the taste. Variations on the baking meat with yogurt theme are found in many pastoral areas around the Balkans, such as Epirus in northwest Greece and Anatolia in Turkey.

*1 1/2 kg (3 lbs) lamb leg or shoulder*
*sea salt*
*2 - 3 garlic cloves, thinly sliced*
*2 tablespoons olive oil*
*lemon juice*
*thyme or oregano*
*freshly ground pepper*
*grape vine twigs if obtainable*
*2 eggs, beaten*
*300 grams (1 1/2 cups) strained*
    *yogurt*

Wash the lamb, rub it with coarse salt and leave to marinate in the refrigerator overnight. Wipe dry, make small slits in the skin of the joint and slip a garlic sliver in each one, drizzle with olive oil and lemon juice and sprinkle on the herbs and pepper.

Preheat the oven to 200°C (400°F) and place vine twigs, if you happen to have any, on the bottom of a roasting pan. Place the lamb on top of them and roast as usual until the lamb is almost ready. If you're a purist, you can bone the lamb at this point (and remove the twigs).

Mix the eggs and yogurt together with the pan juices and pour this sauce over the lamb, whether whole or in slices. Return to the oven for another 30 to 45 minutes. The yogurt thickens and forms a delicious, slightly sour crust. It can also be finished off under the grill. Serves 6.

Vassilis Morakis, the chef at the Araxovoli taverna in Rethymno likes to add 100 grams (3 oz) of honey to the yogurt-egg sauce. This gives it a pleasant sweet and sour quality.

One June Saturday I went to a sheep-shearing in Apokoronas, high in the foothills of the White Mountains. Bleating piteously, eyes rolling like billiard balls, the sheep were herded into a section of unused dirt road that was closed off with a length of wire fencing. There the young priest, Papa Yiorgis, who happened to be the brother of Stavros the shepherd, borrowed a rickety aluminum table from a nearby house and set it with a red plastic bowl for holy water, a few olive branches, and a sheep bell with its heavy leather strap. From this makeshift altar he conducted the full service for blessing the flock, which he concluded by turning his back to them and lobbing the bell over his shoulder as if he were a bride tossing her bouquet. After that, it was a rough and tumble affair. The sheep tapped with the bell was tackled, fore and hind legs bound together before it knew what was happening and its fleece hacked away in great clumps by clicking shears. About ten men joined the fray – brawny and mustachioed with a surprising number of blue eyes among them. Trading insults and jokes, bursting out with the occasional oath, for which the priest who'd shed his cassock for jeans rebuked them with a grin, they grappled with sheep until the stroke of noon.

After a quick wash with the hose, they sat down at the long table outside the nearby house for "kollatsio" – a snack to them, to me a full course meal. Ignoring the salads, homemade bread and cheese, bowls of succulent sautéed pork in winey gravy and liver, they started stabbing large chunks of cold, almost black meat streaked with ivory fat. Dispensing with forks and knives, they gnawed, chomped, guzzled and smacked their greasy lips until the platter was empty. I speared the smallest piece I could find and cut a sliver. Tough, fatty and strong tasting was my verdict and I returned to the sweet tomatoes and bread dunked in pork juices.

Three hours later, after every sheep had been sheared and the wool stuffed into large garbage bags, we repaired to the home of the two brothers' parents for a real feast. There some forty of us sat at long tables arranged in a H shape, waiting for the legendary pilaf, made this time from three post-adolescent sheep, whose heads soon arrived on a large platter, along with more of their black stringy meat. The rice, cooked in what looked like a sawed off smokestack over an open fire in the courtyard by Yiorgis and Stavros's father, was sublime, but the mutton is perhaps an acquired taste.

# Wedding pilaf
## *Gamopilafo*

**This is the traditional pilaf served at weddings and baptisms in western Crete, modified for home use. Its every grain symbolizes a wish for the young couple's wealth and prosperity. Whenever Cretans talk about this dish, they become even more animated than usual, as if it triggers a host of wonderful memories. Although no seasonings are added, the dish is made in such quantities that the broth in which the rice is cooked is a heady extract. For example, a pilaf made with seventeen chickens is not considered out of the ordinary. In the past, when chickens were still a luxury, they were preferred over lamb by those who could afford them. Now some people make the pilaf with a combination of chicken (free range, if possible) and year-old kid (*tzigouri*) or lamb, but broth from many animals is more the norm at large celebrations. Adding to the extravagance, several spoonfuls of bubbling staka (see Cheeses, page 44) are swirled into the pilaf before the hungry guests, who may number high in the hundreds or even into the thousands, tuck in. You will have to omit this luxury, but crème fraiche, mascarpone or even hot clarified butter makes a reasonable substitute.**

*With thanks to Katerina Farandaki for sharing this recipe.*

*1 lb (1/2 kg) lean lamb*
*1 2 kg (3-4 lb) free range chicken*
*2 liters (8 cups) chicken or meat stock (optional)*
*2 cups (400 g) rice, preferably medium grain (Arborio, Valencia, Nyhaki)*
*60 ml (1/4 cup) lemon juice and an extra lemon*
*salt and freshly ground black pepper*
*2-3 tablespoons warmed staka, crème fraiche, mascarpone (optional)*

Place the meat and chicken in a large soup kettle and cover with cold water or stock. Bring to the boil, season with salt and skim well. Simmer for 1 hour or longer until you have a rich stock (skim off the fat if you wish) and remove the meat to a platter.

Pour 1440 ml (6 cups) of the stock into a clean saucepan and bring to the boil. Add the rice and simmer until the rice has absorbed most of the stock. Stir in the lemon juice and salt and pepper to taste. Cover the saucepan with a clean dish towel and the pan's lid and remove from the burner. Let stand 5 minutes, pour in the staka, and serve. Slice the meats, sprinkle with more lemon juice, and serve them separately. Serves 4 to 6.

You'll get a richer broth if you bring chicken to the boil from a cold start, but you'll get whiter, better looking meat if you add it when the liquid is boiling.

# INGREDIENTS FOR A TRADITIONAL WESTERN CRETAN WEDDING

*Between 500 to 2,000 close relatives and intimate friends.*

Up to 100 friends and neighbors to help with the cooking, pilaf stirring, lamb basting, sausage and vine leaf stuffing, pie frying, pastry twirling, etc. on the day and well in advance.

*As many freezers as can be mustered.*

A village square or large open-air taverna on a summer evening.

*Gallons of raki poured into minute glasses as the guests leave the church.*

Bowls of piquant graviera cheese cubes.

*Platters heaped with morsels of roast pork.*

Baskets of bite-sized chunks of fresh bread.

*Tulle-wrapped bonbonieres – sachets of white candy-coated almonds, sometimes known as "bride's eggs – tied with a white ribbon.*

A pale pastry rosette or *xerotigano* for each guest, wrapped in cellophane.

*A Cretan lyra or fiddle to play*
*while the bride dances with the bachelors –*
*the prize her kerchief (not a blue garter)*

One large bowl of honey and walnuts and a mother-in-law waiting on the doorstep of the couple's new home with a spoonful to "sweeten up the bride" and one for each of the bachelors to "sweeten up their prospects."

*A little finger dipped in the honey for tracing a cross on the lintel and*
*A red pomegranate for the bride to smash on her spotless floor*
*(to ensure wealth and babies, preferably sons).*

Long tables set with immaculate white linen and bowls of peanuts roasted in salt-encrusted shells and tiny coriander-scented rusks for nibbling with raki before the mezedes are paraded in. Trays piled with fried lamb's liver, home-made sausages, olives, pickles, marble-sized meatballs, miniature pies encasing creamy myzithra cheese or herbs and greens gathered from the mountains, stuffed vine leaves and salads, to tease the appetite before the pièce de resistance, the wedding pilaf, is served, followed by the boiled meat.

*Course number three, the patatada, baby lambs roasted in the oven with potatoes or, less traditionally, on the spit. Required for show but often barely touched.*
*Barrels of strong tawny wine, one perhaps as old as the bride or groom.*
*Case upon case of soft drinks; neither home-made nor home-grown, this can be the most expensive item on the menu.*

A lyra and two lutes to set the stage for *mantinades* – traditional couplets, half-sung, half-spoken, some centuries old, some made up on the spur of the moment: "Today the eagle is united with the dove," "The sun and the moon are crowned," and in a lighter vein, "Bride, where you are going, watch your step, love your father-in-law, but give your mother-in-law the boot."
*And for dancing, dancing, dancing till the next day.*

*Hundreds of extra plates for throwing at the dancers' feet, not to mention a few flower pots and chairs.*
*Shotguns for firing exuberant, deafening volleys into the air and/or large signs declaring "Shooting on these premises is strictly forbidden! By order of the police and the management."*

Traditional wedding presents: cash-stuffed envelopes to help the couple set up house.

OPTIONAL
The *proikologi* or dowry bearers, young men to carry the furniture, kitchen equipment, linen and blankets to the new home.
The nuptial mattress – to be made fruitful by rolling a baby, preferably a boy, on it, once it's made up.
Several old shirts to be worn by the bridegroom at "the small wedding," the party the night before the actual wedding, and torn off by his friends in a ritual shedding of old bachelor habits.

Oh, and I almost forgot! The bride and groom, the priest, and the all important *koumbari* – the best man and bride's attendant, who handle details like the ring, wedding crown and church.

# Kid with artichokes in egg-lemon sauce

*Katsikáki avgolémono me angináres*

1 kg (2 lbs) boneless kid (or baby
  lamb), cut in large cubes
120 ml (1/2 cup) olive oil
1 large onion, coarsely chopped
60 ml (1/4 cup) lemon juice
6 artichokes, cleaned (and halved or
  quartered, depending on size and
  left to soak in acidulated water)
1/2 cup chopped fresh dill
1 bunch green onions, chopped
salt and freshly ground pepper, to
  taste

FOR THE EGG-LEMON SAUCE
60 ml (1/4 cup) lemon juice to taste
2-3 eggs, at room temperature

**This is a classic dish, eaten all over Greece, but in Crete the artichokes that gastronomes consider the most delicious are more covered in spines than any I've seen elsewhere. They are round rather than pear-shaped and resemble a mace or some other medieval weapon of torture. You have to attack them with thick gardening gloves or suffer the consequences. But they are the ultimate in taste.**

Heat the oil in a large stewpot and brown the meat on all sides, a few pieces at a time. Remove it to a platter, lower the heat and sauté the onion gently until very soft, stirring from time to time with a wooden spoon so it doesn't burn. Add 240 ml (1 cup) water and the lemon juice, scraping up any bits stuck on the bottom, and return the meat to the pot. Bring to the boil and simmer, covered, until the meat is half cooked, about 30 minutes. Add the artichokes, dill, spring onions and seasonings, and simmer till tender. Pour in a little more water if necessary.

Make the egg-lemon sauce at the last minute. Beat the eggs and lemon together until frothy. Slowly add several tablespoonfuls of broth from the stew to the mixture, whisking while you pour to prevent the eggs from curdling. Stir the contents back into the stew pot, off the heat. Mix thoroughly, reheat very gently to avoid scrambling, and serve at once. Serves 4-6.

In this dish, 1 kg (2 lbs) of wild greens, shredded romaine lettuce, curly endive or spinach can be substituted for the artichokes. If you like bitter greens, try any of the chicory family. A wild, dandelion lookalike called *stamnagathi* or spiny chicory (even though it is not really thorny) is a favorite addition in Crete. But when using greens, parboil them first in lots of boiling water for about 10 minutes, drain and then add to the lamb.

# Lamb cooked in a sheep's stomach
## *Kléftiko*

**This recipe was inspired by stories of klefts and rebels who managed to cook without pots, pans or telltale odors while on the run. Before Greece won its independence from the Ottomans, a caste of bandit warriors arose whose specialty was harassing the Turks and stealing what they could for their compatriots. Naturally, though the name kleft comes from the Greek verb to steal, thieving from the enemy was a heroic act and the deeds of these guerrillas became legendary. Whether they or the shepherds accompanying their flocks to the high summer pastures in the Cretan mountains originated this practice of concealed cookery, it certainly saves on the washing up. Effie Manoulaki, who gave me this recipe, has a special place in her summer restaurant outside Chania for making this dish. Don't worry, you can use a clay pot instead of the stomach.**

If you are not favorably inclined towards eggs, you can bind and thicken the sauce with *derbiyé*. This is the Turkish word for egg-lemon sauce, but in Crete the original "t" has been replaced with a "d" and flour is substituted for the egg – in this case 1 tablespoon of flour blended with the juice of 1 lemon or more (taste the broth first to see how much additional lemon you'll be wanting). With *derbiyé*, you employ the same technique of blending the sauce in a bowl with a little of the pan liquid before adding the mixture to the pan, but there is far less risk of curdling. In fact, "terbiyé" means "to behave" – an obvious reference to the dangers of egg-lemon sauce misbehaving if you let it boil.

After cleaning the sheep's stomach with abundant water and lemon juice, which Effie maintains takes at least one day to do properly, she stuffs it with the meat, seasonings and cheese. Like the klefts, she has dug a hole in the earth and lined it with stones. She places the filled stomach on top of the stones, covers it with more earth and lights a fire, which cooks the meat slowly for 5 or 6 hours.

The meat is exquisitely tender but if you cannot/do not ever want to find a sheep's stomach, an unglazed clay pot of the sort used to roast a chicken would make a fine substitute. Just place the lamb in it, toss the meat, seasonings, cheese and oil together, and seal the pot with a ribbon of flour-and-water paste. Bake at 130°C (250°F) for 5 hours. Serves 4-6.

*1 leg of baby lamb (1 kg or 2 lbs), boned and cubed*
*1 sheep's stomach or 1 ovenproof clay pot with lid*
*2 tablespoons chopped mint*
*salt and freshly ground pepper*
*1 heaping tablespoon myzithra*
*1 heaping tablespoon feta*
*1-2 tablespoons olive oil*

# Easter meat and cheese pie

*Toúrta Paschaliní*

**This rich confection was and still is made at Easter when the lambs are young and tender, the cheese plentiful and creamy. In the past, though, no one had tasted either meat or dairy products for forty days, while today fewer people have the will or the faith to fast so strenuously. The thin crust, which is not too different from an Arab pitta, soaks up the juices from the filling, which is surprisingly delicate.**

FOR THE FILLING

*1 1/2 kg (3 lbs) spring lamb, preferably shoulder*

*lemon juice*

*salt and freshly ground pepper*

*2 bay leaves*

*1/4 teaspoon cinnamon*

*1/2 teaspoon cumin (optional)*

*450 grams (1 lb) myzithra or ricotta*

*225 grams (1/2 lb) malaka or mozzarella*

*3 tablespoons staka or mascarpone (optional)*

*3 tablespoons chopped fresh mint*

FOR THE PASTRY

*450 grams (1 lb) flour*

*1 envelope instant yeast*

*big pinch of salt*

*240 ml (1 cup) milk at room temperature*

*1 egg, beaten*

Marinate the lamb for a few hours in salt, pepper and lemon juice. Then put it and the bay leaves in a large pot with water to cover, bring to the boil and cook gently for about 1 1/2 hours. Take out the meat, cool, debone and cut into pieces about 5 cm (2 inches) square and 2 cm (1/2 inch) thick. Taste and adjust the seasonings, adding cinnamon and cumin.

Mix the cheeses together in a separate bowl.

To make the pastry, sieve the flour, yeast and salt together and make a well in the middle. Pour the milk and the beaten egg into the well. Slowly swirl the flour into the liquids with your fingers and knead into a firm dough. Cover and put in a warm place to rise while the lamb is cooking.

Preheat the oven to 190°C (375°F). Divide the dough into 2 pieces, the one for the bottom crust somewhat larger than the other. Roll out the larger one to line the bottom and sides of an oiled baking dish (22 x 30 cm/9 x 13 in). The pastry should drape over the edges. The bottom crust should also be a bit thicker than the top (like a pizza in consistency) to absorb all the juices. The top should be nice and thin.

Fill the pastry as follows: cheese, meat, mint, cheese, crust. Crimp the top and bottom edges of the pastry together (wet fingers help), make a couple of slits in it with a sharp knife, paint with beaten egg, sprinkle with sesame seeds and bake for about 30 minutes or until the crust is golden. Serves 8-10.

Save the broth, skimming off the fat, and you'll have the beginnings of the makings of a Cretan festive pilaf.

# Cretan cannelloni with ground beef

*Kanellónia kritiká me kimá*

(EASTERN CRETE)

**Cretan cannelloni? Well, it is not certain whether this recipe is left over from Venetian days or whether it was introduced by Italian travellers in more recent years. Nevertheless, you should approach this version as something a bit different from the cannelloni you may be used to. The filling was described by the testers as "scrumptious," the tops have a delectable crunchiness, and the two of them polished off 14 of the 16 cannelloni!**

FOR THE DOUGH
*450 grams (1 lb) (bread) flour*
*5 large eggs, beaten*
*pinch of salt*

FOR THE FILLING
*2 medium onions, finely chopped*
*3/4 kg (1 1/2 lb) ground beef*
*5-6 tablespoons olive oil*
*salt and freshly ground black pepper*
*1 teaspoon cinnamon*
*2 teaspoons oregano*
*1/2 cup chopped parsley*
*960 ml (4 cups) beef broth or even bouillon from a cube*
*grated cheese*

To make the pasta, make a well in the flour and pour the beaten eggs and salt into it. Using your fingers, gradually mix the flour into the eggs until you have a smooth dough. Add a little flour if it's sticky and knead for 5 to 7 minutes. At first it may seem stiff and unyielding, but just keep at it. Wrap the dough in cling film and set aside for at least 30 minutes (in the fridge if for longer). Don't worry, it will relax after it's had time to rest and will become amenable.

Sauté the onions and ground beef together with 3 tablespoons of the oil, until the onions are soft and the beef shows no signs of pinkness. Just before they get to that point, add the seasonings and herbs. Stir for a minute or two and then pour in 120 ml (half a cup) of broth and simmer for 10 minutes.

Preheat the oven to 180°C (350°F). Divide the dough into 4 parts and roll out into thin sheets of pasta. If using your pasta machine, put each ball first through setting 1 and finish at setting 4. It should go through without any trouble or any extra flour. Cut the pasta into squares about 10 x 12 cm (4 x 5 inches). In the middle of each square place 2 tablespoons of filling and roll them up into cylinders. Place them in an oiled baking pan and oil each one with a little brush. Bake the cannelloni for about 25 minutes until they are lightly browned. Then add the rest of the beef broth, raise the heat to 190°C (375°F) and cook for another 20-25 minutes. If the top threatens to burn, place a piece of aluminum foil over the pan.

Serve the cannelloni hot with grated cheese and their juices. Serves 4, unless you are being greedy.

# Ypapandi's stuffed cabbage leaves

*I  l a h a n o d o l m á d e s   t i s   Y p a p a n d í s*

(AG. NIKOLAOS)

*1 large green cabbage*
*120 ml (1/2 cup) olive oil*
*1 medium onion, finely chopped*
*1/2 kg (1 lb) ground beef or pork*
*200 grams (1 cup) long grain rice*
*1 egg, lightly beaten*
*2 tablespoons strained yogurt*
*2 tablespoons grated feta*
*2 tablespoons chopped dill*
*juice of 1 lemon*

FOR THE EGG-LEMON
SAUCE
*1 tablespoon flour*
*60 ml (1/4 cup) fresh lemon juice or*
  *more*
*2 small eggs, beaten*

**While Ypapandi Velivasaki was showing me how she stuffs vine leaves and zucchini blossoms (see page 154) one afternoon in the kitchen of the Porto Elounda Hotel, she also rattled off her recipe for stuffed cabbage. The unusual addition of yogurt and feta here add an interesting piquancy to this soothing dish.**

**If you are one of those who doesn't trust a skinny cook, you would feel comfortable with Ypapandi. In her mid forties, she's very round, very animated and wears the happy expression of someone who loves her work. I saw that look on the faces of several chefs in Crete. Though she's been working since the age of 8, Ypapandi always enjoyed cooking, and early on discovered she could make things taste much better than her mother could.**

Parboil the cabbage in plenty of water for about 10 minutes. Drain and when cool enough to handle, carefully separate the leaves from the cabbage head. Lay on paper towels or dishtowels to dry and slice off thick ribs near the stem end. Cut the larger leaves in half with scissors. The leaves should be soft and floppy enough to roll. If some of the inner ones have remained crisp, parboil them again for 2 minutes.

Heat 3 tablespoons of olive oil in a large heavy frying pan and gently sauté the onion until soft and translucent. Add the chopped meat and brown until all traces of pink vanish. Let cool and then mix in the other ingredients.

Oil the bottom of a large saucepan and then line it with torn or unstuffable cabbage leaves. To stuff the leaves, put a tablespoon of filling in the middle of each leaf about 4 cm (1 1/2 inches) from the wide end, fold the bottom over the filling and roll towards the top, folding the sides towards the center as you go. Lay the stuffed leaves seamside down in the pan. Repeat the procedure until you have used up all the stuffing. Pour in the remaining olive oil, lemon juice and some water until the liquid is about half way up the dolmades, and strew any unused leaves over them. Place an old plate on top of the cabbage rolls to keep them from unravelling, bring to the boil, cover and simmer for about 1 hour.

Remove the cabbage rolls to a platter, reserving their liquid, and set in the oven to keep warm while you make the egg-lemon sauce.

Beat the eggs with the lemon juice in a small saucepan. Slowly beat in several tablespoons of liquid from the cabbage rolls and then add to it all the remaining liquid. Heat the sauce very gently, stirring all the while, until it thickens to the consistency of thin custard. Serve the cabbage rolls and sauce separately. Serves 4-6.

You can also use the meatless stuffing on page 154 or substitute leftover diced chicken or turkey for the ground beef.

# * Stuffed vine leaves and zucchini blossoms
*Dolmadákia*

This version of one of Greece's best known dishes is a specialty of Archanes, a lovely neoclassical town in what must be one of the oldest wine-growing districts in the world. Lying just up the road from Knossos, not only does it boast many Minoan cemeteries, but it also has two winepresses dating from Minoan times. Many of Crete's finest wines come from this area, so it is only natural that housewives would have plenty of vine leaves to experiment with.

Irini Lyritsaki, who gave me this recipe one June morning, had just prepared a potful of them for a neighbor's dinner party. Community spirit seems a common feature of many Cretan villages. In Krousta, above Agios Nikolaos, Maria Pangalou automatically makes enough for extra portions for her extended family and friends. "Why not?" she says, "They'll do the same when they cook something special."

The amounts may seem large, but when you've made up your mind to stuff vine leaves, there's no point in just doing a dozen. After the first few, you get into a rhythm and the process seems easy. You can count on your guests eating at least 6 each, because they are quite small, and if you have any left over, why not take some next door?

Greek cooks freeze or dry great quantities of vine leaves for use in the off-season. Vine leaves that have been preserved in brine are available at Greek and Middle Eastern groceries. To prepare these, rinse well under running water and then boil for about three minutes in plenty of water. Drain in a colander and then spread out on paper or dish towels to dry before using. Fresh vine leaves need no rinsing but should be similarly parboiled and drained.

*50 vine leaves*

*as many zucchini blossoms as you can lay your hands on*

*1 large onion*

*1 large eggplant*

*2 medium zucchini*

*1 medium carrot*

*1 or 2 tomatoes, grated, skins discarded (for color more than taste) (optional)*

*1/2 kg (1 lb) ground beef*

*olive oil for frying plus 60 ml (1/4 cup)*

*50 grams (1/4 cup) long grain rice, rinsed*

*1/4 cup chopped parsley (optional)*

*1/4 cup chopped fresh mint (optional)*

*salt and freshly ground pepper*

Wash and trim the vegetables and chop them pretty finely in the moulinex or food processor. Fry the meat in a few tablespoons of olive oil until there are no traces of pink and scoop it into a bowl with the vegetables, rice, seasonings and 60 ml (1/4 cup) of olive oil. Mix thoroughly.

Line the bottom of a saucepan with some torn vine leaves. To fill the rest, place a teaspoon of the rice/meat mixture near the top of each vine leaf, fold the two sides over it and then roll it toward the tip, making a small cylindrical packet. Place seamside down in the saucepan. Don't worry about making them perfect. They won't fall apart, since you pack them close together. Repeat until all the vine leaves are filled, except for a few more torn ones for the top. Stuff the zucchini flowers, pushing the tips inward over the filling. Don't bother to remove the stamens, you'll simply tear the flowers.

Cover the stuffed leaves and flowers with any remaining vine leaves and with an old plate a bit smaller than the saucepan, add water to the level of the plate, bring to the boil and cover. Reduce heat and simmer for 20-25 minutes. Remove the plate and pour in the 2-3 tablespoons of lemon juice mixed with a tablespoon of flour (derbiyé), shaking the saucepan to distribute the juice. Serve hot. 8 servings.

Instead of cooking these on top of the stove, many Cretan women arrange them standing up in a nonstick pan and bake them for 45 minutes at 190°C (375°F). Rather than filling the pan half-full with water, they add chicken or beef stock (or broth made from a bouillon cube). In this case of course, you eliminate the plate and cover them with extra vine leaves, sliced tomatoes, breadcrumbs or even sliced potatoes. The resulting dolmades are firmer than the boiled variety.

They are often served with egg-lemon sauce made with 2-3 eggs, lemon juice and about 1 1/2 cups of cooking liquid instead of derbiyé. See page 116 for technique.

For a change of taste and texture try making the same dolmades with bulgur instead of rice.

# Marika Petraki's stuffed vegetables

*Ta diáfora yemistá tis Maríkas Petráki*
(Eastern Crete)

Twice a year my friend Carol Christ the thealogian (sic) takes a group of American women on a Goddess tour of Crete. They visit major and lesser Minoan shrines, peak sanctuaries and caves, places where evidence of Goddess worship has been found. In Eastern Crete, they make a pilgrimage to the Minoan site on the island opposite Mochlos, where in addition to the cemetery there is a shrine with a red kernel or offering stone in the shape of the female triangle with indentations for placing the first fruits. Afterwards they dine at Marika Petraki's taverna on the mainland, where her sublime stuffed vegetables are another reason for coming back year after year.

Greeks everywhere stuff almost everything that comes out of the garden, usually with rice or with meat. These vegetables will be more special if you can find fresh farmer's market produce, do not eat them straight out of the oven, and can find a bottle of white wine from Siteia as an accompaniment. It is worth making this dish in large quantities as the left-overs are even better the next day.

*4 large firm tomatoes*
*4 green peppers*
*4 medium-sized zucchini*
*4 medium-sized potatoes*
*2 small eggplants*
*salt to taste*
*sugar to taste*
*2 + 2 tablespoons olive oil*
*250 grams (1/2 lb) ground beef*
*1-2 large onions, coarsely chopped*
*2-3 garlic cloves, coarsely chopped*
*1 tablespoon cumin*
*1 tablespoon crumbled oregano*
*salt and freshly ground black pepper*
*small bunch parsley*
*1/2 cup fresh (1/4 cup dried) mint*
*1 tablespoon tomato paste dissolved*
  *in 60 ml (1/4 cup) water*
  *(optional)*
*100 grams (1/2 cup) long grain rice*
*vine leaves and zucchini blossoms, if*
  *available*
*240 ml (1 cup) chicken broth or*
  *water*

Wash and dry all the vegetables. Slice the caps off the tomatoes and scoop the insides into a bowl, being careful not to pierce the sides. Take the tops off the peppers and deseed. Trim the zucchini and with an apple corer or potato peeler dig out as much flesh as you can without cutting through the sides. Slice one end off each potato and do the same. Slice the top quarter off the eggplants and using a knife and hollow them out. Save all the vegetable caps near their mates for replacement later. Sprinkle the cavities of the vegetables with salt together with a little sugar in the case of the tomatoes. Place the insides of all the vegetables in the bowl of a food processor, together with the onion, garlic and herbs and pulse quickly, but try not to purée. You may have to do it in more than one dose. (Otherwise, finely chop everything by hand.)

Heat 2 tablespoons of oil in a frying pan and sauté the ground beef until it's no longer pink. Mix together all the ingredients,

This mixture, without the meat, is also used for stuffing artichokes, while grated artichokes are often added to this filling. Stuffed artichokes are sometimes referred to as "kalogries" or nuns, because they are fasting food and eaten one by one, solitary as a nun in her cell. Vegetables in general stuffed without meat are known as "orphans."

including the meat with its oil and juices, the raw rice, the tomato paste and 1 more tablespoon of olive oil, in a large bowl.

Preheat the oven to 190°C (375°F). Stuff each vegetable until it is about 3/4 full and put back their caps. Line the roasting pan with vine leaves, place the vegetables on top of them and place some more vine leaves or zucchini blossoms, if you've found them, on top of the vegetables. If you haven't, you could scatter some bread crumbs over them or just leave them they are. In any case, drizzle a little olive oil over everything, pour in the chicken broth and bake for about 1 hour or more – the potatoes and eggplant may need a little more cooking. Serves 8.

# Smyrna sausages
## *Soutzoukákia*

1/2 loaf "day-old" Italian or Greek "peasant" bread
red wine or half water/half vinegar for soaking the bread
1 kilo (2 lbs) ground beef
1 medium onion, grated
3 cloves garlic, finely chopped
2 tablespoons cumin
salt and freshly ground pepper, to taste
vinegar or milk (optional)
olive oil for frying

**There is no question that these meatballs – *soutzouk* is Turkish for sausage – are among the most delicious of the dishes brought to Greece by refugees from Asia Minor. The woman who gave me this recipe had come to Chania from Smyrna as a child. We met under her grape arbor surrounded by roses and gardenias growing in the same beds and olive oil tins as tomatoes, peppers and hydrangeas. They were all thriving under the touch of her arthritic but still "green" fingers. In between recipes she told me stories of days when oil cost 1 drachma a liter and a piece of land could be had for 1000, of marriage at 16, the birth of numerous children and death of two, an invalid husband, turbulent politics, and a brother who appeared like a ghost from 18 years captivity in Turkey only to see his father expire from shock as he stepped through the front door. But life's sadnesses did not seem to have affected her skill in the kitchen because everyone I met who knew her praised her soutzoukakia to the skies.**

**To get the most taste from the cumin, dry fry the seeds in a nonstick saucepan until they darken and release a wonderful smell. Then grind them yourself in a spice grinder or mortar and pestle.**

*With thanks to Katina Stamataki for sharing this recipe.*

Cut the crusts off the bread and soak it in red wine to cover or in vinegar diluted with water, for 30 minutes. Squeeze out all the liquid with your hands.

Knead together the minced beef, crumbled bread, onion, garlic, cumin and salt and pepper. Make fattish "sausages" about 7 cm (3 inches) long and 5 cm (2 inches) plump – they should taper into round points at the ends – and refrigerate for at least an hour or until ready to cook.

Fry the meatballs in 60 to 120 ml (1/4-1/2 cup) of very hot olive oil. Drain on paper towels and set aside.

Make the sauce by boiling all ingredients together – add the cumin just before the end – until thick. Ten minutes before you're ready to eat, add the meatballs to it along with a few tablespoons of the frying oil and simmer to blend the flavors, adding a little water or red wine if needed. Serves 6 to 8 and goes beautifully with fried potatoes or plain pilaf.

FOR THE SAUCE

*1 onion, grated*

*1 kilo (2 lbs) fresh tomatoes, grated, skins discarded or canned tomatoes*

*1 teaspoon sugar, if the tomatoes need it*

*1 piece dried orange peel (optional)*

*2 cloves garlic, crushed*

*2 tablespoons cumin (or to taste)*

*salt and freshly ground pepper to taste*

*water or red wine (optional)*

*2-3 tablespoons of the frying oil*

# THE FAMILY PIG

In the old days, every family had its pig. And like good farmers everywhere they used everything except the squeal. As I write this I can hear Evrydiki Katsouloudaki telling me what that pig meant to her, growing up in one of the poorest households in Sfakia in the 1920s and 30s. Her father was something of a ne'er-do-well, charming but incurably lazy, so they lived on greens, olive oil, vegetables from the garden, bread and the generosity of their neighbors who would sneak her mother a cheese from time to time. But even they had a pig, for it didn't cost anything and was easy to raise. Feeding on acorns for a year would fatten it to a hefty 120 okes (an Ottoman measurement equivalent to 1,280 grams) (343 lbs), while the meat and fat would last for months.

Besides the hams, sausages, brawn from the head, broth from the bones for pilaf, Evrydiki remembered the treats: "a huge slice of bread spread with two fingers thickness of rendered snow-white pork fat and honey"; and *tsingarides* or crisp rind left over from rendering the fat – "we kids would fill our fists with them and a hunk of bread and be happy." Chitterlings or pieces of crackling were also added to trahana (see page 81) with some sautéed onion or to bean soup for a hint of meaty flavoring and her mother would use the fat around the liver and kidneys to make Easter biscuits "because we never had butter." She also baked *kallitsounia* (little pies) stuffed with crackling in the oven and *glinopittes*, pies made with melted pig fat instead of olive oil. One gasps at the thought of all this fat nowadays, but one has to remember that all these dishes were eaten over a whole year, not all at once, and that they were considered luxuries comparable to our birthday cake, lobster and foie gras, not something to indulge in every day.

The men would cut bacon and long strips of filet from the back bone, which were hung up inside the chimney to smoke, sometimes with fires made from fragrant leaves – sage, lemon, bay or eucalyptus. For days the house smelled glorious, as if the whole mountainside had come indoors. Afterwards the filet pieces which were called *apachia*, literally "without fat," would be washed and stored in earthenware jars covered with fat (*glina*), where "they would keep forever."

The women were busy on slaughtering day preparing *omathies* (see page 130), sausages filled with bulgur if you were poor, rice if more prosperous, together with pork liver and lights "cut up very small like chicken feed," raisins, pepper, cumin and, of course, fat. "You'd blow through the intestine to unstick it, fill it not too tight with the stuffing, and boil it. We could get 5-6 okes worth of *omathies* from one pig. The sausages made from the pig's appendix are the best."

Finally, there were knuckle bones, from the pig's elbow, which the children used for games, while folk doctors extracted an oil from the sow's ovaries to rub down people who were sick.

I have not included a recipe for roast pork here, but it is a Cretan favorite and in some parts of the island is still served at weddings instead of lamb. And a soup made by adding both rice and trahana to pork broth and seasoned only with a hint of tomato and quite a bit of lemon juice is traditionally eaten at Christmas.

# Pork with celery
## Hirinó me sélino

1 1/2 kg (3 lbs) celery, stalks and
   leaves
coarse sea salt
1 kg (2 lbs) pork shoulder, cut into
   chunks about 5 cm (2 inches)
   square
120 ml (1/2 cup) olive oil
1 large onion, chopped
3 garlic cloves, chopped
240 ml (1 cup) red or white wine
2 tomatoes, chopped or
   1 cup canned tomatoes
1 bay leaf
salt and freshly ground black pepper

Greek celery (*selino*) looks more like
flat-leafed parsley than the plump
white stalks found elsewhere. It also
has a stronger taste, but Pascal celery
also works well in this recipe,
especially if you use all the leaves
too.

**Pork with celery is a classic combination found all over Greece, but I had the best version I've ever tasted at Nychterida, a wonderful taverna in Akrotiri. I had a table to myself, with candles and fresh flowers, overlooking Souda Bay, where I couldn't tell if the lights below me belonged to ships or to the stars' reflections. Nychterida is one of Chania's oldest; the man who founded it in the 1930s also taught Anthony Quinn how to dance the *hasapiko* for his role as Zorba. His son, Babis Mastoridis, specializes in traditional home cooking prepared to perfection.**

**Usually pork with celery is flavored with lemon. This tomato-wine sauce is an equally delicious variation.**

Clean the celery carefully, making sure to remove any sand and stripping off all the strings. Macerate in a colander for about an hour sprinkled with a couple of tablespoons of coarse sea salt. Rinse and wring the stalks and leaves as you would a sweater; this helps them to cook more quickly. Cut the celery in 9 cm (4 inch) pieces and parboil for about 10 minutes in a large pot of boiling water. Add the thicker stalks first and cook them about 5 minutes longer. Discard the water and drain.

Parboil the pork, skimming off the scum, for about 10 minutes. Discard the water, drain and dry off the pork. Brown the pork in batches in a large saucepan or stew pot with half the oil. Remove the meat to a plate, add the rest of the oil and brown the onions and garlic over low heat. With a wooden spoon, stir in half the wine, replace the meat, add the tomatoes, bay leaf and salt and pepper and simmer, covered, for about 1 hour.

Add the celery and the rest of the wine and simmer for another hour until both celery and meat are meltingly tender. Serves 6.

# * Brawn/Head cheese

*Pichti*

**Though not everyone will be up to dealing with a pig's head and trotters, I include this recipe because brawn is one of the dishes Cretans delight in at Christmas. More prosaically, women used to make it in little bowls for their shepherd husbands, as it was an easily transportable and nourishing lunch. Among the various innards, sheets of tripe, "unmentionables" and whole animals on display in the markets in Chania and Heraklio, you will always see a great, grinning pig's head staring from the butcher's showcase. They may not be so readily found in the UK and US especially, where during World War II many Greeks and refugees of other nationalities survived in style, dining on the offal, feet and other body parts most Americans would almost rather die than eat. A kilo of boned pork shoulder can be substituted for the head and feet, but then you'll need to add 2 tablespoons of gelatine to the broth after reducing it.**

*With thanks to Danae Malinaki for sharing this recipe.*

*1 small pig's head, washed, shaved (have the butcher do this), cut in pieces, brain discarded*

*4-6 forefeet, well washed*

*2 apples, peeled, cored and seeded*

*1 medium celeriac, pealed and cut in chunks*

*3 carrots, cut in chunks*

*3 medium onions, peeled*

*3-4 garlic cloves, peeled*

*1 tablespoon black peppercorns*

*1 tablespoon juniper berries*

*salt, to taste*

*1 tablespoon olive oil (to clarify the broth)*

*3 garlic cloves, crushed (optional)*

*60 ml (1/4 cup) good white wine vinegar*

*60 ml (1/4 cup) lemon or bitter orange juice*

*1 teaspoon cumin (optional)*

Put the head and feet in a large saucepan together with the apples, vegetables and seasonings. Pour in enough water to cover and the olive oil and bring to the boil. Reduce the heat to as low as possible and simmer until the meat is falling off the bones (about 4 hours). Periodically skim off any scum that accumulates during the cooking.

Remove the pig's head and feet, reserving the broth, and cut away all the meat from the bones. Chop the meat in small pieces, put in a container and refrigerate. Reduce the broth until you have about 480-720 ml (2-3 cups), discard the vegetables, peppercorns and juniper berries, strain and put in a cool place overnight.

The next day scrape off any fat that has risen to the surface and bring the by now jellied broth to a boil. Remove from the heat and stir in the garlic, cumin, if using, vinegar and fruit juice. (Add more vinegar or juice if you want a stronger taste.)

Depending on how you're going to serve the brawn, you can either make it in a mold, loaf pan or individual dishes. Lay the meat on the bottom of the pan/mold and cover with the broth. Place in refrigerator to set for several hours. It will keep for a week or longer. Serves 8-10.

# * Pork liver sausages
## *Omathiés*

1 large pork intestine or sausage
    casings
pork liver, spleen, heart or
1/2 kg (1 lb) lean ground pork
1 medium onion, finely chopped
2 tablespoons olive oil
75 grams (1/2 cup) raisins, coarsely
    chopped
75 grams (1/2 cup) walnuts, chopped
grated rind of 1 lemon
grated rind of 1 orange
salt and freshly ground pepper
1/2 teaspoon cumin or
1/2 teaspoon cinnamon and
    2 tablespoons sugar
200 grams (1 cup) rice or bulgur

The theory is that this was a Byzantine dish that probably had its roots in pagan times. Originally the sausages were made with pig's blood, which was boiled until it thickened and then added to the rest of the ingredients used to stuff the pig's intestines. Their name is a corruption of "Aimathies" from the Greek word *aima* meaning blood. But while foods containing blood may have been smiled upon by the ancients, the church took a different view and forbade its use – perhaps behaving as Brussels does today in trying to outlaw traditional Greek dishes like *kokoretsi* (spit-roasted innards) and unpasteurized French cheeses – "in the interests of health." But the eating habits of centuries were hard to break, so the church instituted dire punishments. As Psilakis says, "whoever was caught eating or selling food prepared with blood would have their head shaved, be paraded through the streets, flogged, and have their fortune confiscated." Such threats tended to make these sausages less appetizing and this bloodless version gradually took their place and the name changed slightly. Though they were mainly eaten at Christmas, they are still part of the festive menu for weddings and baptisms in eastern and southern Crete and with the addition of sugar are even sometimes served for dessert!

I first came upon omathies in a cooking shack in Zakros, a kind of communal kitchen used whenever any village family had to cater on a scale impossible at home. Though it was still morning and the baptism party would not take place until evening, about five women – friends and relatives – were already preparing dolmades, little pies, salads and these sausages, while two men were boiling up the lambs for the broth in which the traditional macaroni would be cooked. Whether the banquet highlights pilaf as in the western part of the island or macaroni as is the case east of Heraklio, the dish is always man's work from start to finish, perhaps because managing those huge cauldrons requires considerable strength.

The sausages, nubbly things in a soft skin and about as long as my little finger though a bit plumper, were simmering in a large basin. I was offered a taste. Aromatic, tender and subtly sweet, they were quite different from any commercial Greek or Italian sausage.

If you don't wish to use pork liver and innards, you may substitute lean ground pork or even beef.

I don't suppose very many readers will be brave enough to use pig's intestine but if you are, ask the butcher to save it for you. Wash it thoroughly under running water and turn it inside out. (Some people knead it with flour to get rid of the slime and wash it afterwards with home-made oil-based soap, before turning it back to its original state.) Then fill a bowl with fresh water and slices of lemon and soak the intestine for 5 or 6 days, changing the water twice a day. Sausage casings are much less bother and only need to be soaked in water to become elastic and flexible.

When you're ready to make the sausages, chop the pork liver and innards into small pieces and sauté with the onion in the olive oil. (If you're using the ground pork, sauté it in the same way until it is no longer pink.) Put the meat in a bowl with the raisins, nuts and seasonings and mix well. In another bowl soak the rice or bulgur in water to cover. Once the water is absorbed, mix in the meat and raisins with your hands to distribute all the ingredients evenly.

Cut the intestine into 10 cm (4 inch) lengths and start stuffing them with a teaspoon, closing off each end afterwards with a white thread. In the meantime, have a large pot of salted water simmering and when you have finished stuffing the sausages, put them in to cook, poking them from time to time with a sharp knife or fork so the insides will cook evenly. They should take around 45 minutes or more if the sausage casing is thick. Test before draining and serve either hot or cold. Serves 8-10.

To get the delicious taste of omathies without the fuss of stuffing them, make the mixture into "mystery burgers," halving the amount of raisins, walnuts and rice/bulgur, and either fry or grill. Serve with a squeeze of lemon.

# Chicken with orange and tangerine juice

*Kotópoulo kokkinistó me portakalózoumo kai mandarinózoumo*

*1 chicken, preferably free range, washed, dried and cut in serving pieces*
*3 tablespoons olive oil*
*1 large onion, chopped*
*1 cup canned chopped tomatoes, (or) 2 fresh tomatoes, chopped*
*4-5 chopped sun-dried tomatoes (optional)*
*240 ml (1 cup) orange juice*
*240 ml (1 cup) tangerine juice*
*grated peel of 1 orange and 1 tangerine*

**Evangelia Dokoumetzidi died before I had a chance to meet her, but several of my friends think of her as the most brilliant home cook they have known. Luckily for me, her children live in Athens and were happy to share her recipes.**

**Like most housewives of her era, Evangelia kept detailed recipes for desserts only. Her savory dishes were just noted in shorthand reminders, but they always bear her trademarks: imagination and simplicity, as in this inventive variation on classic chicken with red sauce (kokkinisto). My addition of sun-dried tomatoes makes the sauce a bit richer.**

Brown the chicken pieces in the olive oil, remove and set aside. Sauté the onion in the same oil until it is dark, but not burned, almost caramelized.

Transfer the chicken and onion to a large saucepan with a cover, add the juices, peel and tomatoes and bring to a boil. Lower the heat to moderate, cover and boil gently for about 30 minutes. Complete the cooking without the lid, so that the sauce reduces and thickens. The total time should be about 1 hour, depending on the origin of the chicken of course. Serves 4-6.

Bulgur, rice or noodles are a good complement to this sweetish sauce.

# Marika's chicken with okra
*Kotópoulo me bámyes tis Maríkas*

**Though this dish is eaten all over Crete, Marika Petraki's prescription for preventing the okra from being either slimy or furry makes it a winner. The vinegar adds a tang, the okra are firm and the chicken, even the breast, is moist. While many people find the task of trimming the tops of okra into little dunce caps a good reason for never cooking them, I have discovered that being lazy and simply cutting a tiny bit off the stem is adequate in all but the toughest cases. You really don't notice any difference in the eating. As always when giving recipes that involve stewing a delicate vegetable, Greek cooks always add James Bond's admonition, "shake don't stir!"**

1 kg (2 lbs) small, fresh okra
120 ml (1/2 cup) white wine vinegar
    plus 3 tablespoons
1-2 teaspoons salt
1/2 teaspoon sugar (optional –
    to bring out the taste of
    the tomatoes)
4-5 tomatoes, grated, skins discarded
1 chicken, cut in serving pieces and
    skinned if the bird is free range
60-120 ml (1/4-1/2 cup) olive oil
1-2 onions, finely sliced
2 cloves garlic, chopped
1/4 cup chopped parsley
1 large potato, sliced and parboiled
    for 5 minutes (optional)
freshly ground pepper

First prepare the okra. Wash them well, trim the stems and place them in a large bowl with the vinegar, salt, sugar and the grated tomatoes. Mix them well and set aside for 1-2 hours (longer will not hurt).

Preheat the oven to 200°C (400°F). Brown the chicken pieces in the olive oil and remove to a platter. Sauté the onion and garlic until lightly browned. Pour in the extra vinegar and with a wooden spoon scrape up all the bits of chicken that may have stuck. Add the contents of the frying pan to the okra/tomato mixture in a roasting pan, place the chicken and chopped parsley and the potatoes (if using) on top. Season with pepper and bake for about 1 1/2 hours. Serves 6.

# Romaniote chicken with okra

*Kotópoulo me bámyes*

250 grams (1/2 lb) okra
3+1 tablespoons olive oil
1 teaspoon turmeric
1 1 1/2-2 kg (3-4 lb) chicken,
    cut into serving pieces
1 large onion, chopped
4 large tomatoes, peeled and sliced
a large pinch ground cinnamon
    and cloves
1 teaspoon ginger, powdered
    or grated fresh
1 teaspoon crushed coriander seeds
2 bay leaves
salt and pepper
chicken stock
juice of 1 lemon

**Up until World War II, Chania had a substantial Jewish community. Some were descendants of Sephardim from Spain and Portugal invited by the Sultan to many cities in the Ottoman Empire after their expulsion in 1492. The others had preceded them by more than 1500 years and called themselves Romaniotes in memory of their once proud association with the Roman Empire (the Greeks, too, referred to themselves as Romans, and the term is widely used even today). Protected by both the Venetians and the Turks, the Jews mingled more with their Ottoman overlords than did the Cretans, to the point of exchanging recipes. Thus many of their dishes are redolent with spices and flavorings otherwise foreign to native Cretan cookery.**

**This recipe is borrowed from Nicholas Stavroulakis's wonderful *Cookbook of the Jews of Greece* and reprinted here with the kind permission of the author and Lycabettus Press.**

At least 2 hours before you want to start cooking the chicken, prepare the okra. Rub each one in a towel to remove the bristles. Carefully cut away the stem without opening the seed pod. Put them in a fairly shallow dish with 120 ml (1/2 cup) wine vinegar and salt and set in the sun, or a fairly warm place, for 2 hours. Just before using, rinse well and drain.

Heat the olive oil in a large frying pan, add the turmeric, then the chicken and fry until it begins to brown. Transfer the chicken to a large stewing pot.

Sauté the chopped onion in the remaining oil until transparent. Add the tomatoes and all the spices. Stir in well and reduce to a thick sauce.

In a separate frying pan gently sauté the okra in 1 tablespoon olive oil for 5 minutes, stirring constantly. Add the tomato sauce and the okra to the chicken. Add stock to cover, and salt and pepper. Simmer tightly covered, over a low heat for 1 hour, or until the chicken and the okra are tender. Add the lemon juice shortly before the chicken is done. Serves 4-6.

Even without the okra, the chicken is glorious.

# Roast chicken with whole lemons

*Kotópoulo psitó me olóklira lemónia*

(HERAKLIO)

I promise that this is the easiest and simplest recipe you'll find in this book. It is also surprisingly delicious; the lemons suffuse the chicken meat with their delicate flavor. Find the freshest (unwaxed) lemons you can for this dish, and don't use anything but a free-range chicken. Another of the surprises from Evangelia Dokoumetzidi's marvellous notebook.

*1 roasting chicken*
*3 lemons, scrubbed*
*salt and freshly ground pepper*
*olive oil*

Preheat the oven to 180°C (350°F). Wash the chicken, dry it and stuff two whole lemons in its stomach cavity. Sew the two sides together with your largest needle. Rub the skin with salt, pepper, a little olive oil and the juice of the third lemon, and roast for 1 1/2 hours (again depending on the chicken), basting from time to time. Serves 4-6.

# Partridge with green olives
## Kóttes me prásines eliés

*4 partridges or 1 small chicken*
*1 small onion, chopped*
*2-3 tablespoons olive oil*
*240 ml (1 cup) red wine*
*3-4 ripe tomatoes, halved, grated*
  *and skins discarded or*
*1/2 can (200 grams / 8 oz) chopped*
  *tomatoes*
*1 piece orange peel*
*1/2 cup Greek green olives, tsakistes,*
  *soaked in water for 30 minutes*
  *if too salty*
*salt and freshly ground pepper,*
  *to taste*

**In the old days partridge were Crete's most common game bird, so common they were given the ordinary name, *kotta* or hen. Nowadays chicken takes the place of partridge in this dish, so I give instructions for both birds. You could also use Cornish game hens or even pigeons, if you're lucky enough to find them.**

*With thanks to Danae Malinaki for sharing this recipe.*

Basically, the procedure is the same for both birds. Only if the partridges are wild will they need more cooking; game farm partridges don't need any special treatment.

First, soften the onion in the olive oil, add the chicken or partridges and brown them. Remove the birds, pour in the wine and scrape up all the bits that may have stuck to the pan.

Return the birds to the pot, add the chopped tomatoes and lots of freshly ground black pepper. Bring to the boil, and cover, lowering the heat to simmer. Cook for about 1 hour.

When the partridges or chicken are ready, add the olives and simmer for another 10 minutes. Serves 4.

# Rabbit with two kinds of cumin

*Kounéli me dío kímina*

**Nada Petrandi who provided this recipe has roots in Asia Minor, where cumin is a popular seasoning. In eastern and central Crete, though, people say "kimino-pipero" when giving a recipe almost as often as they say "alato-pipero" (salt and pepper). Whether they acquired the taste for this distinctive spice as a result of contact with refugees from Asia Minor after 1922 or had already got the habit earlier is still open to debate. No matter, this is a treat for cumin lovers anywhere.**

Pour just enough olive oil in a large saucepan to cover the bottom. Brown the rabbit pieces and pour in the wine, scraping up any bits that may have stuck. Cover and simmer on the lowest heat possible.

After about 45 minutes, add the whole cumin seed, the ground cumin and salt. At this point you could also add the onion, if you are using it, and a little more wine if the rabbit looks dry. Cook for another 15 minutes, until all the wine has evaporated and only the oil remains. Serves 6.

*1 rabbit, cut in serving pieces*
*2-3 tablespoons olive oil*
*240 ml (1 cup) red or rosé wine*
*(a light wine, not a brusco)*
*1 1/2 tablespoon whole cuminseed*
*1 teaspoon or more ground cumin,*
*to taste*
*1 onion, finely chopped (optional)*

---

**Cooking cumin too long will give it a bitter taste.**

# * Rabbit meze

*Kounéli xekafkáloto*

**Despite the simplicity of this recipe, it produces a very succulent dish. The ensuing pan juices cry out for fresh bread to mop them up with and the rabbit is juicy and sweet. I tried adding garlic and oregano to the marinade but in fact they did not improve the flavor.**

*With thanks to Kostanza Gavrilaki for sharing this recipe.*

Wash the rabbit and marinate it overnight in lemon juice and salt. Dry it, heat the oil in a large nonstick skillet and brown the rabbit pieces. When browned on all sides, add a little water (about 60 ml or 1/4 cup) and simmer the rabbit, covered, until only the oil remains and the meat is tender. Serves 4-6.

*1 small rabbit, cut up in small pieces*
*lemon juice*
*coarse salt*
*60 ml (1/4 cup) olive oil*

# Sfakian fried rabbit

*Tsigariastó kounéli*

1 small rabbit, cut in serving
    portions
480 ml (2 cups) red, white or rosé
    wine
2 bay leaves
1 cinnamon stick
3-4 cloves
5-6 whole black peppercorns
1 teaspoon oregano
salt and freshly ground black pepper
    to taste
olive oil for frying

**I was served this treat in Askyfou, a village in the mountains between Chania and Rethymno which is famous for its paximadia (rusks) of all kinds. The cook was Sifis (Iosif) Karkanis, who started cooking aged eight when he went to the upper pastures with his brothers and the family sheep. His first creation used cracked wheat pasta, trahana, which he boiled and then fried along with some chunks of bread in a little olive oil. The bread tasted "as good as meat" but then, remembering how his mother added bay leaves for further flavor, he threw in ten of them just to be sure. He has since learned restraint but reminded us that in those days (not so long ago really, in the 1950s), necessity was indeed the mother of invention and ingredients were extremely basic: oil, flour, greens, cheese. Even salt was a luxury and he sometimes seasoned his meals with a little brine taken from the feta tin.**

**Sifi's rabbit combines the tastes of strong spices, just two bay leaves and good wine.**

Marinate the rabbit for a few hours or overnight in the wine and bay leaves, and other seasonings, except for the oregano.

Remove the meat from the marinade, dry the meat, and reserve the liquid. Brown the meat in a few tablespoons of hot oil, along with the marinade spices, bay leaves and oregano. Reduce the heat to a simmer and cook until the rabbit is tender.

When the rabbit is cooked, remove it from the pan, add 240 ml (1 cup) of the marinade and scraping up the pan juices and bits and pieces, reduce it until you have a thick syrupy sauce. Pour it over the rabbit and serve. Serves 4.

Sifis also makes this dish with kid and enriches the sauce with yogurt at the very end.

# Sautéed rabbit with yogurt

*Kounéli me yiaoúrti*

**This dish is very similar to the lamb baked with yogurt on page 111. This version was suggested by Stamatis Moros, a chef at the Rithymna Beach Hotel, who loves his work so much he happily spends seven day weeks eight months a year cooking and overseeing the hotel's various restaurants. Braising the meat, whether rabbit or lamb, keeps it moist.**

*1 rabbit, cut in serving pieces*
*lemon juice*
*salt and freshly ground pepper*
*1/2 teaspoon oregano*
*3 tablespoons olive oil*
*1 medium onion, chopped*
*2 eggs or 2 egg whites*
*200 grams (1 cup) strained yogurt*
*pinch of nutmeg*
*1 tablespoon grated kefalotyri, regato or pecorino cheese*

Marinate the rabbit in lemon juice, salt and pepper and oregano for 2-3 hours.

Dry the rabbit and heat the oil in a large nonstick skillet. Sauté the onion in the oil until soft and then add the rabbit pieces and brown them along with the onion. Add the marinade to the pan with a little water, cover and braise the rabbit until it is tender and no pink juices flow when pricked with a knife.

Meanwhile preheat the oven to 160°C (325°F). Beat the eggs or egg whites until fluffy and fold them into the yogurt along with the nutmeg. Place the rabbit in a roasting pan, pour the pan juices into the bowl with the yogurt mixture, stir gently and cover the rabbit with the sauce. Sprinkle the grated cheese on top and bake for about 15 minutes or until the sauce puffs up like a souffle and turns an appetizing light brown. Serves 4-5.

The egg yolk is included more for color than taste, so if you prefer the rising action without the yolk, save the yolks for a mayonnaise.

# Quick and easy hare stew
## *Lagós stifádo*

1 hare, rinsed in wine and cut
in serving pieces
360-480 ml (1 1/2 - 2 cups)
red wine
salt and freshly ground pepper
to taste
1 1/2 kg (3 lbs) stewing onions,
peeled and trimmed
2 heads garlic, unpeeled
1 stick cinnamon
1 strip orange peel
peppercorns
2 cloves
2 bay leaves
2-3 allspice berries
2-3 juniper berries
60 ml (1/4 cup) vinegar
1-2 tablespoons grape must syrup
(optional) or
1 teaspoon sugar
240 ml (1 cup) olive oil

Hares along with partridge were Crete's most important game animals until a few decades ago. Now one finds them frozen at the supermarket.

Danae Malinaki who gave me this recipe says that it is important to rinse the hare before cooking it, not in water but in wine. She drains the hare over a bowl and uses the same wine to rinse it two or three times. Since she also cooks the hare in it, there is no waste. She also adds a little grape must syrup or sugar to "mellow the taste of the wine."

Do not be alarmed by the amount of olive oil used here. It will give the dish a lovely sweetness, but you won't actually be consuming it, since before you bring the dish to the table you pour and skim it off. Don't throw it away, keep it for cooking another dish.

Put all the ingredients in a large saucepan – no browning is needed here – simmer, covered, until the hare is tender (at least 2 hours) and no liquid except the oil remains. Serves 6.

Danae, who is very well travelled and an ardent improvisor, recommends that you use American bottled Mixed Pickling Spice if you do not have all the flavorings on hand.

HERE'S A TRICK: When you have a lot of spices in a stew like this one, hollow out an orange and stuff them all in it. Sew the edges together again and boil it along with the rabbit or hare. Discard after half an hour. That way you get the flavor with none of the disagreeable sensations that come with biting into a cinnamon stick or juniper berry.

# SNAILS

## Salingária/Hochlioús

With snails available just for the picking, sometimes so thickly clustered on a branch or leaf you can hardly see what's underneath, it's not surprising that they are a fundamental pillar of the Cretan diet. Some families dine on them as often as three times a week, and what snails are not consumed on the island get shipped off to that other place where they are gourmet fodder, France. The export business has, in fact, been thriving since Minoan times, when snails were among the delicacies requested by the court at Akrotiri on what is now Santorini. The squeamish should try to cultivate a taste for them since many scientists, including Serge Renaud – who has done so much research on the Cretan diet and heart disease – believe that they play a key role in combating cardiovascular problems. In a way, those famous greens are again responsible; the omega-3 fatty acids that make the snails so healthful can be traced back to the greens they eat.

Cretans distinguish between summer and winter snails, the summer variety being more elusive, since after satiating themselves on delicate spring greens, they have to be pried from shady hiding places. But they are easier to clean and don't need to be purged or fattened up. Winter snails, on the other hand, need to be fed on flour or other roughage for a week, a process that hardens their shells as well as purifying their digestive systems.

Cookbook writer Mirsini Lambraki, an authority on greens and other Cretan foods, told me how to know if a snail is ready to eat. "Always look for a hard dry membrane across the opening and a firm shell. And when you've cut that membrane off and the snail doesn't poke its 'nose' out while you're handling it, throw it away. It's probably dead."

There are literally dozens of Cretan recipes for snails – pilaf, with egg lemon sauce, "red" with tomato sauce, plain boiled for Lent, with herbs, stewed with potatoes, with mixed summer vegetables – but snails with bulgur or trahana is the dish most Cretans put at the top of their preferences.

# Snails with bulgur or trahana

*Hochlioús me hóndro i xinóhondro*

1/2 kilo (1 lb) snails
1 large onion, finely chopped
120 ml (1/2 cup) olive oil
1/2 kg (1 lb) tomatoes, chopped
salt and pepper to taste
400 grams (2 cups) bulgur or
    trahana

**This recipe is adapted from the booklet published by the Department of Agriculture in Heraklio, "Don't forget tradition in your kitchen."**

Put the snails in a saucepan with water barely to cover, bring to the boil and cook for 5-8 minutes, skimming all the while. Drain and rinse well.

Sauté the onion with the snails in the olive oil until the onion is translucent and starting to brown. Add the seasonings and tomatoes, stirring. Cover and cook over moderate heat until the tomatoes release their juices. Uncover and simmer until most of the liquid has evaporated.

Test the snails to see if they're done by spearing one and cutting the meat. If tender, remove them from the saucepan and add the bulgur or trahana along with 360 ml (1 1/2 cups) of water. Cover and simmer until most of the water is absorbed (10-15 minutes). Put the snails back in the pan and simmer for another 5-10 minutes. Serves 4-6.

# * Snails boubouristoús

4-6 SERVINGS
1/2 kg (2 lbs) snails
salt
80 ml (1/3 cup) olive oil
4 tablespoons white wine vinegar
sprigs of fresh rosemary

**This is one of the most delicious recipes for snails but its name defies translation. *Boubourisma* seems to be the sound the snails make when they are sizzling in the oil and vinegar. This is wonderful taverna fare, and I admit I'd rather eat it there than have to cope with snails crawling round my kitchen. In case you are more courageous, here's how to go about it, in the words of Despina Rasidaki, who lives in Heraklio but always keeps a bucket of snails in her storeroom.**

"The best season for snails is March, when they come out with the rain, and summer when they gather in the olive trees and bushes.

Then they're fatter and don't need any preparation. The best time to collect them is early in the morning when the dew is still on the ground or in the cool of the evening with a flashlight. If they are winter snails, I keep them in a big bucket in the storeroom with some broken up, uncooked angel hair spaghetti or some bran for about a week. Eating this purifies their systems – you never know, they might have been eating something unclean or a weed that makes them taste bitter. And I always put some wire netting over the bucket so they don't escape, and some vine branches inside for them to climb on.

"Before I cook them, their shells have to be wiped of any dirt or slime with a wet cloth. Then I cut off the little hard "shoe" that closes off the opening to their shell. After that I wash them in lots of water and put them in a colander to drain.

"To make boubouristous I throw some coarse salt into a frying pan, enough to cover the bottom, put the snails in with their 'mouth' facing down, and turn on the burner to medium. Then I wait for about 3 minutes for them to spit out ('boubouristoun') their juices before I pour in the olive oil. After the oil heats up I stir them for about 10 minutes, and then I deglaze the pan with some good vinegar and I scatter some rosemary twigs into it. Yum yum."

Don't throw out the oil, you can use it to fry something else, potatoes, for example.

Chrysanna Karelli gives her snails VIP treatment. First she feeds them on flour for a week to clean them and then she puts them in a box or bucket with herbs – sage, oregano, marjoram – for another week. She scalds them in water till they come out of their shells, drains them and boils them in water with orange and lemon leaves as well as citrus flowers. Then she makes a butter with chopped herbs (as the French do) and stuffs the snails back into their shells with this and bakes them in a medium oven for 20-30 minutes.

*19th century travellers on snails*

When Edward Lear was hiking around Crete with George, his manservant, and his donkey, looking for landscapes to draw in 1864, he often commented on his meals. Like most travellers to the island before the 20th century, he usually stayed in monasteries, where the cooking was reputed to be excellent. But one evening in a village near Heraklio he happened to eat a supper of "snails, herbs [greens] as salad and pastachi, this being flour and milk with oil ... The snails, which George and I ate for the first time, we found really decent, boiled in oil. The herbs in oil also were not bad, and the pastachi capital. We all set to with small forks and the host and the muleteer continually filled glasses, perpetual healths and compliments going on before and after drink; a running fire of ceremony."

Robert Pashley was one of the first Englishmen to explore Crete in search of its ancient past. Besides the ruins, he also had an eye for the living and eating habits of the islanders in the 1830s. He has this to say about snails: "The snails of Crete are highly prized in the Levant, and they are one of the regular exports of the island. The Christian population of Constantinople, Smyrna and Alexandria all enjoy this delicacy during the fasts of the Oriental church... . Snails, a luxury in which the Greek is allowed to indulge even on his most rigorous fasts."

# VEGETABLE DISHES

## Lahaniká

I was introduced to Cretan vegetables one May morning at the Saturday open-air market in Heraklio. To me these markets are among the prime joys of living in Greece. Every neighborhood has one and to be sure the sight of red tomatoes from Ierapetra, oranges and avocados from Chania, and chestnuts from the White Mountains is something I'm used to, even in Athens. Cretan products are always labelled and hawked in capital letters, since their origin is a guarantee of good flavor in addition to good looks – in Northern Europe as well as in the rest of Greece. But it was quite another experience to see them so fresh and abundant in their place of origin.

The Heraklio market must be at least a mile long. Wooden stalls line both sides of the street parallel to the Piraeus ferry landing as far as the eye can see, and shoppers jam the space between them. With elbows as sharp as spurs and their secret weapon, the shopping cart, they jostle for position to prod, poke, pick over and taste whatever they buy. Some have their favorite vendors and exchange greetings and cooking advice, but I was content to simply goggle. Once I got accustomed to the din – the shouts, the banter, the innuendoes – I became aware of the smells. Strawberry essence mingled with the unmistakeable aroma of just-picked tomatoes. Someone crushed some

oregano between his creased hands to demonstrate its pungency. The fragrances of sage and camomile wafted up from another stall.

Though late in the season, leafy greens were still very much in evidence, some already tied into bundles for "yiachni" (stews). A leek, some carrot tops, several stalks of spinach beet and wild fennel kept company with a herb I couldn't identify. Finally, I bought some lethal looking barbed artichokes, my own secret weapon to make headway through the throng. Amidst the "professionals" with lettuces, radishes, spring onions, mushrooms neatly arranged in orderly mounds, the one-crop farmers with nothing but oranges, lemons or broad beans, and the greenhouse purveyors with perfect looking polished eggplants, finger-length zucchini and baby stringbeans, there were the country people. Spry, wiry old ladies sat before a dozen brown eggs and a handful of wild asparagus balanced on a wooden crate, a modest pile of bitter greens, dug from the mountain before sunrise, a basket of energetic snails or even a bunch of fragile-stemmed gladioli gleaned from some field.

It was a foodie's paradise, more fun in its way than Harrods' Food Halls or the gourmet basement at Galeries Lafayette. I could go there every week and never weary of the spectacle, the hubbub, the gusto of shoppers and sellers, the extreme freshness of the glorious produce.

Of course, flavor is something the Cretans take for granted. They have never experienced "the tomato problem" northern city dwellers complain of, and most cooks still like to follow the seasons, even though the greenhouses have blurred the distinction between them. Because vegetables are often the main dish at a meal, not just a side show, they have to be excellent.

Over centuries of fasting, whether prescribed by the Church or by necessity, Greeks and Cretans have perfected techniques of combining simple ingredients to make them both taste good and go further, to feed large families. In this they have been amply assisted by nutritious, delicious olive oil. I can think of no Cretan vegetable dish that does not require it, except for the oil-less lentil soup and bitter greens traditionally eaten on Good Friday. To deny oneself olive oil is to fast indeed.

The vegetable dishes in this book fall into five broad categories: braises, pies, stuffed, fried and salads. You will find them under every heading except Desserts, since it is the rare fish or meat dish that does not include a bit of greenery or a little tomato, even if just for color. Some recipes come in two versions, one with meat, eggs or cheese for every day or holidays, the other without for fasting. Since the number of fast days, observed by previous generations at least, amounted to almost half the year, fasting recipes are plentiful. You may find them even more to your taste than some of the feast day extravaganzas that ooze with creamy staka and four kinds of cheese as well as baby lamb. Just remember what the conditions were like when these traditional dishes were established, and balance them with restraint. And remember not to compromise where quality is concerned; always buy the freshest vegetables you can find, from organic or farmers' markets and you'll get the best out of these recipes.

# Zucchini, potato and myzithra casserole
## *Bouréki*

1/2 kg (1 lb) medium potatoes, peeled

1/2 kg (1 lb) medium zucchini, washed and trimmed

3 medium tomatoes, halved and seeded

3 tablespoons coarsely chopped fresh mint

2 tablespoons coarsely chopped flat leaved parsley

salt and freshly ground pepper to taste

350 grams (3/4 lb) fresh myzithra cheese, substitute ricotta or half feta, half curd cheese, if not available

60 ml (1/4 cup) olive oil

1/2 teaspoon oregano

In most of Greece and even in eastern Crete "boureki" is a word of Turkish origin that means a little pie filled with meat or cheese. However, in Chania boureki is a main dish casserole that may or may not have a crust. Heated arguments arise there about the "correct" way to prepare it and the only thing all cooks agree on is that boureki must have zucchini and myzithra, the fresh white cheese similar to ricotta, and that if it does contain tomatoes, it should not be encased in pastry; their juice will make it soggy. I've tried many versions and include three in this chapter: this excellent crustless recipe from Katerina Farandaki, a Chaniotissa now living near Athens, one with a delicious crust, and one substituting pumpkin for the zucchini.

A busy woman who runs a chain of language schools, Katerina has streamlined the preparation without sacrificing any of the taste. Her combination of vegetables, mint and fresh cheese is very delicate and refreshing, a wonderful choice for a summer evening, or a first course before a meat dish for a party.

Have three bowls handy, two for the vegetables, one for the cheese. Slice the potatoes into thin rounds about 2/3 cm (1/2 inch) thick into one bowl. Slice the zucchini into rounds of the same thickness and place them in the second bowl. Grate the tomatoes over the zucchini, discarding the skins. Add the mint, parsley and pepper and salt (depending on the saltiness of the cheese) and toss until evenly distributed. Crumble the cheese into the third bowl.

Preheat the oven to 230°C (450°F). Oil a round baking tin or ovenproof dish approximately 25 cm/10 inches in diameter and line the bottom with half of the potatoes. Sprinkle 1/3 of the cheese on top of them, followed by 1/3 of the zucchini-tomato mixture. Continue, alternating cheese and zucchini (3 layers in all) and cover them with the remaining potatoes. Drizzle the remaining oil over them and dust with a little oregano.

Place in the oven and when you see the juices bubbling, reduce the heat to 190°C (375°F) and bake for another 30 minutes or until the potatoes are tender. Serves 4 as a main dish or 6 as a side dish to accompany meat or chicken.

Cooked this way the potatoes form a succulent crust, top and bottom. If you were making this dish in Chania, you would add a tablespoon of staka (see page 44) to the top layer of potatoes. Mascarpone, clotted cream or crème fraiche can be substituted, but in fact the dish is fine without this enrichment. The myzithra, though relatively low in fat, provides enough.

# Boureki encased in pastry
*Bouréki me fýllo*

**This recipe comes from Marika Daskalogianni, who grew up in Elos, an area thick with fir trees in the mountains southwest of Chania. Her winey crust has an unusual purply tinge and is especially delicious. This recipe can be doubled to produce a fine party dish.**

First prepare the pastry. Make a well in the flour, add the salt, wine and oil and some of the water and with your fingers mix in the flour, dribbling in more water as you need it. Knead well for about 10 minutes until you have a soft, pliable dough. Cover the dough and set it aside for about 30 minutes. If you want to leave it longer, refrigerate it.

When ready to cook, preheat the oven to 190°C (375°F). Separate the dough into two pieces, one slightly larger than the other. Roll out the larger one first and lay it in a lightly oiled baking tin (22 x 30 cm/9 x 13 inches). As with the first boureki recipe, fill the pastry with alternating layers of potatoes, zucchini and myzithra, sprinkling in a little flour, mint, grated cheese and salt and pepper on top of each layer.

Beat the egg with the milk and staka and pour it over the final layer. Dribble the oil over the whole surface.

Roll out the second piece of dough large enough to more than cover the pan, folding over the edges to seal in the steam. Brush with a little oil and sprinkle thoroughly with sesame seeds. Score the pie into square serving portions and bake for about 1 hour or until the crust is a purply gold (from the wine) and the vegetables are done. Serves 8-10.

FOR THE PASTRY
*280 grams (2 cups) flour*
*1 1/2 teaspoon olive oil*
*1/4 teaspoon salt*
*2 tablespoons red wine*
*120 ml (1/2 cup) tepid water (approximately)*

FOR THE FILLING
*3/4 kg (1 1/2 lbs) potatoes, thinly sliced*
*3/4 kg (1 1/2 lbs) zucchini, thinly sliced*
*1/2 kg (1 lb) myzithra or ricotta cheese, crumbled*
*3 tablespoons flour*
*1 bunch mint leaves, finely chopped*
*100 grams (3/4 cup) grated graviera or other mild cheese*
*salt and freshly ground black pepper*
*1 egg, beaten*
*120 ml (1/2 cup) milk*
*2 tablespoons staka (or crème fraiche or mascarpone)*
*120 ml (1/2 cup) olive oil*
*sesame seeds for the crust*

# Baked pumpkin casserole
*Bouréki me kolokýtha*

1 lb (1/2 kilo) pumpkin, peeled
salt and freshly ground pepper
120 grams (1 cup) myzithra (or
   ricotta) or feta, crumbled
1 large onion, grated or finely
   chopped (optional)
1/2 cup finely chopped fresh mint
2 tablespoons finely chopped parsley
   (optional)
flour for coating the pumpkin

FOR THE BATTER
140 grams (1 cup) flour
240 ml (1 cup) soda water
2 tablespoons olive oil
salt to taste

This recipe comes from Apokoronas, the peninsula between Rethymno and Chania. Vamos, the head village there, is well on its way to becoming a live museum of Cretan traditions carried out in beautifully restored buildings thanks to a small group of dynamic young people sickened by the sight of their birthplace sliding into decay and oblivion. Their vision includes bringing the past back to life through food. Besides olive oil, olives and flavored raki, the refurbished general store sells pasta, preserves and cheeses made by local women too old to pick olives or clean hotel rooms. One of them, Maria Frangiadaki, who gave me this recipe, is so adept that she demonstrates her cooking skills for tourists.

Greek pumpkins are neither as orange nor as sweet as American jack o' lanterns. They are also rarely as round, but come in a diversity of shapes, sometimes with long necks, bulbous bases and a hard caramel-colored skin. If you cannot find pumpkin, hubbard or butternut squash would be a fine substitute.

Cut the pumpkin into slices about 2 cm / 1/2 inch thick, 6 cm / 3 inches long. Sprinkle with salt and pepper and set them in a colander to drain off their excess liquid for about an hour.

Mix the cheese with the onion (if using) and herbs in a small bowl.

Dry the pumpkin slices with paper towels, dust them with a little flour and place them in an oiled baking dish, topped with a layer of myzithra and mint. (Depending on the size of your baking dish, you can have more than one layer of vegetables and cheese.)

Preheat the oven to 200°C (400°F). Mix the ingredients for the batter, which should be medium thick, and cover the vegetables and cheese with it. Bake for 30 minutes or until the top is nicely browned. Serves 8 as a side dish.

# * Eggplant-pumpkin rolls
*Melitzánes me kolokýtha pouré*

(RETHYMNO)

**This is by no means a traditional recipe; it is an invention of Stamatis Moros, a chef at the Rithymna Beach Hotel, who loves thinking up new combinations for wonderful Cretan vegetables. Adventurous cooks in the Puglia region of Italy wrap thinly sliced eggplant around sweet preserves as though they were crepes, so why not a pumpkin filling? Not only are these delectable, they are also very presentable.**

*1 large eggplant*
*salt*
*olive oil for frying*
*1 medium onion, finely chopped*
*250 grams (8 oz) pumpkin, rind and*
  *seeds removed and cubed*
*1 tablespoon chopped parsley*
*freshly ground black pepper*
*1 tablespoon flour*
*4 full tablespoons grated kefalotyri or*
  *graviera cheese*

Slice the eggplant as thinly as you dare (about 1 cm/1/3 inch), sprinkle with salt and set in a colander to drain for at least 30 minutes. Rinse and pat dry between 2 dish towels.

Heat a few tablespoons of oil in a large frying pan and fry the slices quickly until they are fairly soft and malleable. Drain well on paper towels.

In the same oil (add a little if necessary), sauté the chopped onion until it starts to brown, then add the cubed pumpkin. When the pumpkin is soft, add the chopped parsley and pepper, and sprinkle the flour into the pan. Simmer, stirring for a minute or two. Remove from heat and mix in 2 tablespoons of the grated cheese.

Preheat the oven to 190°C (375°F). Line up your eggplant slices and place a spoonful of pumpkin mixture at the end of each one and roll up. Place the rolls seamside down in a barely oiled pyrex dish, and sprinkle with the rest of the grated cheese. Bake the rolls for about 10 minutes or until golden. Serves 4.

# Pumpkin dressed up as liver or red mullet

*Kolokýtha savóri*

(MARGARITES, NEAR RETHYMNO)

*1 500 gram (1 lb) piece of pumpkin, rind removed*

*flour for dredging*

*salt and freshly ground pepper, to taste*

*60 ml (1/4 cup) or more olive oil*

*60 ml (1/4 cup) good white wine vinegar*

*sprig of rosemary, fresh or dried*

*handful of black currants (optional)*

Margarites, one of Crete's loveliest villages, is smothered in greenery in the hills above Rethymno. Doors and shutters in mellow shades of green and blue glow like gems set into soft stone arches and lintels. Apart from its prettiness, however, Margarites is known for its pottery. It even boasts two potters who still use the wheel to turn out vases, jugs and storage jars that look so much like ancient ceramics that the BBC recently filmed an episode for a series on life in classical Greece in one of the workshops. During World War II Manolis Tsiragopoulos, who collects his clay from the riverbed on donkeyback, used his pots (loaded onto a previous donkey) to carry provisions up to British soldiers hidden in the mountains. We talked for hours and then he sent me to his wife Maria for recipes.

Maria was making pumpkin cut in slices, fried and sauced like red mullet with vinegar, rosemary and currants. It is thought that savori, with its sweet and sour tastes, dates from Byzantine or even earlier times; it is also found in Venetian cooking, somewhat modified, under the name "saor". The vinegar preserves the fish for up to a month, but there's no point in keeping pumpkin around for that long. Pork liver is also treated in the same way. This dish would make part of a light supper on an autumn evening with stewed greens and a big slice of feta sprinkled with oregano.

Cut the pumpkin into slices about 2.5 cm (an inch) thick, dredge them in flour seasoned with salt and pepper, shake off the excess flour and fry on both sides in hot but not smoking olive oil. Lower the heat to prevent charring. They will become, in Maria's words, "crisp outside and creamy inside like loukoumi" (Turkish delight).

Place the pumpkin slices on paper towels to drain and pour the vinegar into the frying pan. With a wooden spoon scrape up the bits and pieces to make a sauce, add the rosemary and currants if using, and simmer for a minute ot two. Place the pumpkin slices on a platter, drizzle the sauce over them and serve. Serves 4.

# * Eggplant stuffed with vegetables, cheese and olives

*Melitzánes yemistés me kefalotýri*

(Istron Bay Hotel)

This is a creation of Panayiotis Delvenakiotis, the creative young chef at the Istron Bay Hotel in Eastern Crete. Panayiotis received his culinary training and most of his experience in Germany. When he took over the post at Istron Bay, he had a kind of epiphany. "Here in Crete, I've learned so much. About the taste of fresh produce, about the importance of simplicity, and about how much can be done with vegetables, with pulses and wonderful olive oil." His love of the island's summer vegetables shows up in this recipe. Here Panayiotis has certainly achieved his three main aims as a chef: arranging a natural marriage of flavors, clean tastes and attractive, colorful presentation.

Moreover, the stuffing is so exquisite that when I have no eggplant, I use it as a sauce for pasta. It could also serve as a kind of warm dip or salsa accompanied by crisp bite-sized rusks. If you make more than you need and omit the cheese on the extras, you'll also have a superb treat the next day.

*6 long thin or small round eggplants*
*sea salt*
*olive oil for frying*
*1 large onion, chopped*
*2 cloves garlic, thinly sliced*
*2 medium-sized ripe tomatoes, chopped*
*30 black and green olives, pitted and chopped*
*3 tablespoons chopped parsley*
*3 tablespoons chopped basil*
*freshly ground black pepper*
*6 thin slices kefalotýri or pecorino cheese*

Slit the eggplants in half lengthwise and score the cut side diagonally, both vertically and horizontally. Place them in a colander and sprinkle with coarse salt so that they will exude some liquid and become less absorbent when fried. Set aside for at least 30 minutes.

Rinse the eggplant halves and pat dry with paper towels. Heat 4 to 6 tablespoons of olive oil in a large skillet and quickly fry the eggplant for 4-5 minutes on each side. Drain on paper towels and when cool enough to handle spoon out about 1/3 of the eggplant flesh and chop it coarsely.

Make the stuffing. Sauté the onion and garlic in 2 or 3 tablespoons of oil over medium to low heat until barely soft, add the chopped eggplant and sauté for another 2-3 minutes. Add the tomatoes, raise the heat and cook them quickly so they give up their liquid but remain somewhat firm. Add the olives and cook 2 more

minutes and then stir in the herbs and pepper. You may not need to add any salt as the olives and cheese will provide that.

Preheat the oven to 180°C (350°F). Put the eggplant cases in an oven-proof baking dish, stuff with the vegetables and bake for 15 minutes. Place the cheese slices on top of the stuffing and cook for another 5 minutes or until the cheese is melted. Serves 6.

# * Ypapandi's stuffed vine leaves and zucchini flowers

## Dolmadákia

(AGIOS NIKOLAOS)

FOR THE FILLING
*300 grams (1 1/2 cups) Carolina rice, rinsed and drained*
*1 medium potato, peeled*
*2 small onions*
*2 small zucchini*
*2 big ripe tomatoes*
*3-4 garlic cloves*
*6-7 sprigs of fresh mint*
*6-7 sprigs of parsley*
*salt and 1/2 teaspoon freshly ground pepper*
*1/2 teaspoon cumin*
*120 ml (1/2 cup) olive oil (Ypapandi used a whole cup)*

*1 potato, peeled and sliced (optional)*
*30-40 vine leaves, washed and patted dry*
*20 zucchini flowers, washed and drained*

Ypapandi Velivasaki (photo) is one of the cooks at the Porto Elounda Hotel. Her face radiates delight in what she is doing and her round figure proclaims her delectation in her own cooking. She says these dolmadakia are eaten for the first time each spring on Maundy Thursday, a welcome treat during Holy Week where stringent fasting is customary. In Crete they tend to be at least half the size of those commonly found in tavernas or cans elsewhere.

She showed me how to make them in the hotel kitchen one afternoon in that moment of relative quiet after lunch had been cleared away and preparations for dinner had not yet begun. She had picked the zucchini blossoms, vine leaves and vegetables in her own garden that morning and proceeded to grate them with lightning speed into a bowl where the rinsed rice was waiting. She added the seasonings, poured in what looked like a tremendous amount of oil and then mixed everything with her pink, plump right hand, chatting all the while and bantering with a few kitchen helpers who had gathered round for the show. When the dolmades were cooked, in just 20 minutes, she passed them round and we all smacked our lips with approval.

Put the rice into a large bowl. Grate all the vegetables into it, including the tomatoes (discard the skins). Chop the mint and parsley and add them, the other seasonings and the olive oil. Mix thoroughly

with a wooden spoon if you don't like the "hands on" approach.

Line the bottom of a saucepan with the sliced potato or some torn vine leaves. Place a teaspoon of filling near the top of each vine leaf, fold the two sides over it and then roll it toward the tip, making a small cylindrical packet. Place seamside down in the saucepan. Don't worry about making them perfect. They won't fall apart, since you pack them close together. Repeat until all the vine leaves are filled, except for a few more torn ones for the top. Stuff the zucchini flowers, pushing the tips inward over the filling. Don't bother to remove the stamens, you'll simply tear the flowers.

Cover the stuffed leaves and flowers with any remaining vine leaves and place an old plate a bit smaller than the saucepan on top of them. Add water to the level of the plate, bring to the boil and cover. Reduce heat and simmer for 20-25 minutes. Remove the plate and pour in the 2-3 tablespoons of lemon juice, shaking the saucepan to distribute the juice. Serve hot or tepid. They will also be good the next day. Serves 8 as a main course.

For tips on using brine-preserved vine leaves, see page 121.

You can prepare vine leaves with assembly line rapidity if you lay them all out, rough side up, on the table first rather than trying to fill and wrap them one by one.

# Molded okra for parties

*Bámyes se kaloúpi*

1 kg (2 lbs) okra, fresh or frozen
60 ml (1/4 cup) lemon juice
120 ml (1/2 cup) olive oil
4-5 garlic cloves, finely chopped
4 medium tomatoes, chopped
1 teaspoon sugar
1 large bunch parsley, finely chopped
salt and freshly ground pepper, to
    taste

**When Nada Petrandi gave me her recipes one sparkling morning in early April, I had difficulty concentrating because her living room windows looked directly over the port of Heraklio. I could not see the yachts tied at the quay, just the round fortress with the Lion of St. Mark emblazoned against the grey stones.**

**Nada's family came to Crete from Asia Minor, and this very pretty dish has the attention to detail and aesthetics characteristic of its place of origin.**

First prepare the okra, if fresh. Wash them well, trim the stems and place them in a large bowl with 2 tablespoons of the lemon juice, salt as desired, and set aside for 1-2 hours (longer will not hurt). Rinse and drain.

In the meantime make the tomato sauce. Heat the olive oil in a saucepan and sauté the garlic for 1 minute, add the chopped tomatoes and sugar and cover for a few minutes so that they exude their liquid. Remove the lid and simmer until the sauce begins to reduce and thicken, about 15 minutes. Stir in the chopped parsley and salt and pepper and set aside.

Preheat the oven to 180°C (350°F). Take a round shallow mold or baking dish and arrange the okra in it, tails facing the center, stem ends facing out. Place the larger ones first, filling in the gaps with the smaller ones, tapering a bit towards the center as you build. Pack them tightly so they'll stay in place. When you've finished, pour the tomato sauce through the hole left at the top and around the okra. Cover and bake for about 45 minutes or until the vegetables are tender.

Remove the lid, sprinkle some lemon juice over the okra and let sit a few minutes before unmolding. To unmold hold your serving dish firmly on top of the mold and invert the contents onto the dish. Sprinkle with the rest of the lemon juice. Serves 6-8.

# Spinach with green olives
## Spanáki me prásines eliés

**Though dishes with cooked olives are not as common as you might expect in a country where they are so plentiful, they are no rarity in western Crete. Dill is the usual herbal accompaniment to spinach, but it wasn't available in the mountains of Crete until fairly recently, so cooks made do with parsley.**

*With thanks to Marika Daskalogianni for sharing this recipe.*

*1 large onion or 2 small ones, finely chopped*
*3 tablespoons olive oil*
*2 tomatoes, grated, skins discarded (optional)*
*1 bunch parsley, leaves chopped*
*1 kg (2 lbs) spinach, washed, trimmed and thickly sliced*
*1/4 cup cracked green olives (tsakistes)*

Sauté the onions in the olive oil until they become soft and translucent, add the tomatoes, parsley and spinach and cook over moderate heat until the spinach is tender and the juice from the tomatoes, if you are using them, has almost evaporated. The water from the spinach leaves and the tomato juice should be sufficient liquid, but add a little water if it seems too dry.

Add the olives and simmer for another 5 minutes. Serves 4.

This dish can also be made without the tomatoes, substituting a little lemon juice.

# Spinach or amaranth sautéed with "garlic oil"

## Spanáki i vlíta me skordólado

**Stamatis Moros, one of the chefs at the Rithymna Beach Hotel, recommends sautéing spinach or amaranth in olive oil, which you have blended with one clove of garlic, and a tiny amount of chicken broth. No precise quantities are necessary here.**

# Artichokes and broad beans

*Anginarokoukiá*

(ALL CRETE)

8 fresh smallish artichokes, leaves
    closed not unfurled

2-3 lemons and their juice

1/2 kg (1 lb) fresh broad beans, pods
    discarded unless they are very
    tender

1 large onion, finely chopped

5-6 tablespoons olive oil, for sautéing

120 ml (1/2 cup) dry white wine
    (optional)

2 tablespoons finely chopped wild
    fennel or the feathery tops of
    cultivated fennel

**Artichokes stewed with broad (fava) beans is a classic spring dish eaten all over Greece. It is so delicious that I couldn't resist including it here.**

Peel off the outer leaves of the artichokes, down to the very tender heart. If the artichokes are young, they might not even have any choke. Many cooks use only the bottoms, but I can never bring myself to discard all those delicious inner leaves, so I quarter the artichokes, cutting off the tough, inedible segments of leaf. While you're working, rub the surface of the artichokes with half a lemon and keep them in bowl of water to which you have added more lemon juice until you're ready to cook them. This keeps them from turning brown and unappetizing.

Mix together the artichoke hearts or bottoms, the beans and the chopped onion and sauté gently in a large pan with a little olive oil so that they simmer in their own juices. If you need more liquid, add water or the white wine. When the vegetables are tender, add the chopped fennel tips and the juice of one lemon. Serves 4.

This dish can also be made with an egg-lemon sauce (see note on page 116).

# WILD CRETAN GREENS
*Hórta*

M. Tournefort produced his two-volume opus *A Voyage into the Levant* in 1718. A botanist-physician, he had much to say about the Cretans' predilection for eating wild greens. "The Greeks don't much mind [lean meat]; they quicken their Appetite with Roots: and this is what gave occasion to the Proverb, which says, that a Greek would grow fat on what would starve an Ass. And this is literally true, the Asses eating none but the Leaves of Plants, whereas the Greeks devour the very Root. We often wondered at their way of living."

While many visitors to Crete have wondered about the copious amounts of greens consumed daily by the islanders, very few made the connection between health and diet until fairly recently. One exception was an Ottoman physician posted to Crete during the reign of Sultan Abdulhamid II (1876-1909). Apparently his practice was so uneventful he sent a note back to Constantinople requesting a transfer. As quoted in Paula Wolfert's *Mediterranean Grains and Greens*, his message read as follows: "Everyone here is his own doctor. The people eat only greens, herbs and olive oil. They don't need me." Less observant travellers would sigh with relief as they tucked into the fowl or mutton procured for them by their hosts during fasting periods, little dreaming that the bowl of greens they confined themselves to was anything but a hardship.

Now the secret is out and I suppose if we had any sense, we too would be eating greens several times a week and pressuring our markets to stock more and different varieties. But why are greens so good for us? As Ed Blonz, a California nutritionist, told me, "If you consider that plants and vegetables weather the sun and the elements, take nourishment from the earth and still survive and thrive, they must have something in them that enables them to do this. People are beginning to figure out that this goodness is contained in anything exposed to the sun, and maybe one day we'll be eating a vitamin supplement prepared from olive leaves. For the moment, though, wild greens and, to a lesser extent, cultivated vegetables and greens contain plenty of antioxidants that are just waiting to combine with the free radicals our own cells produce. Free radicals are those nasty rogue electrons that bombard DNA molecules repeatedly in their search for a partner and damage them until eventually they start making copying mistakes. These mistakes are responsible for the aches and pains of aging, tumors, hardening arteries and other unpleasantnesses. But the even better news is that cooking greens and vegetables with olive oil makes their minerals, vitamins and antioxidants soluble. Olive oil is the medium which makes them accessible to us. So even if we can't all get hold of wild greens from Crete, making a habit of eating fresh vegetables, olive oil and fruit will still benefit us."

Many Cretans and indeed many Greeks are so passionate about greens that they may devote their Sundays to gathering horta, much as other people go mushrooming, berry picking or hunting game. It is a demanding, back-breaking occupation, for you must keep your eyes to the ground, stoop to extract the precious weed from the soil with your special knife, and then knock off the earth and trim off the yellowed or tough leaves. Only then can you add it to your basket or plastic bag. Some passionate horta pickers have special aprons with separate pouches for sweet and bitter. A field with several apparently headless figures, bottoms aimed at the sky, is a very common sight from the moment the rains begin in the autumn until late spring when everything starts to shrivel. But collecting the greens is only the beginning. Then come the sorting, the washing and the storing, if you're not going to cook them at once.

Although I would rather just take a walk and be given a bag of cleaned horta, I love being able to choose from the huge raggedy mounds of greens offered at the various stands in Greek farmers' markets. Here you can buy both wild and cultivated greens and get recipes for them at the same time (see list on page 235). Greens are usually grouped according to taste: sweet – Swiss chard, nettles, beet tops; piquant – arugula, mustard greens, watercress; sour – sorrel, summer purslane, vine leaves and shoots; and bitter – dandelion, chicory, curly endive, escarole, broccoli rape (a kind of turnip top despite the name). Bitter greens are always made more palatable by blanching in plenty of boiling water before you add them to the rest, and some people may find that a little is too much. Try to experiment, choose something unfamiliar – even the choice in supermarket bins is becoming more exciting – and add it to your pies, stews, casseroles and salads. You'll find selecting them gets easier as you learn, it's fun and they're tasty besides being healthy.

Almost three hundred years after Tournefort's comment, Cretans still have a mania for a certain root called *Askolimbrous* (Lat. *Scolymus*), a very unfriendly looking, prickly thistle, which is actually a type of salsify. From when it appears with the first rains in late October until its disappearance in late spring, the trimmed roots and tender shoots command a price higher than any meat on the market because of the difficulty of cleaning away the thorny leaves.

# Sautéed winter greens
*Tsigariastá hórta*

(ALL CRETE)

**There are two versions of this ever popular dish, one for winter greens and one for the things that come up in your summer vegetable garden along with what has actually been planted. It may be hard to find the greens used here, but a Cretan cookbook without a recipe for greens would be like a Greek meal without bread, they are that basic. I will try to give equivalents or Latin names where possible. Combine the greens so that they amount to about a kilo (2 pounds); a larger quantity is hard to handle.**

*With thanks to Katerina Farandaki for sharing her knowledge of Cretan greens.*

All these greens have slightly different flavors and textures, which only a person who has been initiated into their mysteries would be able to combine to perfection. Still, planning along general lines, you will probably wish a predominance of sweetish greens, such as spinach beet or Swiss chard, spinach, nettles, with some peppery overtones from a bunch of arugula, mustard greens or watercress, and a slightly bitter touch from dandelions, any of the chicory family, curly endive, escarole or broccoli rape.

Wash and trim the greens, discarding any yellow or bedraggled leaves. Coarsely chop the larger leaves.

Sauté the greens in a large pot with the olive oil (a Cretan would use a whole cup). When they are thoroughly coated and have begun to shrink, add a little water and boil until the greens are tender. If you are left with too much liquid, remove the greens and boil it down quickly. The reduced juices make a lovely sauce and it would be a pity to have it too watery.

Serve with lemon juice or vinegar, as desired. (Alternatively, you could drink the broth, which many Greeks do, for its medicinal qualities). Serves 4.

Cretans like to add salt cod to this (see page 98), substituting it for potatoes and thickening the sauce with lemon and flour. Octopus is another variation, but it is cooked separately and added at the end along with a handful of green olives.

*60-120 ml (1/4-1/2 cup) olive oil*
*3 cloves garlic, chopped*
*1 medium onion, chopped*
*kafkalithres (Lat. caucalis, tordylium) – a sweet green*
*ahártzikous (chervil)*
*striftoúlia (bladder campion)*
*lagoudóhorto (salsify)*
*séskoula (Swiss chard)*
*skordaloúdia (wild garlic)*
*spinach*
*wild fennel*
*akournópodous (plantain, a bitter flat leaved plant)*
*paparoúnes or koutsounádes (wild poppies)*
*kapsóvrouves or kapsanthó (mustard greens)*
*2-3 small new potatoes, quartered (optional)*
*salt and freshly ground black pepper, to taste*

# Sautéed summer greens
*Tsigariastá hórta, kalokairiná*

120 ml (1/2 cup) olive oil
1 bunch spring onions, chopped
2 garlic cloves, chopped
6 baby zucchini, left whole
4 baby carrots (optional), left whole
    or halved
6 tiny new potatoes, left whole
1 cup string beans, runner beans (cut
    into 6 cm / 2 1/2 inch pieces) or
    fresh borlotti beans
1 bunch zucchini blossoms
small bunch tender tomato leaves
a few tender zucchini leaves,
    deveined and trimmed
a few klouvida or solanum tips
    (a plant with the ominous name
    of strychnine but which is not
    poisonous, just pleasantly bitter)
    (optional)
500 grams (1 lb) amaranth (vlita),
    blanched for 1 minute in boiling
    water
2 tomatoes, chopped
1 cup finely chopped parsley
salt and freshly ground black pepper
2 tablespoons finely chopped basil

**The ingredients for this dish will be easy to round up if you have a vegetable patch. Otherwise, if you can't get hold of zucchini leaves or tomato plant tips, don't worry, add more parsley or more beans or anything else that takes your fancy. This is an anything goes recipe.**

**All the vegetables should be washed, trimmed and coarsely chopped unless otherwise noted.**

Heat the oil in a deep stewpot and gently sauté the onions and garlic for about 2 minutes. Add the zucchini, carrots, potatoes and beans and roll in the oil for another 3 minutes. Add all the greens, toss them in the oil, mix in the chopped tomatoes and parsley and 120 ml (1/2 cup) water. Bring to the boil, reduce heat to moderate and cover. After about 10 minutes, stir gently, and add a bit more water if necessary. Just before all the vegetables are as tender as you like them (20-30 minutes), season with salt and pepper and sprinkle in the basil. Serves 4.

In most of Greece, basil, *vasilikos*, the royal herb, is ignored in cooking because of its religious associations. St. Helen, mother of Constantine the Great, who proclaimed Christianity the official religion of the Roman empire, journeyed to the Holy Land in search of the True Cross. She is said to have stumbled upon it surrounded by a bed of this fragrant peppery herb. Since then priests sprinkle holy water with it when they bless houses and boats, and no balcony or terrace will be without several pots (some say to keep mosquitoes away), but rarely does it find its way into salads or sauces. Western Crete is an exception to this rule (as is Corfu), and there basil turns up in mixed vegetable stews, baked fish, stuffed vegetables and summer salads.

# Mixed summer vegetables
## *Zarzavatiká kalokairiná*

(ELOS, WESTERN CRETE)

**This unusual old recipe calls for chunks of corn on the cob, which in Greece is almost always simply roasted over charcoal, either at home, or more frequently on the street by the same vendors who roast chestnuts in the autumn and winter months. Marika Daskalogianni who gave me this recipe maintains that Greek corn is much tastier than the variety sold nowadays, grown from imported American seeds, even though it is very chewy.**

60 ml (1/4 cup) olive oil or more, to taste
1 large onion, thinly sliced
3 garlic cloves, finely chopped
1 big ripe tomato, grated, skin discarded
salt and plenty of freshly ground pepper
1 kg (2 lbs) amaranth (vlita), washed and trimmed
1 small bunch parsley, finely chopped
2-3 ears of sweet corn, cut into 3 or 4 pieces, depending on size
1 bunch zucchini flowers, closed if possible

Sauté the onion in the oil for about 5 minutes, add the garlic and sauté a minute or 2 more, add the grated tomato and salt and pepper and simmer, covered, for a few minutes. Stir in the rest of the vegetables, except for the zucchini flowers, and coat them with oil and tomato. Add a little water, 240 ml (1 cup) should be enough, cover and stew over low heat for about 15 minutes or until the amaranth and corn are tender. Add the zucchini flowers just before the end and cook until they wilt. Serves 4.

Try this dish without the corn and zucchini flowers but with as much garlic as you like, 2 or 3 tomatoes and 1 or 2 cubed potatoes. Marika grinds lots of pepper over it and splashes in a bit of red wine along with a little water. It's an easy dish for a lazy summer's supper.

# A mixed casserole from the garden
## *Sofegáda or Sympetherió*

4-5 small new potatoes

3-4 skinny eggplant

6-7 tiny whole zucchini (or large ones, sliced)

1 large onion, thinly sliced

60 ml (1/4 cup) olive oil (though Cretans would use more)

2-3 green peppers, thinly sliced

3-4 small tomatoes, chopped or grated, skins discarded

1 head garlic, finely chopped

1/2 kg (1 lb) sweet greens, spinach or amaranth, well washed and coarsely chopped

1/2 cup chopped parsley

1/4 cup chopped basil

salt and freshly ground black pepper

**In Greek your *sympetheri* are your inlaws. You're thrown together with them whether you have anything in common or not and the same is true for this stew which could contain anything that happens to be growing in your kitchen garden at the height of summer, or especially towards the end, when there are only a few specimens of each vegetable left. On the other hand, *sofegada*, the name for this dish in Eastern Crete, comes from a Venetian word meaning drowned or suffocated and apparently originally referred to a meat stew. There is definitely no trace of meat here in what could be considered the Cretan version of ratatouille, differing only in that potatoes and greens are added. In any case, it is a homey, satisfying dish, easy to prepare and even better the next day. Obviously you can vary the amounts and ingredients depending on what you have on hand. This is definitely one instance when the Cretan cook's rule – VOV = vale oti vreis = put in whatever you can find – would apply.**

Cut the potatoes, eggplant and zucchini (if larger than finger length) into slices that are roughly the same size, about 3 cm/1 inch thick. Sauté the onion in the oil over medium heat until soft, add the potatoes, cook another 5 minutes, then the zucchini and finally the eggplant and peppers. When all the vegetables are thoroughly coated with oil and beginning to get a little color, add the chopped tomato and garlic, cover, and boil gently while you prepare the greens.

Half fill another saucepan with water, bring it to the boil and toss in the greens. Parboil until they are reduced in size, drain (reserving a little of their liquid) and add them to the other vegetables. Stir, replace the lid, and lower the heat to a simmer.

Stir a couple of times during the next 15 to 20 minutes and add a little of the reserved broth if necessary. Sprinkle in the parsley and basil a few minutes before you turn off the stove. Good hot or at room temperature the next day. Serves 4.

Cooking times will depend greatly on the freshness of your vegetables and whether you like them al dente or very tender, Cretan style.

# Borlotti beans with leeks

*Barboúnia me prássa*

**Pink and white borlotti kidney beans are sold fresh in their wrinkled pods in summer in Greek and Italian farmers' markets. The Italians like to put them in minestrones, the Greeks in salads or baked as in this recipe. They get their name from the red mullet fish, also called *barbounia*, because their color is so similar. Disappointingly, their delightful candy-cane patterns fade in cooking, but their nutty taste still rates as superior.**

*500 grams (1 lb) fresh borlotti beans or dried Greek giant beans (gigantes)*
*120 ml (1/2 cup) olive oil*
*3 medium leeks, white part only, finely chopped*
*2 green peppers, finely chopped*
*1/2 bunch celery, finely chopped*
*1/2 cup finely chopped parsley*
*3 medium tomatoes, grated, skins discarded*
*salt and freshly ground black pepper*
*1 tablespoon dried oregano*

If you're using giant beans, soak them overnight before boiling. Fresh beans need no soaking and should just be boiled in plenty of salted water for about 20 minutes or until almost tender. Drain in a colander and place them in a large shallow baking dish.

For giant beans, bring them to a boil in a large pot of water and discard the water after the first boiling. With new, salted, water bring them to the boil again and cook for about 1 1/2 hours. Drain and place in baking dish.

Preheat the oven to 190°C (375°F). While the beans are cooking, sauté the leeks in the oil for about 5 minutes. Add the peppers, celery and parsley and sauté another 2-3 minutes before adding the tomatoes. Season with salt, pepper and oregano, pour the mixture over the beans, toss and bake for about 30 minutes until a light crust forms on top and the beans are tender and juicy. Serves 8.

---

A dish of beans may sound humble, but listen to this description by J.E. Hilary Skinner, who was touring Crete in 1867 during one of the many insurrections. "The good old bishop [of Preveli] … marshalled us into supper. He was so courteous in the dignity of his deputed hospitality and poured out the tiniest drop of wine with such an air, that the rough table, the dish of beans, and the one drinking cup, which was handed around, seemed the proper belongings of a banquet: and a banquet it was, compared to what we afterwards experienced. There were dishes of cheese and honey to flank the dish of beans, whilst as to pieces of soaked biscuit, there was as much as we could desire to eat." His later meals with the rebels seem to have consisted solely of cheese and paximadia, with a very occasional roast lamb or "cheese cake" [Sfakian pie].

# Roasted chestnut stew

*Kástana fournistá stifádo*

1 kg (2 lbs) chestnuts
1 kg (2 lbs) stewing onions
60 ml (1/4 cup) olive oil
1 tablespoon tomato paste
120 ml (1/2 cup) dry red wine
piece of dry orange peel (fresh peel
　　will do)
bay leaf
salt and freshly ground black pepper

**This old recipe from the mountains is very rarely made today when meat is so readily available. But the woman who provided this recipe says that she remembers this and other dishes her grandmother used to make as being much more delicious than many modern treats. It is even better the next day when the chestnuts have absorbed some more of the sweetness of the onions and the sauce.**

Preheat the oven to 200°C (400°F). With a sharp knife slit a cross in the shell of each chestnut and roast them in the oven for about 1 hour. During this time, turn them over 2 or 3 times to make sure they cook evenly. They will be better if they are well browned.

While the chestnuts are still warm, peel them and take off all the inner skin as well. Put the chestnuts in a bowl. Lower the onions into a pot of boiling water and keep them there for about 30 seconds. Drain and when they're cool enough to handle, slip off the skins and make a little cross at the base of each onion.

Heat the olive oil in a deep saucepan and when the oil is hot, roll the onions in it to brown a bit. Dilute the tomato paste in the wine, pour it over the onions, cover and boil gently for about 5 minutes. Add 240 ml (1 cup) of water and the salt and simmer, covered, until the onions are half cooked. At this point add the chestnuts, bay leaf, orange peel, salt and pepper, and simmer for another 20 minutes. Pour in a little more wine or water if necessary. Serves 4-6 as a main course.

As a side dish this would go beautifully with roast pork, chicken or turkey.

# PRESERVES

## Homemade tomato paste
*Domatopoltós spitísios*

**One thing you have to have on hand for this traditional way of making tomato paste is an old pillowcase!**

Choose firm, ripe tomatoes with a lot of taste. Wash, dry and quarter them and let them sit in a colander over a basin for 2-3 days. Then with your hands squeeze out as much juice as you can. Next put them in the clean pillowcase and hang them up overnight with a bowl underneath to catch any more liquid. When they seem to be fairly dry, place them in the sun for 4-5 days to eliminate any trace of moisture. Now add the salt, 2-3 tablespoons for every kilo (2 lbs) of tomato paste, mix well and press into clean sterilized jars, making sure there are no air bubbles. Top with olive oil, put on the lids and store in a cool dark place. It should keep all winter.

# Pickled hyacinth bulbs

*S k o r d o u l á k i   o r   v o l v í*

FOR 1/2 KG (1 LB)
WILD HYACINTH BULBS OR MORE

*1 bunch dill*
*2 cloves garlic*
*60 ml (1/4 cup) good quality vinegar*
*120 ml (1/2 cup) olive oil*
*1 tablespoon sea salt*

**The piquant bulbs of wild hyacinths (*Muscari comosum*) are a great delicacy in many parts of Greece, southern Italy (Puglia) and Crete. The English name for them is tassle hyacinth because of the amethyst fringe that bursts from the top of its beaded stalk from early to late spring. The ancients prized them for their reputedly aphrodisiac qualities (perhaps a consequence of their shape) and had dozens of recipes for them. Nowadays they are pickled in olive oil and vinegar and eaten as a meze, especially during Lent, when their sharp crunchiness contrasts with blander, softer foods such as taramosalata and puréed split peas or broad beans. Ready pickled in small jars, they can be found in some Italian or Greek specialty shops; in their raw state – looking very similar to daffodil bulbs – you might see them piled in small mounds at farmers markets in Greece, Italy or elsewhere. In case you should happen to come across some, this is how they should be prepared. You can also roast them in the embers of a barbecue fire, as you would onions or potatoes.**

Peel off the dry outer skins and carefully wash the bulbs, trim off the roots, then make a cross at the base as you would with stewing onions and put them in a bowl of cold water to soak for 48 hours. Change the water 2 or 3 times a day. Afterwards boil them for 5 minutes, drain, rinse in plenty of cold water and reboil in fresh water for another 5 minutes. Repeat a third or even a fourth time, if they are still too bitter for you. They should however remain fairly crisp.

Drain the bulbs in a colander and place them in a clean, dry jar with a little finely chopped dill and sliced garlic.

Beat together the vinegar with the olive oil and salt, pour this over the bulbs. Let the flavors mellow for a week or so before you eat them. Will keep about 8 months in a dark cool place.

# Olives in bitter orange juice

*Kolymbádes se nerantzóhymo*

**This is how Danae Malinaki makes her olives. She uses tiny black *kolymbades*, but any ripe fleshy olive can be substituted. After preparing a brine with water and enough salt to float an egg in a large bowl, she puts the washed olives into a crockery or glass jar and pours the brine over them, followed by enough olive oil to seal the brine. She screws the lid on and leaves the olives on a dark shelf in her pantry until August 15th, about 8 months! Only then does she open the jar, empty the brine, rinse the olives and pour in enough juice from bitter oranges and lemons to cover them. They have become incredibly sweet from sitting in the brine so long, while the juices give them a delightful tang.**

Few of us would have the patience to wait that long and uncured olives are not easily available outside the Mediterranean, so I suggest the following treatment for 1/2 kg (1 lb) store-bought black olives, either the large round Amphissa type or the streamlined pointed ones from Kalamata.

Make a "sauce" with 240 ml (1 cup) extra virgin olive oil, the juice of two fat lemons, several thin lemon slices and a teaspoon of oregano. Shake vigorously, pour the mixture into the jar or crock where you'll store the olives and if it does not cover them, add some salted water (to taste). They must be completely covered with liquid or else they'll spoil. Let sit at least a week before using.

# HARD TIMES

One evening in late October, when the first snowfall had already dusted the peaks of Psiloriti, I peered into a taverna window in Anoyeia, saw a fire blazing though no tables were occupied and went in to get warm. The couple who owned the place were chatting with an elderly shepherd and I sat down with them next to the hearth on a bench padded with thickly woven rugs with geometric designs in soft reds and burgundies. The antlered skulls of long-dead deer and mountain goats decorated the walls. This far into autumn, the tourist season with its day trippers to Zeus's birthplace in the cave higher up the mountain was over and they hadn't expected anyone but a few locals to pass by. Soon we were talking about why I was there and the conversation quickly shifted from politics to food, particularly "nostalgia food," the things they had loved as children and the treats that had kept them going during the war.

Anoyeia, where some of Crete's finest musicians have come from, is often hailed for its traditions, but people in search of picturesque houses and charming town squares hugging this romantic, steep mountain setting are likely to be disappointed. Anoyeia was a hotbed of resistance and when the Germans discovered General Kreipe's kidnappers had hidden their prize here briefly before spiriting him off the island, they retaliated with terrible vengeance – murdering every male regardless of age and levelling every building. Only the church survived, the rest of the buildings are contemporary concrete blocks on stilts, without a single redeeming feature. Nevertheless, the women still weave and embroider, a couple of bakeries still specialize in decorated loaves for weddings and baptisms (see pp. 174-175), and several tavernas serve makaronia with staka and great chunks of meat smoke-roasted in soot-blackened outdoor cooking shacks.

As we talked that night, younger men came in for a raki and joined us, eager to listen to memories not of the black side of war and poverty but of the moments that made them bearable. The dishes described with such fondness will never be found in a taverna, many have probably not been prepared since those days of necessity. Certainly the majority do not sound very appetizing, but most of us have never been as hungry as those villagers. On the other hand, these were the meals that kept them healthier than their American counterparts, who even though rationed during the war still managed to sink their teeth into white bread, red meat, refined sugar and, if not butter, then the newly invented margarine.

Here are some of the treats of *cucina povera* at its poorest. Anoyeia did not recover from the war until the early 60s. It was only then that enough prosperity trickled in to make coffee readily available and my hosts no longer had to sell their eggs to buy salt and pepper; otherwise, except for cigarette paper, they had been self-sufficient.

**Bazina:** "My mother used to feed this to us kids. She made a batter with some flour, salt and water, and stirred it in the frying pan with some olive oil. That was all there was to it. We didn't have sugar or even honey to sweeten it."

**Mangiri:** You'll find a recipe for this delicious plate of boiled and fried homemade pasta on page 76. Making pasta can be a long drawn out process, but on a winter evening with no TV, it became a game the whole family could play.

**Ladouridi:** This sounds like dumplings. "We'd mix a handful of flour with olive oil and salt in a plate with a little water, stirring it with our fingers until it crumbled into little balls. If we were lucky we'd have some sheep's milk instead of water. Then we'd boil some of it and fry the other half, like mangiri, and eat it with a spoon like soup.

**Kavroma:** The basis for this is sheep's or kid's stomach, well washed and marinated for 2 hours in lemon and salt, and washed again. After that it was cut in small pieces, brought to a boil in plenty of water to tenderize and then sautéed in olive oil with lots of onions, tomato, bay leaf, pepper and sheep's liver. Described as being finger-licking good, it must have been quite a luxury compared to the other fare.

**Psarokollyva:** This "fake" *kollyva*, as opposed to the dish served at memorial services (see p. 228), is a simpler mix of wheat, chick peas, beans, soaked overnight, boiled and drained and dressed with some olive oil and chopped onion like *papoudia* (p. 87).

**Skirozoumi:** This wartime dish was nothing more than water seasoned with olive oil and salt into which paximadia (rusks) were crumbled.

**Potatoes with xinohondro (trahana):** Having no prejudices about adding starch to starch, Cretan villagers would try to fill their

tummies with potatoes sautéed in oil with grated tomatoes, "stir until it smells good," to which a little water would be added. Trahana, soaked in a bowl of water to soften it, would be thrown in at the last minute, after the water had been absorbed or evaporated. "Stir 5-6 times and it's done." This would be a good simple supper dish even in peace time.

**Skoudourakous:** There was no price on volvi, wild hyacinth bulbs pickled in oil, vinegar, salt and garlic; you just had to know where to find them.

**Bahoudi:** Bulgur dressed with oil.

**Eggplant with potatoes, tomatoes and onions:** This simple "yiachni" was such a fancy dish for poor Anoyeia, it was served at weddings up to thirty years ago.

From this list, you can see that as long as you had wheat and barley to make flour and olive oil to season and cook with, you would never starve. Meanwhile with a little *zestari* – hot wine in a clay jug – set on one side of the hearth and another clay pot filled with fava beans or split yellow peas simmering with an onion in the coals, you could even think yourself lucky.

# BREAD & FLOUR

## "All the joy in the world"

They say that Greeks eat more bread than any other nationality. A meal is not a meal without it, as I soon found out after inviting disgruntled Athenians to stir-fry or curry parties with only rice to mop up sauces. In fact, I have one friend who boasts, "The only thing I don't eat bread with is bread." "Give us this day our daily bread" is a prayer the Greeks take literally; it is most definitely the staff of life. In pre-war Crete, however, one could have modified that prayer to "daily dose of flour."

Evrydiki Katsoulidaki is typical of many Cretans born in the first half of the 20th century in the countryside. Although she grew up in the White Mountains near Sfakia, a district known for its sheep and goats, her father had no animals of his own and she rarely tasted meat. "But we were never hungry because we had flour, and because we had that, we had all the joy in the world." Flour naturally meant bread, often *migadi* – a mixture of wheat and barley – and rusks, but it also was used in many other ways: to make noodles (*hilopittes*), pancakes, and dozens of the simplest combinations of flour, olive oil and water, which were kneaded into dumplings and boiled, stirred together and

*"Better to have olives and paximadia at home than to have foreign sugar fed to me by others."*

fried or baked on an iron griddle (*plaka*) over the fire to make a meal. Some of them must have been like porridge, or a soupy gruel, not terribly appetizing to us today. *Plakopitta*, a kind of unleavened bread, on the other hand, was so delicious it inspired a rhyme: "*Plakopitta kai lahana, tou kosmou ta katakala* – Griddle pie and cabbage, nothing better in the world." Of course, the fact that the flour was ground from the family's own wheat, sometimes in a handmill if bulgur or trahana was desired, must have made it that much more tasty and nourishing than the bleached, factory-milled flour of the cities.

In normal times the Cretans had four types of homemade bread: ordinary loaves for everyday, which were likely to be whole wheat or a mixture of wheat and barley or even oats, and either eaten fresh or baked a second time into enduring rusks; holiday breads made with white flour and aromatics, spices, juices, spirits and sometimes studded with fruit and nuts, for Easter, Christmas, New Year's or a name day; white bread for the church, called *artos*, the ancient Greek word, as opposed to *psomi*, stamped with the initials ΙΣ ΧΡ ΝΙΚΑ (JESus CHRist CONQUERS); and decorated breads to commemorate life's milestones – birth, motherhood, baptism, betrothal, marriage and death. When I read about all the occasions on which these breads were made in the Rethymno Historical and Folk Museum's wonderful publication, *Traditional Bread of Rethymno*, I could not help feeling that in some households it must have been a nearly full-time occupation. There were also breads made in the shape of the five-pointed Star of Solomon, a corner of which was held to cure illness; breads dedicated to St. Fanourios, the St. Anthony of the Orthodox, who is the finder of lost things; portrait breads meant to resemble a relative recently deceased, which were baked on Lazarus Saturday before Palm Sunday; and little Easter rolls for children in the shape of barnyard animals.

Most extraordinary, though, are the milestone breads. These usually took the form of wreaths (*koulouria*), always contained sugar, and were decorated with symbols appropriate to the event. In some parts of Crete they were so intricate that not an inch of dough was left unadorned and involved so much work that shaping and applying the ornaments, of dough also, was often a group effort – by a bread team of friends and relatives. At a wedding or baptism, there were small wreaths for the guests, slightly larger ones for the closer friends and relatives and a full-sized one for the best man or godfather, bride and groom. The decorations changed with the occasion. A baptism wreath always had at least one bird with spread wings, symbolizing the child's health and happiness, while the godfather's was a collage of various leaves, flowers, a lizard, a string of worry beads, a *lyra* (the archetypal Cretan fiddle), in addition to birds in flight, all applied with special tweezers. Fertility symbols formed the motifs for the wedding loaf or koulouri: vines and bunches of grapes, pomegranates, pine cones, and even snakes, together with lemon blossoms and roses, but a bride's birds would be snuggled in their nests.

Some breads could only be prepared by a certain individual. For example, besides knitting tiny garments an expectant mother had to bake dozens of sweet rusks called *kalopsykia* (good souls?) which she would offer to visitors once the baby was born. In turn, her mother-in-law would present her with a loaf with the figures of mother and child in the center, surrounded by posies and foliage, as well as the indispensable birds. Engaged couples would exchange koulouria decorated with their initials, squeezed in amongst the other tokens of love, fidelity and fecundity. All these loaves are far too beautiful to be eaten, and surely many were kept as mementos until they turned moldy, for other less ornate breads were served at the party table.

Nowadays few people can spare the time, fewer still have preserved the knack and events are more likely to be celebrated with sweets ordered from the pastry shop – tiered western wedding cakes with a miniature bride and groom stuck on top – than with masterpieces of folk art. Nevertheless, I know of at least one bakery, in Anoyeia, which takes orders for them. Nonedible facsimiles, made with salt-laden flour and varnished, are turned out for tourists in the markets of Chania and Rethymno. They can never be as beautiful or as meaningful as the real thing, but for those of us who may never see, touch or eat from a loaf decorated for a specific person or ceremony, they capture the essence of a delightful custom.

Linked as it is to life, bread also had a role at funerals. People close to the bereaved family would make a large wreath, naturally devoid of ornaments, to be shared among the mourners. In addition, ten small loaves adorned with a laurel leaf and three large ones were baked for the poor, the latter for needy friends, the former to be given along with clothes. It was thought that this act of charity would help bring the deceased forgiveness for his sins.

# RUSKS OR PAXIMADIA

Whether you become addicted to Cretan rusks as I have or view them with exasperated intolerance as "uneatable biscuit knobs" like the painter Edward Lear, they are an undeniable fixture in a Cretan's diet. The archetypal rusk is the doughnut-shaped barley dakos or koukouvayia (owl!), which still has bits of bran mixed into the flour and serves as a "plate" for chopped tomatoes drenched with olive oil and a dollop of myzithra cheese, a favorite meze. But a snoop around Chania's bakeries, for instance, will reveal many more types of paximadia than fresh bread. First of all, every kind of bread can be and is baked twice into a hard, virtually indestructible rusk, from the white – polytelias or luxury – bread, to country bread from unrefined flour, to half and half mixtures of bran and wheat, and so forth. But there are also flavored rusks – with coriander, anise, cinnamon and orange juice, nuts and currants – almost every combination you can conceive of. People will go far out of their way to find the best rusks – I go to a baker in Askyfou, halfway to Hora Sfakion when I have the time, and to Hari Bonatos, who has a stall in the Chania market in addition to his fourno near the waterfront. In the old days, paximadia were even served at weddings, dolled up with coriander, cloves and mastic.

Paximadia must be almost as old as the hills. In *Siren Feasts*, Andrew Dalby speculates that they may have taken their name from a certain Paxamus, author in the early Roman era of numerous handbooks on such disparate subjects as cooking, dyeing, sexual postures (!) and farming. The barley rusk has certainly been around since that time, feeding armies on the march to the farflung corners of the empire and countless generations of rural families from the Middle East to Venice. Though it was an excellent way of preserving bread, you might think that nowadays with a baker in every village, electric ovens and freezers, rusks would have lost in popularity to the fresh loaf. But not at all, Cretans go on dipping them in a little water, sweetening them with thick green olive oil, mopping up salad dressings and gravies, and crunching away. Even children appreciate their value. The tooth fairy being unknown in Crete, when a baby tooth falls out, the child pokes it into a hole in an old wall, chanting, "Here, mouse, take my tooth and give me back an iron one so I can chew up our paximadia."

Never touch any greenery on Easter Monday or your bread will get moldy!

# Seven-times kneaded bread
*Psomí eftázymo*

This bread, which is leavened with fermented ground chick peas, is cloaked in mystique. Apparently the dough is so sensitive that it may not rise if subjected to noise or the slightest draft. So conditioned are some women that they even whisper when they tell you how they make it. It is also vulnerable to the evil eye – spells cast by jealous neighbors – and extravagant steps are taken to prevent them from discovering that one is baking. I had learned about some of the precautions used on the island of Zakynthos, where one should have a black-handled knife, a red blanket and a prayer book near by to keep evil spirits away and prevent the devil from getting at it. But it was not until I sat down with Viktoria Athanasiadou-Tzanidaki in Chania that I discovered that it most certainly is not kneaded seven times. Viktoria, who has a regular radio program with two other women on Cretan foods and traditions, believes that the word "efta" (seven) "zymo" (*zymono* = to knead) is a corruption of *autozymo* or self-rising. She also remembered how her mother behaved while making this bread.

"When she was baking, we had to tiptoe round the house, quiet as mice. She didn't even like us to ask whether we could wash our hair with laurel water [the dough is kneaded with water in which bay leaves have been soaking], and she refused to let anyone watch her. She used to cover the dough with wool blankets and take a quick peak to see if it was rising. It was so sensitive it could even spoil in the oven. So to prevent the delicious smells from leaving the house and alerting the neighbors to her baking, she used to take some coals from the oven and put them in an old shoe. This made such a horrible stink that no one could smell the bread and cause it to fall. There was one silly woman who figured this out and used a shoe herself to prove she was as good a cook as my mother!"

Presumably there is no danger of the bread attracting the evil eye when made in a non-Greek kitchen, but there are numerous pitfalls, from grinding the chick peas without spraying them all over the kitchen to finding the right combination of durum wheat and barley flour and kneading, which requires a heavy duty mixer. This is the recipe as given in the little booklet prepared by the Department of Agriculture in Heraklio, "Don't forget tradition in your kitchen."

*1/2 kg (1 lb) chick peas*
*half a handful of salt, approximately*
*a little mastic or cinnamon and*
    *cloves*
*a few bay leaves*
*about 2 liters (8 cups) water*
*30 kg (66 lbs) flour*

Prepare the starter as follows:

Grind the chick peas in the hand mill until they are as fine as flour. (Some say that if you crush them in a mixer, they won't swell and froth.) Heat the water in a saucepan until it is as hot as your hand can bear. Throw in the chick peas and the salt and mix well. Cover the saucepan and set it in a warm spot where it will remain at a constant temperature. One good place is a sack filled with straw; put the saucepan with the starter in the bag, wrapped in a wool blanket. This is usually done in the evening and one can normally count on the starter taking about 7 to 8 hours to rise. When it is ready mix about 5 kilos (11 lbs) of flour with the starter, knead well and set aside for about 1 hour until it rises a second time.

Next, add the rest of the flour, the mastic or cinnamon and cloves and knead with hot water to which you have added a dozen bay leaves until you have a soft dough. Shape it into small round loaves, with or without a hole in the center, and cover carefully so they will rise again. As soon as they have risen, bake them for about 1 hour. [As this is presumed to be an old-fashioned wood-burning oven, no temperatures are given.]

Take the bread out of the oven, cut into large pieces and return to the oven to become rusks.

For a more manageable recipe and advice on how to make this temperamental but very flavorful bread, I suggest you turn to Paula Wolfert's, *Mediterranean Grains and Greens.* Paula devotes several pages to the making of this bread in a modern Western kitchen.

If you are flabbergasted by the quantity of flour given in the preceding recipe, you should bear in mind that Cretan women used to bake once or twice a month, saving just a few loaves to be eaten as bread and the rest to be preserved as paximadia. Before electricity came to the mountain villages (during the 1960s), it was simply too much work and too expensive to light the outdoor, wood-burning oven very often; most cooking was done in the fireplace. But even today there are many families who wouldn't dream of buying bread from a commercial baker, and when they bake, they don't just knead a few loaves.

I came upon one such family in Zakros, a largish village linked to the Minoan palace on the coast by a paved road, naturally, but also by a path through the Gorge of the Dead, so-called because so many Minoan graves have been found there. I had walked up the gorge to meet Mary Daskalaki, owner of a wonderful taverna at Kato Zakros, who gave me dozens of recipes before sending me to her sister, Alexandra Nerolidou, who was baking bread that summery October day.

By the time I wandered into the courtyard with the big soot-blackened oven and a set of five tall wooden paddles and rakes leaning on the whitewashed wall just beside it, Alexandra had already kneaded 30 kilos (66 pounds) of flour with her sour dough starter to make 40 loaves of bread.

It was definitely a family operation with three generations present, including Alexandra's *sympetheri* or co-inlaws, her daughter's husband's parents. Irini (photo), a very bouncy 77 year old woman in a pink-flowered, short-sleeved dress, white hair tied back in a bright red kerchief, was clearly in charge. Though not even 1.5 meters (5 feet) tall, she was a bundle of energy, telling her husband when to inspect the bread or how many branches to stoke the fire with, and keeping up a running patter of funny stories and village gossip. When they started shoveling the loaves out of the oven, lining them up on wood panels on the ground, she was the first to squat down, as nimble as her toddler granddaughter, and with asbestos hands tear the scored loaves into five or six thick slices. Most of the bread was returned to the oven where it would remain for another 24 hours to become hard rusks to be eaten, dipped in a little water, sauces or salad juices, for the next two months.

When the last of the loaves was set back in the oven, I said my

thanks and started to make my departure. Nothing doing. Alexandra took hold of my arm and together we marched to Irini's house for lunch. More of the family appeared, a son, a daughter, another grandchild, and we sat down to a spread of fried anchovies, roast chicken with okra and potatoes, tomato, ònion and cucumber salad and the new bread, with raki and wine, followed by grapes.

Then Irini and her husband Yannis started to reminisce. About the war, first, how he used to have to fetch supplies from Siteia for the Germans and Italians, which meant a five- to six-hour hike barefoot leading the mules. The Italians had to have white bread, the Germans preferred theirs sour and black. Even after the war all trade with Siteia was in the hands of muleteers until the road was built in the early 1950s. It was around that time that Yannis "stole" Irini. They were in love, her parents did not approve, so they ran away … on foot. "And when we came to the river, I picked her up and carried her piggyback across it, we spent the night in a cave, and when we came back no one could argue any more, so we got married." And lived happily ever after, by the looks of it.

The next morning, before leaving Zakros, I stopped by Alexandra's to have a coffee and say goodbye. As she opened her fridge to get out some sweets, I noticed a strange jar. "What's that?" I asked. "Oh," said Alexandra, a handsome, dignified-looking woman in her sixties, "those are barley grains. I use them when someone asks me to cast out the evil eye (*ksematiasi*). They're hard to find nowadays since we don't grow barley around here anymore, so I store them in the fridge. You put nine in a glass of water, recite the story from the Bible about Christ casting out evil and the curse is lifted. You could do the same thing with earth dug from under an untrodden stone, but I prefer barley."

Alexandra told me that undoing spells (and I have heard countless tales – of orange groves shrivelling overnight for no reason, inexplicable malaises, husbands enchanted by sorceresses, for example) is an art passed down from generation to generation but that a man must learn from a woman and vice versa. But she left me wondering about the role of the ancient grain in this mysterious process.

Mastic: The crystallized resin from the *pistacia lentiscus* tree which grows only in southern Chios is pounded into a powder to flavor a few Cretan sweets and breads. The courtiers of both the Sultan and the Sun King used to chew mastic crystals to sweeten their breath in the days before toothpaste and the Chiots say that the search for another source of mastic drove Columbus across the Atlantic. Today it is becoming recognized as a natural cure for stomach ulcers. Some Greek grocers may stock mastic crystals, chewing gum, liqueur or jars of the gooey white spoon sweet known to all Greek kids as a submarine (*ipovrihio*) because they dunk it in a glass of ice water between licks.

# Christmas bread

*Christópsomo*

**The dough for Christmas bread, baked all over the island and a tradition in the rest of Greece as well, is so filled with nuts, spices and raisins that it more resembles a cake. Coated with sesame seeds and sometimes walnuts, the crust often bears a cross or X in Greek which stands for Ch(rist). It is an attractive addition to the festive table, along with the New Year's cake (*Vasilopitta*), *melomakarona* and *kourambiedes* that no house is without during the holiday season. (See Desserts for recipes.)**

The day before you want to bake, prepare the starter with 115 grams (4 oz) flour, the yeast and a little warm water (about 120 ml or half a cup) in a large bowl, cover and set aside.

In the morning add 100 grams (1/2 cup) sugar, half the oil and 140 grams (a cup) of flour, knead well, cover with a cloth and leave to rise in a warm place.

When the mixture has doubled in size, stir in the rest of the ingredients and knead for about 15 minutes on a lightly floured surface, adding flour if you have to, until you have a smooth, non-sticky dough.

Cover the dough and let it rise again, covered with a cloth, in a warm place (about 1 1/2 hours). Punch the dough back to its original size and form into a round loaf. Place on a lightly oiled baking tin. Let it rise again (about 45 minutes) and brush the surface with a little oil, and sprinkle on the sesame seeds and walnut halves. Preheat the oven to 200°C (400°F) and bake for 15 minutes. Lower the heat to 150°C (300°F) and bake for another 35 to 40 minutes.

FOR 1 LARGE ROUND LOAF

*900 grams (2 lbs, 6 cups) (bread) flour*
*60 grams (4 tablespoons) active dry yeast or 2 tablespoons instant yeast*
*300 grams (1 1/2 cup) sugar*
*120 ml (1/2 cup) olive oil*
*250 grams (2 cups) raisins softened in*
*240 ml (1 cup) red wine, warmed*
*1/2 teaspoon salt*
*1 teaspoon crushed mastic*
*200 grams (1 1/4 cups) walnuts, coarsely chopped*
*1 teaspoon cinnamon*
*1 teaspoon ground cloves*
*grated peel of 1 orange*
*120 ml (1/2 cup) fresh orange juice*
*60 ml (1/4 cup) brandy*

FOR DECORATION:

*1-2 tablespoons sesame seeds, 10-12 walnut halves*

# Stella's biscuits

*Paximadákia tis Stéllas*

240 ml (1 cup) olive oil
200 grams (1 cup) sugar
120 ml (1/2 cup) fresh orange juice
grated peel of 1 orange
1 teaspoon ammonia (optional)
2 tablespoons brandy
1/2 teaspoon baking soda
2 tablespoons fresh lemon juice
grated peel of 1 lemon
1 teaspoon powdered cinnamon
about 800 grams (5 1/2 - 6 cups)
    (cake) flour
150 grams (1 cup) walnuts or
    almonds, chopped
75 grams (1/2 cup) raisins, chopped
    (optional)

**The Greeks call these sweet rusks "dunking biscuits" and dip them in their morning and afternoon coffee, but they also go well with fruit salads and compotes or an after dinner liqueur.**

Preheat the oven to 180°C (350°F). Put the olive oil and sugar together in a large bowl and beat with the electric beater for at least 5 minutes. Dissolve the ammonia in the orange juice and the baking soda in the brandy and add these liquids, along with the lemon juice and grated orange and lemon peel and continue beating.

Sift the flour with the cinnamon into another bowl and stir the flour, a cup at a time, into the liquid with a wooden spoon. Fold in the nuts (and raisins if you use them) before the dough gets too stiff.

When you can handle the dough without sticking to it, knead it with your hands as you add the rest of the flour. Roll out the dough into cylinders 7.5 cm (3 inches) wide and slice off pieces about 2.5 (1 inch) thick. Sprinkle each piece with sesame seeds, place on a lightly greased baking sheet and bake until lightly browned (about 25 minutes). Remove the pan from the oven and when cool enough to handle, separate any rusks that have stuck together. Return them to the oven at a very low setting (135°C or 275°F) and leave them there for at least 1 hour to harden. Makes about 50 rusks.

# SWEETS & DESSERTS

## Glyká

For an island with such a long history of poverty, rebellion and fasting, Crete has an enormous number and variety of succulent sweets. Some are exceedingly simple combinations of flour and water embellished with a spoonful of honey; others have a long list of ingredients and require several steps. But most of them represent inventive, creative uses of what the land provided – walnuts, almonds and chestnuts, soft fresh cheeses, sesame seeds, grape juice syrup and raisins, pumpkin and quince, orange and lemon juice. What is surprising to a westerner brought up on blackberry pies, baked apples, strawberry shortcake and peach ice cream is the total absence of traditional desserts made with cooked fruits. For the Greeks and the Cretans, in particular, fruit is something that is eaten raw, as is, occasionally dried and frequently in the form of preserves – spoon sweets – during a visit to another's home, but never, traditionally at any rate, encased in pastry or folded into a pudding.

In fact, dessert is a fairly recent addition to the Cretan meal and even today is not a standard conclusion to it. Sweets were certainly not consumed on a daily basis; instead with the exception of simple treats like *tiganites* (pancakes) for children, most of the pies, biscuits and cakes described here were reserved for special occasions – weddings and baptisms, holidays, namedays – and thus the original recipes for them call for enormous quantities. There are also several recipes containing no eggs or dairy products, which were intended to cheer up the fasting periods.

Despite any preconceptions you may have about making a cake or pastry with olive oil, you'll find them to be light, delicate and definitely not "oily." Because some of these recipes call for what may seem a large amount of oil, you may not want to use your best extra virgin. Look for a mild olive oil that does not have a pronounced taste but do not succumb to the temptation to substitute corn, sunflower, peanut oil or anything else for good olive oil.

*A backward look at Cretan sweets*

In the past few years there have been several books published on the foods of antiquity as well as reprints of the great ancient food writers, Athenaeus, Apicius and so forth. Now that archaeologists sift through every particle of earth and subject even invisible molecules to scrutiny rather than targeting their interest on structures, potsherds and gold, they are able to describe Minoan or Classical eating habits in such detail you'd think they had been present at the meals. Of course, the cooking methods and final result are not always possible to ascertain, but the same ingredients appear over and over again: flour, sesame seeds, nuts, honey. In their *Classical Cookbook*, Andrew Dalby and Sally Grainger even have two or three versions of little cheesecakes that seem remarkably akin to the sweet cheese pies of Heraklio and Chania. Even more remarkable is the comparison Maria and Nikos Psilakis (*Traditional Cretan Cooking*) point out between an ancient Cretan confection called *gastrin*, mentioned by Athenaeus (*Deipnosophists*, XIV, 57, 647-648), consisting of a thin layer of pastry made of crushed sesame seeds, a filling of almonds, walnuts, hazelnuts, poppy seeds, pepper and honey and a second thin sheet of pastry, which looks like being an ancestor of the baklava. In time, the poppy seeds and pepper were abandoned but there are still dozens of biscuits which preserve the notion of thin pastry folded around chopped nuts (see the recipes for *patouda, zournadakia, mamoulia*, among others), quite apart from the baklava-type sweet found all over the eastern Mediterranean.

Interspersed amongst the very traditional sweets prepared for specific occasions, you will also find some western-sounding cakes and desserts. City women, particularly, would compete to outdo each other with the latest tastes as well as the latest foreign fashions. Unfamiliar procedures and ingredients like chocolate ripples, fruit icings, coconut and sprinkles began infiltrating treasured notebooks between the wars, sometimes copied from a ladies' magazine, more often accompanied by the name of a friend. Social gatherings in towns could be sophisticated affairs where it was essential to surprise with something new. There was at least one circle in Chania, for example, in the 1950s and 60s that met every Sunday evening in a mansion in the elegant Halepa quarter to listen to chamber music, sip tea or whiskey, and chat in English and French as well as Greek.

A uniformed maid would pass the delicacies.

One staple in virtually every pantry was the spoon sweet. Talent in converting fruits, flowers and even baby vegetables into a luminous jewel supended in syrup was a quality that separated a superb housewife from a competent one. The average visitor might never taste her stuffed vine leaves or kid with artichokes but a spoon sweet proclaimed its creator's expertise, rather like the embroideries hanging in her windows and draped over every surface in her salon. It is difficult for a westerner to grasp the social significance of what looks to us as little more than jam. The name alone is a stumbling block. The spoon sweet, *glyko tou koutaliou*, is so called to distinguish it from the *glyko tou tapsiou* – the baked sweet – which is eaten by the portion or plateful, not measured out in coffee spoons like Prufrock's life. For there was a strict etiquette surrounding the administering of these preserves. Said to have been invented during the Byzantine era, and customary in Jewish and Muslim cultures as well, they became synonymous with hospitality. Other cultures have a piece of cake, a cup of coffee or a drink, embedded in their welcome rituals; the Greeks, Cretans included, had and to a lesser extent still have spoon sweets. Offered neither too soon nor too long after the guest's arrival, they were served from special crystal bowls from whose rim dangled delicate silver spoons. The bowl and matching crystal plates, too small for any other use, occupied a doily-covered tray, along with tall glasses of cold water and tiny glasses of the Cretan national spirit, raki.

Nowadays, spoon sweets can be bought in supermarkets but many housewives still take pride in making their own. Some are comparable to our jams and jellies, but for the most part the syrup is less dense and often the fruit is whole, impossible to spread on a piece of bread. There are preserves for every season: fresh almond, rose petal, strawberry in the spring, sour cherry, apricot a bit later, walnut, watermelon, baby eggplant, grape, the whole range of citrus fruits – sometimes just the peel, sometimes a whole green bitter orange the size of a pingpong ball – and finally the wonderful quince, for which no better use exists. Though the ritual is dying out, many of them are wonderful toppings for ice cream or yogurt. And you might even acquire a taste for a spoonful of sweet to jolt you awake from a summer siesta, as so many of us have here in Greece.

# PASTRIES

## Fried pastry coils
*Xerotigana*

(HERAKLIO)

**Literally called "dry fries," these ineffably delicate pastry spirals
are what tradition-minded Cretans invariably serve instead of cake at
weddings and baptisms. Some women are in such demand for their
pastry-making skills that they are given orders for one thousand of
these at a time and are kept busy all summer long turning out these
delicacies for friends and relatives. They calculate that a kilo of flour
will make 70 xerotigana, and that when working with 20 kilos (44
pounds) of flour, 8 kilos (17.6 pounds) of honey and 2 kilos (4.4
pounds) of sugar will be needed for the syrup. When you add to that
the amount of oil required to fry them all, you realize the expenses
and labor involved. One expert I talked to, Alexandra Nerolidou in
Zakros, longed for the wedding season to end.**

**The traditional xerotigana resemble a loose roll of hair ribbon
or a coiled spring. Making them is an art that usually demands two
people. I describe it here in case you want to try, but I also give the
simpler method used on less formal occasions.**

FOR THE PASTRY
*60 ml (1/4 cup) raki or grappa*
*60 ml (1/4 cup) lemon juice*
*60 ml (1/4 cup) olive oil*
*240 ml (1 cup) water, approximately*
*about 900 grams (2 lbs) flour*

FOR THE SYRUP
*400 grams (2 cups) honey*
*400 grams (2 cups) sugar*
*360 ml (1 1/2 cups) water*

FOR THE GARNISH
*300 grams (2 cups) finely chopped
    walnuts and browned sesame
    seeds*
*1 teaspoon cinnamon powder*

*2 liters (1 qt) ordinary olive oil for
    frying*

Pour the liquids into a large bowl and mix in the flour gradually
with your fingers – about a cup or so at a time. Knead until all the
flour is absorbed and you have a tough dough. This can take up to 20
minutes, but you could also use the dough attachment on a heavy
duty mixer if you have one.  You may have to add a little water or
flour. Cover the dough and let it rest for about 1 hour.

While you wait, make the syrup by bringing all the ingredients to
a boil. Lower heat and simmer for about 15 minutes, stirring
occasionally, or until you have a medium syrup. Set aside.

Divide the dough into several pieces about the size of a tennis
ball, flatten them as you would a hamburger pattie in the palm of
your hand, and put each one through the largest slot in a pasta

machine a few times, working gradually up to the narrowest opening. (As you work, keep the other balls covered with a damp cloth.)

The final "sash" of dough should be about 60 cm/24 inches long. Lay it on a floured work surface and with a pastry wheel cut each band into strips about 4 cm/1 1/4 inch wide.

This is really a two-person operation; one puts the dough through the machine, the other cuts, twirls and fries the pastry.

Heat 2 liters (8 cups) of olive oil in your deep fryer or largest stew pot. Now comes the tricky part; hook one end of a pastry ribbon on the tines of a fork and dip it into the bubbling oil, holding the other end with your other hand. Twirl the fork so that the pastry coils around it like a spring. Try to get the whole ribbon wrapped around itself evenly. Leave for about a minute to cook through, but lift out before it burns or even browns. Drain on a platter with absorbent paper. Repeat until you have finished frying all the ribbons.

A less time-consuming way to make a nest is to hold the ends of two ribbons in your left hand and loosely coil the pastry around your fingers. Drop the coil into the bubbling oil (without burning your fingers), press the pastry to the edge of the pan if it starts to unravel and fry quickly (about a minute for each side).

After you have fried all the xerotigana start dipping them into the syrup and then onto a serving platter. Sprinkle them with the chopped nuts and sesame seeds and cinnamon. If you're not going to eat them within a few days, don't add the syrup and topping. They'll keep for at least a month in a dry place. (You can reheat the syrup if it becomes too sticky.)

Makes about 70 pieces.

If this procedure seems too daunting, simply cut the dough into squares about the size of an ordinary paper napkin, twist into bows, knots or cylinders, fry quickly and add syrup and nuts as before.

Made this way, they are very similar to the so-called diples or pleated pastries of the mainland. Under the name of cartellate or carteddate, they appear as a Christmas favorite in Puglia, yet another of the dishes and customs that stretch between that easternmost part of Italy and Crete. The only difference is that there the dough is prepared with a little yeast and white wine.

With or without the addition of eggs, they are also found all over the Middle East and in Provence, where they are called "oreillettes" or "little ears."

# Fried pastry "reeds"

## *A v g o k a l á m a r a*

These fried pastries, made with eggs (*avga*) as their name implies, are a favorite sweet at baptisms and weddings on this part of the island. They do not require the elaborate, painstaking procedure of *xerotigana*. The traditional shape resembles a reed (*kalami*), but as with the *diples* mentioned above, you could give them other shapes. The original recipe calls for 1 cup of *alousia*, wood ashes boiled with water, which produces a very light, crunchy texture. Lacking fireplaces modern cooks have tended to substitute soda water.

In a large bowl make a well in the flour and add the raki, juice, oil, salt and the eggs. Mix in the flour and slowly add the soda water until you have a tough dough. Knead for about 10 minutes so that it is smooth but remains on the tough side. Cover and set aside to rest for about 1 hour while you prepare the area where you'll roll out the dough, fill a large frying pan with olive oil (about 8 cm – 3 inches – deep), and combine the ingredients for the crushed nut topping.

Roll out the dough, a little at a time to prevent it drying, so that it is as thin as possible and about the same width overall (easily achieved with a pasta machine, if you have one). Cut the dough in squares about the size of a cocktail napkin (10 cm/4 inches) or into strips 10 cm (4 inches) long and 5 cm (2 inches) wide. If you choose strips, fold them into bows, triangles and pleats. Heat the oil until boiling but as you cook regulate the heat so the pastries don't burn and fry only a few at a time, using 2 forks. Lift out and drain on several layers of paper towel, and proceed to the next. As the woman who told me this recipe says, it helps to have someone else preparing the squares while you fry.

On the other hand, they don't have to be a specific shape to be good. Once all the pastry is cooked, make the honey syrup, which should be very thick, taking it off the heat when big bubbles start to form. Dip the pastries one by one into the hot syrup, let excess drops drain over the saucepan and then place on a serving platter. Sprinkle them all with the crushed nuts and serve. Makes about 45 pieces. They will keep for about 10 days.

FOR THE PASTRY
*420 grams (3 cups) (bread) flour*
*60 ml (1/4 cup) raki or brandy*
*60 ml (1/4 cup) orange juice*
*2 tablespoons olive oil + more for frying*
*1/2 teaspoon salt*
*2 eggs plus 1 egg white, lightly beaten*
*120 ml (1/2 cup) soda water*

FOR THE SYRUP
*360 grams (1 1/2 cups) honey*
*100 grams (1/2 cup) sugar*
*120 ml (1/2 cup) water*
*1 cinnamon stick*

FOR THE GARNISH
*150 grams (1 cup) each crushed almonds and walnuts*
*3 heaping tablespoons sesame seeds*
*1 teaspoon powdered cinnamon*
*75 grams (1/2 cup) crushed hazelnuts (optional)*

# Spiced nut rolls
## *P a t o ú d a*

FOR THE FILLING

350 grams (2 1/2 cups) chopped
 walnuts and/or almonds
3 heaping tablespoons sesame seeds,
 browned quickly in a heavy
 frying pan
1 full teaspoon ground cinnamon
1/2 teaspoon nutmeg
1/2 teaspoon ground cloves
2 tablespoons dry bread or rusk
 crumbs
60 ml (1/4 cup) olive oil
4 tablespoons honey dissolved in 6
 tablespoons hot water

FOR THE PASTRY

about 420 grams (3 cups) (cake)
 flour
3 teaspoons baking powder
240 ml (1 cup) olive oil
70 grams (1/3 cup) sugar
80 ml (1/3 cup) soda water
60 ml (1/4 cup) raki or brandy
grated peel of 2 lemons
confectioners' sugar for dusting

**This confection from Eastern Crete combines a lemony, shortbread-like crust folded around a filling of crushed nuts; even the confirmed non-sweet eater will find the smoky taste of the sesame seeds and the hint of honey hard to resist. Because these offer consolation to the rigors of fasting, they contain no butter, milk or eggs. Using olive oil instead produces a stiffer dough that needs no resting time.**

Mix the filling ingredients thoroughly in a bowl.

Sift the flour with the baking powder into a medium-sized bowl. In a separate, larger bowl, beat the olive oil and sugar together until the mixture is smooth and then slowly add the soda water, raki or brandy and lemon peel. Finally, beat in the flour gradually, using the pastry hook attachment if you have one, until dough begins to form. When the electric beater gets too sluggish to have any effect, take out the dough and knead on a floured surface until it is soft and pliable. Roll it out immediately into four strips about 26 cm long x 12 cm wide (11 x 5 inches), as thin as possible.

Preheat the oven to 200°C (400°F). Lay the filling on one side of the first strip and fold the other side over it, pressing the edges together to close the seam. Repeat with the other three. Place them on a lightly oiled baking sheet and bake until golden, about 10-15 minutes. When cool, dust with confectioners' sugar and cut each "loaf" into slices about 2.5 cm (1 inch) thick, on the diagonal. Makes about 48 pieces that can be kept up to a week or more in a biscuit tin.

You can also shape the dough into circles (with a glass or cookie cutter), placing a spoonful of filling in the center and folding the dough over to make crescents. But then you will have some filling left over.

## Honey

Cretan honey, among the most highly prized in Greece today, was famous even in antiquity, when the bee was an emblem on the coins of some city-states. In 1718 the French traveller Tournefort described it as "transparent as crystal and as perfumed as flowers" in his two-volume work, *A Voyage into the Levant*. The Turkish writer, Evliya Celebi, who visited Crete at the end of that century, reported the presence of 75,000 bee hives and forty different kinds of honey. It is also possible that Cretan honey has special properties because of the herbs the island's bees frequent. It is delicate and fragrant. If you get hold of some, save it for your toast or yogurt and use a cheaper honey for the syrups poured over some Cretan sweets.

Two or three teaspoons of honey before retiring after a night of excesses are a better antidote to a hangover than Aristotle's "hair of the dog" since they prevent it from even occurring.

## Petimezi

Petimezi or grape must syrup is similar to *vino cotto*, which can be substituted, and like it is made by boiling down unfermented wine must until it is syrupy. Sometimes the Cretans (and the Turks) boil down the must until it is even thicker, almost solid, and dip a "necklace" of strung walnut halves into it repeatedly until they have a sausagelike sweet called *kefteria*. You can find this in some Greek and Anatolian specialty shops. Laying the dense must on trays to dry in the sun also produces a sweet very similar to Turkish delight (*loukoumi*) with less trouble that will keep all winter.

# Spice cake with grape juice syrup
## *Petimezópitta*

(HERAKLIO)

about 420 grams (3 cups) flour
3 teaspoons baking powder
1/2 teaspoon powdered cloves
1 teaspoon cinnamon
1/2 teaspoon nutmeg
240 ml (1 cup) olive oil
200 grams (1 cup) sugar
240 ml (1 cup) petimezi, grape juice
    syrup, or vino cotto
60 ml (1/4 cup) brandy
60 ml (1/4 cup) fresh lemon juice

**Crete's answer to gingerbread, this spicy cake calls for grape juice syrup which can also be found in specialty shops/health food stores under the name *vino cotto*. In September when the grapes are harvested, many housewives rescue a few liters of the must (unfermented grape juice) before it gets to the barrels and use it to make various sweets. One of them, *moustalevria* is boiled and stirred for hours with a little flour until it thickens. Then it is poured into bowls, dusted with cinnamon and left to set into a rather solid jelly. *Moustokouloura*, biscuits made with must instead of milk or wine, are another seasonal favorite.**

Preheat the oven to 180°C (350°F).

Sift the flour into a bowl with the baking powder, cloves, cinnamon and nutmeg.

Using an electric mixer, beat the olive oil and sugar together in a separate bowl until creamy and then add the petimezi, brandy and lemon juice a little at a time until thoroughly blended. Add the flour, again gradually. When all the flour has been absorbed and there are no lumps, pour the batter into an oiled springform cake pan (24 cm – 9.5 inches – in diameter) and bake for 40 to 45 minutes until the cake is a golden brown and a tester poked into the center comes out clean. Serves 8 -10.

# Lenten sesame paste cake
## *Tahinópitta*

(HERAKLIO)

**This recipe is from the handwritten notebook of Evangelia Dokoumetzidi, a renowned home cook. Although she and her family left Heraklio for Athens in 1960, she continued to produce her famous Cretan specialties. There has been so much demand for them**

over the years that her daughters, Lila Tsantila and Maro Kallimani, copied them down in their own notebooks after her death and Lila's son, Spyros, has entered them in his computer. Luckily, because the original pages are now in tatters.

Because it has no eggs, the cake does not rise much. Its dense texture is similar to that of gingerbread and as you eat, you become aware of the subtle blend of tastes – of the spices, the orange peel and the underlying hint of tahini. Soup made with sesame seed paste was a staple during the Second World War and the pious still eat it during Lent, but used in this way tahini loses all connotations of deprivation.

Preheat the oven to 180°C (350°F).

Sift the flour into a bowl with the baking powder, cloves, cinnamon and nutmeg.

In a separate bowl, using an electric mixer, beat the sesame paste with the sugar, 180 ml (3/4 cup) of water and juices, alternately, a little at a time until thoroughly blended. Beat in the brandy and orange peel. Add the flour, again gradually. When all the flour has been absorbed and there are no lumps, stir in the raisins and walnuts. The batter will be fairly liquid.

Pour it into an oiled springform cake pan (24 cm – 9.5 inches – in diameter) and bake for 40 to 45 minutes until the cake is a golden brown and a tester poked into the center comes out clean. Serves 8 - 10.

*280 grams (2 cups) flour*
*1 1/2 teaspoon baking powder*
*1/2 teaspoon ground cloves*
*1 tablespoon cinnamon*
*a few gratings of nutmeg*
*120 ml (1/2 cup) tahini (sesame paste)*
*200 grams (1 cup) sugar*
*120 ml (1/2 cup) fresh orange juice*
*2 tablespoons lemon juice, added to the orange juice*
*grated rind of 1/2 orange*
*1 teaspoon baking soda, dissolved in the orange juice*
*2 tablespoons brandy*
*150 grams (1 cup) raisins, chopped and dusted with flour*
*a handful of walnuts, chopped*

# Raisin cake
## *Stafidópitta*

(SITEIA)

This recipe was given to me by a woman lucky enough to use her own raisins when she bakes this. The cake has a toffee-like crunchiness on the outside, while the inside reminds me of old-fashioned wedding cake though moister and even more succulent.

Having been invented to perk up fasting periods, this cake contains no eggs or milk but uses extra virgin olive oil for

**shortening. It makes a scrumptious snack for winter afternoons and evenings. Leftovers can be turned into delicious rusks for dunking into coffee or tea. Leave the cake a day or two, cut it into neat pieces and bake them in a low oven for an hour or so until they are hard. They will keep indefinitely.**

*300 grams (2 cups) golden raisins*
*60 ml (1/4 cup) raki or brandy*
*about 420 grams (3 cups) flour*
*1/2 teaspoon ground cloves*
*1 teaspoon ground cinnamon*
*240 ml (1 cup) olive oil*
*200 grams (1 cup) sugar*
*120 ml (1/2 cup) fresh orange juice*
*1 tablespoon baking soda, dissolved in the orange juice*
*grated peel of one orange*
*120 ml (1/2 cup) soda water*
*150 grams (1 cup) chopped walnuts (optional)*

Preheat the oven to 180°C (350°F).

Soak the raisins in the brandy for about 10 minutes and then chop them in the food processor.

Sift the flour and spices together into a bowl. In a separate, larger bowl, using an electric mixer if you have one, beat together the olive oil and sugar until creamy and slowly add the orange juice along with the grated peel, soda water, brandy-soaked raisins and chopped walnuts. Stir in the flour, a little at a time, until you have a thick batter.

Slide it into a lightly oiled springform cake pan (24 cm, 9.5 inches in diameter) and bake for about 1 hour. Serves 10.

**Siteia, the largest town in Eastern Crete, must be the raisin capital of Greece. Whether blond or black, its raisins are large and juicy and have inspired dozens of original and delectable cakes and sweets.**

# Filled raisin-almond biscuits
*Stafidotá*

These biscuits look like fig newtons, but there the resemblance ends. They are much crisper and finer than those cookies we used to munch on during recess. This recipe comes from the pretty village of Myrsini, which overlooks Mirabello Bay from the mountains opposite Agios Nikolaos. I had stumbled into the studio of Nikos Makrynakis, a talented potter whose glazes in all shades of turquoise and blue shone in the October light. As we chatted I told him I was hunting down recipes; fifteen minutes later I was talking with his mother, Despina. Warm and gracious, she had a sadness about her. In between recipes and tales of old-time weddings, her story emerged. Twenty-nine years ago when Nikos was only five, his father had had a stroke, which left his speech blurred and his mobility limited. They left Agios Nikolaos and returned to Myrsini, where she supported Nikos, his brother and her invalid husband with the help of a small pension. Nevertheless, she still wears a smile and has raised her sons well; Nikos is head of the village cultural association.

With these biscuits, Despina says "the more almonds you add the merrier," so if you like them as much as she does, do increase the amount suggested.

FOR THE DOUGH

1 teaspoon baking soda
80 ml (1/3 cup) orange juice
240 ml (1 cup) olive oil
70 grams (1/3 cup) sugar
2 tablespoons raki or brandy
420 grams (3 cups) flour

FOR THE FILLING

450 grams (1 lb) chopped raisins
200 grams (7 oz) chopped almonds
3 heaping tablespoons sesame seeds
80 ml (1/3 cup) olive oil
1 teaspoon cinnamon
1/2 teaspoon nutmeg
1/4 teaspoon cloves

Mix all the filling ingredients together.

Dissolve the baking soda in the orange juice. In a separate bowl beat the olive oil and sugar together with an electric beater for about 5 minutes. Pour the orange juice and brandy into the bowl and continue beating. Add the flour to the liquids gradually, stirring all the while with a wooden spoon or beating with the pastry hook, until a dough forms. Knead well until you have a pliable dough.

Preheat the oven to 180°C (350°F). Roll out the dough in strips about 30 cm (12 inches) long and 20 cm (8 inches) wide and then place the filling on one side (looks like a strudel), close, and slice on the diagonal. Place the pastry on a lightly oiled baking tin and bake for 45 minutes or until the crust is golden. Makes about 4 dozen pieces.

# Sweet open-faced cheese tarts
## *Kallitsoúnia*

*300 grams (2 cups) fresh unsalted myzithra, ricotta or curd cheese*

*3 tablespoons sugar*

*1 1/2 tablespoons melted butter*

*1 egg, at room temperature*

*1 tablespoon chopped mint (optional)*

FOR THE PASTRY

*2 tablespoons unsalted butter*

*100 grams (1/2 cup) sugar*

*2 eggs, at room temperature*

*1/2 teaspoon crushed mastic (optional)*

*(1/2 teaspoon vanilla if you can't find mastic)*

*1 teaspoon baking powder dissolved in 4 tablespoons brandy or raki*

*3 tablespoons milk*

*1/2 teaspoon ground cinnamon (optional)*

*about 350 grams (2 1/2 cups) flour*

*1 egg, beaten, for brushing on the filling*

*cinnamon for sprinkling (optional)*

**These cheese tarts are among Crete's best known pastries. You find them in bakeries everywhere; around Heraklio they are called *kallitsoúnia*, which means a little fried pie in the west of the island, where they are called *lychnarakia* after the miniature oil lamp (*lychnari*) they resemble. Delicately flavored with mastic, extracted from the resin of a pistachio-related tree that grows only in southern Chios, these tarts are a wonderful snack any time of day or they could be served for dessert along with fruit. Traditionally they are eaten at the post-midnight meal after the mass on Easter Eve (well into Sunday by the time one actually sits down at the table).**

To make the filling: If the cheese is very fresh and soft, spread it on paper towels on top of some newspapers so that the excess liquid will drain off. Then put it in a bowl and beat in the remaining ingredients.

To make the pastry: Beat the butter and sugar together until creamy, beat in the eggs one at a time, add the flavorings, brandy and milk. Stir in the flour, a little at a time, and then knead it after stirring becomes too difficult. The dough will be fairly stiff. Cover and let rest for up to half an hour.

Preheat the oven to 180°C (350°F). Pinch off a little ball of dough at a time. Roll out to about 1/2 cm (1/4 inch) thick and using a mug or saucer cut out round shapes about 10 cm (4 inches) in diameter. Put 1 tablespoon of filling in the center and pinch the edges between two fingers as you'd flute a pie crust.

Paint the surface with beaten egg and sprinkle with cinnamon. Place the tarts on a lightly buttered baking sheet and bake for 15-20 minutes. Makes about 18 tarts.

# Easter cheese tarts

*Kallitsoúnia paschaliná – Lychnarákia*

(CHANIA)

**This recipe, given by Marika Daskalogianni, is a variation on the same theme, with slightly different ingredients, which make for slightly sweeter pies with a lighter crust. The oil lamp itself, with from one to three wicks, was a prominent feature of rural life until the 1960s when the Cretan countryside finally got electricity. Zakros was just one village where as many as ten or fifteen young women would sit around the kitchen table spinning, embroidering and weaving by its flickering light, telling stories and wondering which boy they'd end up marrying. Eventually this little dishlike lamp was replaced by kerosene lamps with glass attachments, but many women I talked to remember the cosy atmosphere with nostalgia, especially when they compare it to the TV-induced isolation of today's evenings.**

Dissolve the yeast in the milk, adding a little flour (about 1 teaspoonful), and set aside to let it rise. Or, if using instant yeast, simply add it to the flour and proceed with the recipe.

Beat the oil with the sugar in a large bowl until creamy, then add the egg, salt, yogurt and the yeast/flour mixture. Mix well and slowly add the rest of the flour, with your hands. Knead the dough on a lightly floured surface for about 5 minutes. Cover and let it rest while you prepare the filling.

Pass the cheese through a food mill if you have one. Otherwise, mash it with a fork or potato masher. Stir in the egg yolk, vanilla, honey, lemon peel, half the cinnamon and the butter until thoroughly blended. Then add the sugar gradually, stirring all the while.

Preheat the oven to 180°C (350°F). Roll out the dough and cut into circles (10 cm, 4 inches in diameter) with a teacup or cookie cutter. Using a wet tablespoon, place a spoonful of filling in the center of each pastry circle and then crimp the edges of the pies into about 8 ruffles; they look like stars.

Brush the pies with the egg yolk/water mixture or with a little milk and dust with the rest of the cinnamon. Place the pies on a buttered baking sheet and bake for about 30 minutes. Makes 24-26 tarts.

FOR THE PASTRY
*2 teaspoons active dry yeast or*
*  1 packet instant yeast*
*4 tablespoons tepid milk*
*500 grams (4 cups) (cake) flour*
*120 ml (1/2 cup) olive oil*
*140 grams (2/3 cup) sugar*
*2 small eggs, beaten*
*pinch of salt*
*3 tablespoons strained yogurt*

FOR THE FILLING
*480 grams (4 cups) sweet myzithra,*
*  ricotta or farmer's cheese*
*2 egg yolks*
*1 teaspoon vanilla extract*
*2 tablespoons honey*
*2 tablespoons grated lemon rind*
*1 tablespoon cinnamon*
*2 teaspoons unsalted butter*
*6 tablespoons sugar*
*1 egg yolk diluted in a little water*
*  (for brushing the pies)*

# Easter biscuits
## *T s o u r e k á k i a*

*300 grams (10 oz) concentrated
   butter*
*150 grams (3/4 cup) sugar*
*2 yolks, whites reserved (use small
   eggs)*
*60 ml (1/4 cup) brandy*
*1 tablespoon baking powder,
   dissolved in*
*60 ml (1/4 cup) milk*
*450 grams (3 1/2 cups) flour,
   approximately*
*sesame seeds (optional)*

**Tsoureki is the traditional, brioche-like sweet Easter bread made all over Greece but with origins in Constantinople. Referred to in the diminutive, these Easter biscuits contain the same ingredients – eggs, milk and butter which in theory have not been tasted since the beginning of Lent. To make them richer, Kostanza Gavrilaki, whose baking talents are renowned in certain circles of Heraklio, uses "voutiro galaktos," which is a form of clarified butter sold in Greece in jars. I used Dutch Mayflower concentrated butter, which is specially recommended for pastries and cakes. It comes in a tall cylindrical tin and can be found in the dairy section of supermarkets.**

Preheat the oven to 180°C (350°F). Cream the butter and sugar together with an electric mixer until fluffy – the more you beat the lighter the biscuits will be – then add the egg yolks, one at a time, followed by the liquids.

Add the flour slowly, sifting it directly into the bowl. When the mixture becomes too thick to beat with the electric mixer, remove it to a lightly floured surface and knead until you have a smooth, pliable dough. Let the dough rest for up to half an hour.

Break off small pieces of the dough and roll them into "S" shapes as thin as a finger. Make each biscuit with two of these squiggles, lining them side by side and pressing them slightly together. (You can, of course, make them in any shape you want to, but try to make sure they are all the same thickness.)

Place them on a lightly buttered baking sheet. When you have used up all the dough, paint the surfaces with the beaten egg whites and sprinkle with sesame seeds. Bake for 15 to 20 minutes. Makes about 4 dozen.

# New Year's Cake
## *Vasilópitta*

Though an established tradition, which takes a variety of forms depending on which part of Greece it is made, the *vasilopitta* – named after *Ai Vasili* (the Greek Santa Claus) – does not appear to have arrived in Crete until the late 19th century; it took another few decades to reach the countryside. The use of olive oil rather than butter is unusual here – it is not a fasting recipe – but it does not make the cake taste "oily." Instead, it has a light, spongy texture and a delicate flavor. Any leftovers will make delicious rusks (just slice and leave in the oven at a very low temperature, turning once until both sides are hard).

*600 grams (4 cups) flour,
   approximately*
*3 teaspoons baking powder*
*120 ml (1/2 cup) olive oil*
*400 grams (2 cups) sugar*
*grated peel of 1 lemon*
*grated peel of 2 oranges*
*120 ml (1/2 cup) milk*
*120 ml (1/2 cup) orange juice*
*60 ml (1/4 cup) fresh lemon juice*
*3 eggs, at room temperature*

Preheat the oven to 190°C (375°F).

Sift the flour and baking powder together and set aside. Beat the olive oil and sugar together in a bowl at high speed together with the grated orange and lemon peel for 3-4 minutes. Add the other liquids and beat for another 2 minutes. Add the eggs one at a time, beating well each time. Stir in the flour gradually with a wooden spoon until smooth. You should have a thick batter.

 Lightly oil a cake tin, about 25 cm (9.5 inches) in diameter, pour in the batter and bake for about 1 1/2 hours until lightly browned and cooked through.

# Xenoula's New Year's cake
## *I vasilópitta tis Xenoúlas*

This is a more traditional version of the classic New Year's cake, using butter instead of olive oil as the shortening, but the addition of ground almonds and brandy makes it quite distinctive and rich. There is a special ritual observed in the cutting of this cake, which like the English Christmas pudding has had a good luck charm or coin inserted into it. The head of the household makes the sign of the cross over the cake three times with the knife, cuts it in four and then starts slicing it. The first slice goes to the Christ Child, the second to St. Basil ("Ai Vasili"), the third to the poor, the next for any absent relatives. Only then does he portion out the pieces for himself followed by the family members in order of age.

*With thanks to Mary Panethymetaki for sharing this recipe.*

420 grams (3 cups) flour
1 teaspoon baking soda
1 teaspoon citric acid
220 grams (8 oz) unsalted butter
400 grams (2 cups) sugar
4 eggs, at room temperature
150 grams (1 cup) blanched
    almonds, finely ground
grated zest of 1 lemon
240 ml (1 cup) milk, scalded and
    cooled to warm
120 ml (1/2 cup) brandy

Preheat the oven to 190°C (375°F).

Sift together the flour, baking soda and citric acid.

In a separate bowl cream the butter, and adding the sugar slowly, beat until the mixture is light and fluffy. Add the eggs one at a time, beating until each egg is completely absorbed. Stir in the crushed almonds and grated lemon peel. Then beat in the flour and the milk, a little at a time, alternately. When you have finished the milk, start trickling in the brandy.

Scrape the batter into a buttered cake tin (24 cm – 9.5 inches – in diameter) and bake 40 minutes to 1 hour. The cake is done when a knife stuck into the middle comes out clean.

## Almond butter cookies

### *Kourambiédes*

Several people I met in Heraklio praised these almond shortbread biscuits made by Kostanza Gavrilaki as the best they had ever tasted. In Crete they are in great demand for weddings and christenings, as well as being a traditional Christmas sweet. When Kostanza visits her younger daughter in Detroit, all her friends ask if they may borrow her for their parties. *Kourambiedes* are traditionally served at Christmas but are welcome all year round. This recipe can be halved easily.

Kostanza uses "*voutiro galaktos*," which is a form of clarified butter sold in Greece in jars. I used Mayflower concentrated butter, which is specially recommended for pastries and cakes (see p. 198).

One of the secrets to making successful kourambiedes is prolonged beating of the butter and sugar until the mixture gets white and fluffy. Kostanza does this by hand but I use an electric beater. After it has reached this stage, mix in the rest of the ingredients, and add the flour slowly until you have a tough dough. The dough should be fairly crumbly but malleable enough to be molded into shapes, either crescents or slightly flattened balls.

To make the shapes of your choice, break off small bits of dough and roll them between your palms until they are fairly smooth and line them up on greased cookie sheets. Don't worry if there a few cracks; the confectioner's sugar you will dust them with after baking will cover up any minor defects.

Preheat the oven to 180°C (350°F). Bake for 15-20 minutes on the middle rack. Keep a close watch over them since they must not brown. Let cool to barely warm and then, using a sieve, shake confectioners' sugar over the biscuits.

Later, when they are completely cool, have the remaining sugar on a platter or large piece of waxed paper and gently roll each biscuit in it, patting the sugar with your fingers to make it stick. Kourambiedes should be completely white, with no pastry showing. Makes about 80 small biscuits.

*1/2 kg (1 lb) concentrated butter, softened*

*2 tablespoons confectioners' sugar*

*1/2 kg (1 lb) almonds, blanched and browned a bit in oven, chopped fairly finely*

*2 egg yolks*

*1 teaspoon powdered cinnamon*

*2 tablespoons brandy*

*600 grams (6 to 6 1/2 cups) sifted flour*

*1 kg (2 lbs) confectioners' sugar for covering*

In this diet-conscious age small biscuits are the most appealing. Your guests can convince themselves that they can't do much harm and, therefore, will have more than one.

# Akrivi's Christmas cookies
## *Melomakárona*

**FOR THE DOUGH**
*about 450 grams (3-4 cups) flour*
*1/2 teaspoon baking powder*
*240 ml (1 cup) olive oil*
*50 grams (1/4 cup) sugar*
*1/2 teaspoon baking soda diluted in*
*120 ml (1/2 cup) fresh orange juice*
*60 ml (1/4 cup) brandy*
*grated peel of one lemon*

**WALNUT FILLING**
*1/2 kg (1 lb) walnuts, coarsely*
*    chopped*
*3 heaping tablespoons honey*
*1 tablespoon cinnamon*
*1/4 teaspoon ground cloves*
*1/4 teaspoon grated nutmeg*

**SYRUP (OPTIONAL)**
*150 grams (3/4 cup) sugar*
*120 ml (1/2 cup) honey*
*120 ml (1/2 cup) water*
*60 ml (1/4 cup) brandy*

**FOR THE TOPPING**
*finely chopped walnuts*
*    roasted sesame seeds*

**Akrivi Mouzouraki is the proprietress of the Albatross taverna at Gournes on the coast near Heraklio. Open all year around except for December, seven days a week, lunch and dinner, hers is one of the most popular and successful restaurants in the area. All the recipes she gave me are a bit different from the norm; and she only gave them to me "because the book was going to be published in English." She wouldn't dream of giving away her secrets to a Greek!**

**Every Greek housewife makes melomakarona for Christmas. Some like Akrivi stuff them with chopped walnuts. It is the syrup that makes these sweet; if your sweet tooth is not as pronounced, you can omit it and still have delicious biscuits.**

Sift the flour with the baking powder into a bowl.

In a larger bowl beat together the olive oil and sugar with the electric mixer for 3 or 4 minutes and then beat in the other liquids, adding the grated lemon peel at the end. Slowly stir in the flour until a soft dough forms. Remove the dough from the bowl and knead it on a lightly floured surface until it is smooth and malleable. Add more flour if the dough seems sticky. Cover with cling film and set aside to rest for about 30 minutes.

For the filling mix all these ingredients together with your hands or a wooden spoon to distribute the spices evenly. Preheat the oven to 180°C (350°F). Pinch off a walnut-sized piece of dough and roll it into a ball. Make a hole in it with your thumb and fill it with some of the walnut mixture. Close the hole and place the ball, which should look like a small egg, onto an ungreased cookie sheet. When all the dough has been shaped into biscuits, bake for about 30 minutes or until golden.

To make the syrup boil the ingredients together for 3 minutes, skimming off the foam. Dip the biscuits in the syrup when it has thoroughly cooled or the next day. Sprinkle finely ground walnuts and roasted sesame seeds on top. Makes about 2-3 dozen, depending on how large you want them.

# Red wine biscuits

*Krasokoúloura*

**Simple to make, these biscuits are in the great fasting tradition. No eggs, no butter and only lightly sweetened, they are light, crunchy and difficult to resist. A good accompaniment to a fruit salad, compote or ice cream. Left straight, they resemble grissini and make for excellent nibbling at the end of a meal with raki, the last glass of wine or a liqueur.**

*With thanks to Mary Daskalaki for sharing this recipe.*

180 ml (3/4 cup) olive oil
150 grams (3/4 cup) sugar
1 tablespoon baking powder
1/2 teaspoon baking soda
1 tablespoon powdered cinnamon
120 ml (1/2 cup) dry red wine
420 grams (3 cups) flour,
   approximately
1/2 cup sesame seeds

Beat the olive oil and sugar together in a large bowl until the sugar is no longer grainy.

In a separate bowl, mix the baking powder, soda and cinnamon with the wine and then beat this into the sugar and oil. Add the flour to the bowl slowly, beating until a dough forms and the beater gets bogged down. Stir in the remaining flour with a wooden spoon and finally knead with your hands until you have a medium dough.

Brown the sesame seeds quickly in a heavy frying pan and turn off the heat when they start to pop.

Preheat the oven to 180°C (350°F). Break off bits of the dough about the size of a chestnut and roll them between your palms or on a flat surface until you have "ropes" about 15 cm (6-7 inches) long. Try to get them all the same thickness so they will cook evenly.

Leave them as sticks or loop them into circles, roll each cookie in the sesame seeds and place them on an oiled baking sheet. Bake for up to 25 minutes, depending on how brown you want them. Makes about 34 pieces.

# Spicy beer-leavened biscuits

*Tsourekákia me bíra*

(ZAKROS)

420 ml (1 3/4 cup) olive oil
200 grams (1 cup) sugar
1/2 teaspoon soda
1 tablespoon baking powder
1/2 can (130 ml) beer
1 teaspoon cinnamon
1 teaspoon nutmeg
1 teaspoon powdered cloves
700 grams (5 cups) flour,
    approximately
sesame seeds for sprinkling

**Like the preceding red-wine biscuits, this recipe was given me by Mary Daskalaki, who became famous in archaeological circles because of her taverna in Kato Zakros, one of the few unspoilt seaside spots in Crete. Every summer Mary would cook marvellous meals for the dusty, parched men and women who were sifting through the rubble of one of the last great Minoan palaces to be discovered, just a few minutes walk from the coast. By the time I arrived on her doorstep she had retired and her son was running the taverna, but Mary gave me a typical Cretan welcome. She devoted a whole morning to sharing her wonderful recipes with me, introduced me to the team of friends and relatives who were cooking for a baptism party that evening, filled my arms with bags of handpicked marjoram and thyme, and sent me up to her sister who was baking bread with her family, where I was most cordially invited to lunch. At that point I could have spent the rest of my life in Zakros!**

Beat the olive oil and sugar together in a large bowl for about 5 minutes. Dissolve the soda and baking powder in the beer and then beat this liquid into the oil-sugar mixture, together with the spices. Add the flour to the bowl contents, a cup at a time, beating with a wooden spoon and eventually kneading with your hands, until you have a medium dough.

Treat as in preceding recipe.
Makes about 40 pieces.

# Shortbread biscuits filled with nuts
*Mamoúlia*

**This is another of Evangelia Dokoumetzidi's fabulous recipes. Her notebook contained 129 of them, some just listing the ingredients because she needed no reminders as to procedure or oven temperature, others impeccably precise with quantities given in the drams and okes of pre-WWII measurements. Like so many of the recipes I was given all over Crete, hers for sweets seem intended for, if not an army, then a batallion. I'm sure this reflects the generous custom of most housewives to make enough for their next door neighbors and the philosophy that "baking is such an effort, you might as well cook for a crowd and besides you never know who might stop by."**

**I do not know whether these wonderful nut-stuffed biscuits are connected with any celebration; they obviously have nothing to do with fasting. Though making the dough is easy, filling each cookie is time-consuming, so if you decide to double the recipe (ie go back to the original quantities) I suggest you do it with a friend. If you do double it, use 3 large eggs instead of 2 small ones.**

FOR THE DOUGH
*225 grams (8 oz) unsalted butter*
*120 ml (1/2 cup) milk*
*150 grams (3/4 cup) sugar*
*1/2 kg (3 1/2 cups) (bread) flour*
*2 small eggs at room temperature*
*1/2 teaspoon baking soda dissolved in*
*60 ml (1/4 cup) brandy*

FOR THE FILLING
*250 grams (1/2 lb) walnuts, finely*
   *chopped*
*1 teaspoon cinnamon*
*2 tablespoons brandy*
*100 grams (1/2 cup) confectioners'*
   *sugar, approximately*

FOR COATING
*rosewater or orange blossom water*
*icing sugar*

To make the dough melt the butter in a large nonstick saucepan over low heat. Heat the milk in a smaller saucepan and then stir in the sugar. Pour this into the melted butter, stirring constantly, and when it starts to foam begin adding the flour, a little at a time, stirring all the while with a wooden spoon. Keep adding flour even after the dough forms and comes away from the sides of the pan, but if you think you can't add any more, stop, remove the pan from the heat and place it in a basin of cold water to cool. When the mixture seems coolish, stir in the eggs one at a time and then the brandy. At this point you can gradually mix in the rest of the flour. You should have a soft golden dough.

To make the filling, chop the walnuts in a food processor until they are in fairly small pieces but not powdered. Mix in the cinnamon and brandy in a medium-sized bowl and stir in the sugar. The mixture will start to cohere. If you think it should be "stickier" add a tiny bit of water. This cohesiveness makes the filling easier to handle.

Butter a large baking sheet and preheat the oven to 150°C (300°F).

Pinch off a walnut-sized piece of dough, roll it into a ball between your palms and flatten it against the palm of one hand. When the pastry is quite thin, add a teaspoonful of filling and fold the sides over it, pressing down to seal it. Mold it a little as if you were playing with plasticine into the shape of a large raindrop or rounded pyramid and set it on the baking sheet. Repeat until you have used up all the dough and filling. (I can't promise you won't have a little of one or the other left over.) Bake for 25-30 minutes until they turn a light beige; don't let them brown.

In the meantime, have ready a small bowlful of rose- or orange-blossom-water and a larger bowl with icing sugar. As soon as you can handle the biscuits, dip each one in the scented water and then roll it in the icing sugar. You might think this step excessive but it makes the crust crisper as well as prettier, and heightens the taste. Makes about 3 dozen.

# Yogurt cake
*Yiaourtópitta*

80 grams (1 cup) rusk or digestive biscuit crumbs
300 grams (1 1/2 cups) sugar
225 grams (1 cup) unsalted butter, softened
4 eggs, separated
420 grams (3 cups) flour
400 grams (2 cups) strained Greek yogurt
grated rind of 1 lemon
1/4 teaspoon ground cinnamon
1 teaspoon baking powder dissolved in 1 tablespoon lemon juice

**The recipe for this light, delicious cake comes from the notebook of the Dokoumetzidis family. This cake is somewhat like an American cheesecake, with a golden crust and a moist centre. Delicious on its own, it would be even more festive served with a sauce made of sour cherries, apricots or plum compote.**

Butter a baking pan 24 cm (9.5 inches) in diameter and 4-5 cm (about 2 inches) deep and line it with the finely ground crumbs. Preheat the oven to 180°C (350°F).

Beat the sugar and butter together until smooth and fluffy. Beat in the egg yolks, one at a time. Stir in the flour and the yogurt alternately, until you have a smooth, thick batter.

Whip the egg whites until they form peaks and fold them into the batter. Sprinkle in the lemon rind and cinnamon and stir in the baking powder/lemon juice. Pour the batter into the baking pan and bake for about 45 minutes. Let the cake cool and invert onto a serving dish. Serves 10-12. Keep refrigerated.

# Yogurt souffle

*Yaoúrti soufflé*

(RETHYMNO)

This exquisite feather-light dessert was served to Hillary Clinton when she came to Greece for ceremonies connected with the lighting of the Olympic Flame for the Atlanta Games in 1996. It was preceded by rack of baby lamb filets no bigger than walnuts in a sauce containing orange juice and sweet red wine. This souffle is far easier to prepare. It goes well with a sauce made from puréed fruit – raspberries, strawberries or sour cherries.

*With thanks to Grecotel chef Dimitrios Staikopoulos for this recipe.*

3 egg yolks

200 grams (1 cup) sugar plus a little extra

275 grams (1 1/4 cups) strained yogurt

2 tablespoons cornstarch

5 egg whites

1 tablespoon butter

Beat the egg yolks with the sugar in a bowl until pale and stir in the yogurt and cornstarch gradually. In a separate bowl beat the egg whites until they form stiff peaks and fold them gently into the mixture.

Preheat the oven to 180°C (350°F). Grease a souffle dish (21 cm/8 inch) with butter and dust with sugar to prevent sticking. Set the dish in a slightly larger pan half-filled with water and bake for about 25 minutes until the souffle puffs right up and turns golden. Serves 6.

# Bite-sized doughnuts

*Loukoúmia*

(EASTERN CRETE)

In most of Greece, loukoumia is a term meaning Turkish delight – squares of firm jelly scented with rose water, mastic or pistachio and sometimes studded with pistachio nuts. In Crete, however, these puffy sweets resemble more the fritters known as *loukoumades*. They are a specialty of Eastern Crete, where they are made during the Christmas holidays, but in Kritsa, a large village in the hills above Agios Nikolaos, the bride traditionally offers them to her wedding guests at her new home after the ceremony. There they are called "wedding bells." This recipe is among those published by the Heraklio Department of Agriculture in their booklet, "Don't forget tradition in your kitchen."

*2 tablespoons olive oil*
*50 grams (1/4 cup) sugar*
*60 ml (1/4 cup) raki or brandy*
*juice and grated rind of 1 orange*
*1/2 teaspoon cinnamon*
*1 teaspoon active dry yeast dissolved*
*    in 1 cup warm water or*
*    1 envelope instant yeast or*
*1 teaspoon soda and 240 ml (1 cup)*
*    warm water*
*250 grams (2 cups) flour*
*    (approximately)*
*oil for frying*

Mix together the oil and sugar together in a large bowl and beat with the electric beater at top speed for about 3 minutes. Add the raki and orange juice and beat for another 2 minutes. Add the grated rind, cinnamon and yeast or soda, and stir in the flour little by little until it forms a dough.

Take it out of the bowl and knead with the heel of your hand until you have a smooth soft dough, adding more flour if it remains sticky.

Pinch off chestnut-sized chunks and roll them into ropes about 3 cm (1.5 inches) thick. Cut them into 6 cm (2 inch) pieces and set them aside on a tray to rise for 30 minutes or more.

Deep fry a few at a time in a lot of hot but not smoking oil until they are brown. Drain them on paper towels before arranging them on a platter, sprinkle with sugar mixed with cinnamon or honey and serve. Makes about 40 pieces.

## Akrivi's batter-dipped cheese balls

*Loukoumotyrópittes tis Akrivís*
(ALBATROSS TAVERNA, GOURNES)

Just about everyone loves loukoumades, which might be described as doughnut "holes" fried in bubbling oil and dripping with cinnamon-sprinkled honey. But they cannot be compared with these. I'd been sitting in the Albatross taverna one afternoon after the lunch customers had departed, prying recipes out of Akrivi Mouzouraki, a stately red-head of generous proportions and proprietress of one of Heraklio's best known eating spots. After discussing her techniques of preparing lobster, rabbit, seafood pilaff and Christmas biscuits, I felt as though I'd eaten a ten course dinner but still had room for that "bit of sweet that makes the meal complete." As if she suspected as much, Akrivi ordered her kitchen help to bring her the wide bowl with the batter she keeps on hand for this house specialty and another bowl filled with sweet myzithra cheese. After the helper heated up the oil, she deftly rolled little balls of the cheese between her plump palms, dipped them into the batter and quick as a wink dropped them into the deep fryer. When I bit through the crunchy coating into the cool creamy interior, I knew I'd found the dessert of my dreams. Akrivi beamed with pleasure and a certain smugness as if she'd known it all along.

Akrivi's batter provides an extremely light, crisp crust which could be used to coat other things besides sweetened cheese, such as summer fruit or even savory cheese.

Whisk the batter ingredients, liquids and egg yolk first, adding the flour and baking powder slowly until you have a batter that resembles a thick custard.

Mash the myzithra with the sugar and cinnamon until it is smooth. You can use an electric beater for this. Both the cheese and the batter can be made ahead of time.

Have ready a saucepan filled with boiling oil for frying. Make little balls out of the cheese mixture. Dip each ball in the batter and brown a few at a time quickly in the hot oil. Lift them out with slotted spoon, drain on paper towels, and serve with honey or sugar. Because they cook so quickly, you would do well to have someone removing them as you prepare them. Makes about 40 balls.

The batter will keep in the refrigerator for several days; dilute it with a little milk if it seems too thick.

FOR THE BATTER
*180 ml (3/4 cup) milk*
*2 tablespoons brandy or raki*
*2 tablespoons olive oil*
*1 egg yolk*
*210 grams (1 1/2 cup) flour*
*1 tablespoon baking powder*

FOR THE FILLING
*1/2 kg (1 lb) sweet myzithra (or ricotta)*
*2 tablespoons sugar (or more, to taste)*
*1 teaspoon cinnamon*
*480 ml (2 cups) olive oil for frying*

# Unorthodox moist walnut cake

*Asynithisti karydópitta*

150 grams (2/3 cup) butter plus 1
    tablespoon
80 grams (1 cup) dry breadcrumbs
5 cups (650 grams) chopped walnuts
    and a few walnut halves for
    decoration
1 teaspoon baking powder
1 teaspoon baking soda
1 teaspoon ground cinnamon
1 teaspoon grated nutmeg
200 grams (1 cup) sugar
4 eggs, well beaten
1 large apple, peeled and grated (save
    the peel)
60 ml (1/4 cup) sweet red wine,
    preferably Mavrodaphne
60 ml (1/4 cup) milk
2 teaspoons vanilla essence
1 tablespoon sesame seeds

SYRUP
400 grams (2 cups) sugar
360 ml (1 1/2 cups) water
6 cloves
piece of orange peel
apple peel
2 tablespoons honey

**One evening I was sitting in the Anaplous taverna in Chania before any customers had arrived. As Effie the owner was telling me a few of her tips, her mother and a friend dropped by and in no time, they were rattling off recipes so quickly I could barely scribble them down. This walnut cake was one of them. Walnut cake is a favorite winter sweet all over Greece, but this version is by far the moistest and most interesting I've come across, perhaps because it contains no flour.**

*With thanks to Irini Manolaki-Kalavretsou for sharing it.*

Preheat the oven to 200°C (400°F). Butter a round cake tin (26 cm, 10 inches in diameter) and roll the breadcrumbs around it to coat the sides and bottom.

Mix together the walnuts, the rest of the breadcrumbs, the baking powder, baking soda, cinnamon and the nutmeg. With an electric mixer beat the butter and sugar together until light and fluffy. Add the beaten eggs gradually, using a wooden spoon to stir in a little of the walnut mixture with each dose.

Stir in the rest of the walnut mixture together with the apple, and slowly add the liquids, stirring all the while. Slide the mixture into the prepared baking pan, sprinkle with the sesame seeds, and decorate with halved walnuts. Bake for 20 minutes in a hot oven, lower the temperature to 190°C (375°F) and cook for a further 20 minutes.

To make the syrup boil the ingredients except for the honey for 10 minutes, stirring until the sugar melts. Then strain the syrup and stir in the honey, returning it to the heat until it dissolves.

Pour the hot syrup over the cooled cake and serve. This cake is so moist and scrumptious it can be eaten without the syrup. Serves 10.

# Cretan pancakes
*Tiganítes*

**When my son was little, our Greek housekeeper used to make him tiganites, named for the frying pan (*tigani*) in which they are cooked. The batter was nothing more than flour and water. Little did I know then that this was a food enjoyed in Classical Athens, where vendors used to sell them on the street. Topped with thick Greek yogurt (or unCretan whipped cream), this sophisticated version could even be served at a dinner party. In years past they were a must on St. Andrew's day, when it was said that the *kallikantzari* (the Greek equivalent of hobgoblins) would steal your frying pans or poke holes in them if you didn't put them to use. Children would bang the pan like a drum the night before, pretending they were the evil spirits.**

*1 teaspoon baking soda, dissolved in 180 ml (3/4 cup) fresh orange juice*
*ground cinnamon and cloves, to taste*
*grated rind of one orange*
*35 grams (1/4 cup) chopped raisins (optional)*
*1 tablespoon olive oil plus oil for frying*
*1/2 teaspoon salt*
*250 grams (1 2/3 cups) flour, approximately*
*chopped walnuts (optional)*

In a medium-sized bowl mix the spices, orange peel, raisins, salt and olive oil with the orange juice. Gradually stir in the flour until you have a thickish batter (these are not crepes!). If the batter is too thick, add a little water. Let rest for 1 hour or more to let the flavors mingle.

Heat a few tablespoons of oil in a frying pan and drop in as many tablespoons of the batter as will fit comfortably without touching. Flip them over when you see bubbles forming on the surface. Drain the pancakes on paper towels and serve them, with a little sugar or honey, and sprinkled with chopped walnuts if desired. Makes 24 small pancakes.

# Cretan apple fritters
## *Tiganítes me míla*

250 grams (1 2/3 cups) flour
pinch of salt
1 tablespoon cornstarch
1 teaspoon  instant yeast
600 ml (2 1/2 cups) warm water
1-2 apples, peeled and thinly sliced
240 ml (1 cup) oil for frying
ground cinnamon and nutmeg for
    sprinkling

FOR THE SYRUP
200 grams (1 cup) sugar
120 ml (1/2 cup) water
1 tablespoon honey

**These wonderfully light puffy fritters are another of Irini Manolaki-Kalavretsou's inventions, ideal for nibbling by the fire on a cold, wintry day.**

First, prepare the syrup. Boil the sugar and water together for 10 minutes, being careful to stir the sugar with a wooden spoon until it melts. Stir in the honey.

Mix the flour, salt, cornstarch and instant yeast together in a large bowl and slowly add the warm water. Stir until smooth, cover with a cloth and leave to rise in a warm place for about a hour. Stir the apples into the batter.

Heat some oil in a frying pan and drop in tablespoons of the mixture, a few at a time to keep the heat constant. Brown on both sides and drain on paper towels.

To serve, sprinkle with cinnamon and nutmeg and pour a little syrup over the fritters. A squeeze of lemon juice will heighten the flavors. Makes about 12 fritters.

The batter mixture can be kept in the refrigerator for about three days.

## Cretan breakfast

There are no hard and fast rules for a Cretan breakfast. It might be as simple as a rusk dunked in a large cup of red wine (which could be rationalized if a man were going out to his fields at the crack of dawn) or a bowl of trahana boiled in water. Some villagers remember eating left-overs – anything from bean soup to vegetable stew or the inevitable greens drenched in olive oil that were and still are a daily staple in some homes. In winter tiganites – thick pancakes – doused with *petimezi* – grape juice syrup – kept you warm and fortified against the snowy mountain blasts that penetrated through your many layers of clothes right to your marrow. Nowadays, Cretans like most Greeks are not big breakfast eaters. A thimbleful of coffee, a biscuit dunked in it, might be all a person might grab on the way out to work. Given a bit more time, a mug of herbal tea, a rusk drizzled with olive oil and *petimezi*, a piece of feta or anthotyro and a few olives would keep one going for quite a while.

## Fyllo

Also known as strudel pastry, 500 gram (1 pound) packets of these paper thin sheets of dough are to be found in the freezers of many large supermarkets in European and American cities. Before you intend to use it, after defrosting it, let it come to room temperature. Cold fyllo will be too brittle to work with.

Instructions for using fyllo: 1. There are generally 12 sheets per packet. Unless otherwise specified, allocate half for the bottom of the pie and half for the top. 2. Each sheet should be brushed (a wide paint brush speeds up the process) with olive oil or melted butter, one at a time. Keep the remaining sheets covered with a damp cloth to prevent them drying out. This is true whether you're making many individual pies or one large one. 3. If the latter, score the pie surface in square or diamond shapes before baking and sprinkle the top with a little water to prevent the pastry from splitting.

In the Venetian district of Rethymno not far from the mosque/conservatory there is a hole in the wall of a "factory" which produces fyllo and *kataifi* ("shredded wheat") the old-fashioned way. Sheets of fyllo big enough to cover a double bed and thinner than the best percale are stretched by hand, as if they were being readied for the laundry line, and then placed between damp burlap mats. Most of the customers are hotels and pastry shops, but individuals are also welcome.

# Nut-filled pastry twists
## *Zournadákia or Hanoúmisses*

FOR THE FILLING
*450 grams (3 cups) chopped walnuts
or half walnuts, half almonds,
chopped, skins left on
1 teaspoon cinnamon
pinch of ground cloves
2 tablespoons sugar
grated peel of 1 lemon*

FOR THE PASTRY
*1/2 packet fyllo
220 grams (1 cup) melted butter*

FOR THE SYRUP
*400 grams (2 cups) sugar
320 ml (1 1/3 cup) water
1 cinnamon stick*

**The village of Vamos in Apokoronas between Chania and Rethymno is beginning to attract attention for its efforts to preserve and revive traditions as well as beautiful old buildings. In addition to its taverna and its grocery shop where local cuisine and local products can be sampled and taken home, Vamos SA, the group of ten young Cretans bent on using the past to give their village a future, also sponsors cooking demonstrations. The mother of one of them, Maria Fragiadaki, is so famous for her version of these crinkly oriental pastries that she is a frequent performer. She wields a long thin rolling pin, thinner even than the one many country women still use when they make their own fyllo, and winds up a whole sheet of fyllo as if it were a large and supple kerchief, defying it to disobey her wishes. She then cuts it into four pieces. Other cooks have found it easier to divide each fyllo sheet into four from the start, and that's the method I've suggested here, especially since few western households are equipped with a meter-long rolling pin.**

First, make the syrup. Boil the sugar and water together with the cinnamon stick for about 10 minutes. Stir the sugar constantly with a wooden spoon until it melts. Remove the cinnamon stick before serving.

Mix the filling ingredients together.

Lay each sheet of fyllo on a flat surface, paint it with the melted butter and then cut it in four squares. Leaving a margin of 1 cm/1/3 inch around it, put a tablespoon of filling at the edge of the square, place a thin stick such as the handle of a wooden spoon, or a pencil, on the fyllo and roll the fyllo around it. Then push the ends of the roll towards the middle until it is all crumpled – as if you were threading a rod through a curtain – and pull out the stick. Do the same with each sheet of fyllo until the filling is used up.

Preheat the oven to 190°C (375°F). Lay the pastries in rows on a buttered baking sheet and bake until crisp (about 25 minutes). When they've cooled down, douse them with the syrup. Makes about 48 sweets.

# Pumpkin baklava

*Baklavá apó glykiá kolokýtha*

(CHANIA/ASIA MINOR)

The Cretans eat a lot of pumpkin during the winter and have learned to do a lot of simple but very tasty things with it. Most Greek pumpkins will not make great jack o' lanterns; more often than not they are pale brown and come in diverse shapes, like grandiose gourds. Their flesh is paler, too, and takes longer to cook than the standard American variety. In Greece you can have the greengrocer cut off as little or as much as you like.

This recipe's roots are in Asia Minor, but its name is misleading because each sheet of fyllo is wrapped around a bit of filling rather than layered in a baking pan. However you want to call it, this inspired pumpkin classic will have your guests sneaking thirds.

Bring the pumpkin to a boil with 120 ml (1/2 cup) of water and a pinch of salt. Simmer until the pumpkin cubes become mushy. Drain them overnight in a colander.

The next day, heat 60 ml (1/4 cup) of oil in a saucepan and add the pumpkin, stirring from time to time with a wooden spoon until you have a purée. Let cool. Add the crushed walnuts, semolina, sugar and spices and mix everything together thoroughly.

One by one lay the sheets of fyllo on your work space, paint the surface with olive oil and spread a little of the mixture on the long side of each sheet, leaving 5 cm (a couple of inches) as margin on either side. Roll up each sheet as you would a strudel and cut the pastry into lengths of about 9 cm (3 inches) (about 4 pieces from each cylinder). Repeat with the rest of the filling and fyllo, laying them side by side on an oiled baking sheet. Preheat the oven to 200°C (400°F).

When you have finished making the pastries, heat the remaining olive oil to boiling and drizzle a teaspoonful of the hot oil over each of the rolls. Bake for 30 minutes. While they are baking, make the syrup. Bring the sugar, water and honey to the boil in a small saucepan, lower the heat to moderate and boil slowly for about 5 minutes. Add the lemon juice a minute or two before the end.

Let cool and then pour the syrup over the pies while they are still hot. Makes about 30 pieces.

500 grams (1 lb) cleaned pumpkin, cut into large cubes
salt
120 ml (1/2 cup) olive oil, plus oil for brushing the fyllo
75 grams (1/2 cup) walnuts, chopped
70 grams (1/2 cup) fine semolina
150 grams (3/4 cup) sugar
1 teaspoon powdered cinnamon
1 teaspoon ground cloves
1/2 packet fyllo

FOR THE SYRUP
200 grams (1 cup) sugar
240 ml (1 cup) water
1 tablespoon honey
1 tablespoon lemon juice

# Fyllo-encased cheese pie

## *Bouréki me myzíthra*

(HERAKLIO)

THE FILLING

450 grams (1 lb) myzithra, ricotta or
    fresh farmer's cheese
140 grams (3/4 cup) sugar
1 teaspoon cinnamon
1 tablespoon honey
3 eggs, at room temperature

THE CRUST

1 packet fyllo
220 grams ( 1 cup) melted butter

THE SYRUP

240 grams (1 1/4 cups) sugar
200 grams (1 cup) honey
240 ml (1 cup) water
lemon peel
1 cinnamon stick
1 tablespoon fresh orange juice
2 tablespoons fresh lemon juice

**Just another example of the linguistic confusion in Crete. This is a sweet cheese pie traditionally eaten on the last Sunday before Lent, which is called Cheese Sunday (*tis Tyrinis*). It bears no resemblance at all to the Boureki of Chania, the zucchini and potato casserole described on pages 148-149 (though they both contain fresh myzithra cheese), nor to the eggplant croquettes also known as *bourekakia* in other parts of Greece. Because this is the last time fasting Cretans will eat cheese and eggs until Easter, they go a bit overboard. I have halved this recipe, which originally called for 7 eggs and a kilo of cheese.**

**In this pie, the cold aromatic syrup is a superb complement to the hot flaky crust and soft filling. A sauce made with fresh-picked blackberries also won raves from the "testing committee" on the night I served it, though of course that could not be said to be traditionally Cretan.**

**In Italy, particularly Puglia, where wonderful, flavorful sheep's-milk ricotta is so prevalent, pies like these, with or without a crust (but not with fyllo), are also common.**

Make the syrup. Bring the sugar, honey and water to a boil in a medium saucepan and boil gently until sugar dissolves. Add the cinnamon stick, lemon peel and juices and simmer for about 10 minutes, stirring constantly with a wooden spoon. (The longer it boils, the thicker it will become.) Set aside.

Using an electric mixer cream the cheese until there are no more lumps and add the sugar, a little at a time, with the cinnamon and the honey. Add the eggs one by one and continue beating until the mixture is as smooth as a custard.

Preheat the oven to 180°C (350°F). Line the bottom of a 22 x 30 cm (9 x 13 inch) baking pan with 6 buttered fyllo sheets (3 cut in half). Spread the filling evenly on top of the fyllo and then add 4 more buttered fyllo sheets (2 in half). Lightly cut through the top 2 sheets with a sharp knife into serving portions and bake for about 20 minutes or until the crust is a burnished gold.

Serve the hot pie with cold syrup or a sauce made of fresh or frozen berries, a little sugar and 60 ml (1/4 cup) of water. Serves 8.

# Evangelia's custard pie
## *Bougátsa*

**Evangelia Dokoumetzidi's recipe for custard pie can be made as one large dessert or as individual pies. Bougatsa is such an enduring favorite that Iordanis in Chania has thrived for 60 years making nothing else but these exquisitely flaky, barely sweet pastries, which they serve dusted with granulated sugar on wax paper. With its golden crust and creamy interior, this pie makes quite an impression at a dinner party. The custard will be even creamier if you use half evaporated, half fresh whole milk.**

*140 grams (1 cup) fine semolina*
*200 grams (1 cup) rice flour*
*100 grams (1/2 cup) sugar*
*3 eggs*
*1200 ml (5 cups) milk*
*6-8 sheets fyllo pastry*
*110 grams (1/2 cup) melted butter*
   *for painting the pastry*

Mix together the ingredients, except for the fyllo, and simmer in a nonstick pan, stirring continuously with a wooden spoon, until it starts to bubble. Set aside.

Preheat the oven to 190°C (375°F). Keep the fyllo sheets under a damp kitchen towel as you work. Paint each sheet with melted butter and line a buttered baking tin or large rectangular pyrex dish (22 x 30 cm or 9 x 13 inches) with 4-5 sheets of buttered fyllo. Spread the custard over the topmost sheet and cover with another 3 buttered sheets. Brush the final sheet with melted butter, score the surface with portion-sized squares or diamonds and sprinkle generously with confectioners' sugar and cinnamon. Bake for 20 minutes or until the crust is golden. Serves 8.

To make into individual pies, cut each sheet of fyllo in 3 strips lengthwise, butter each one with melted butter. Put a heaping tablespoonful of cooled custard at the bottom of the strip and fold over, first to the right then to the left so that you have a triangular pie at the end. Place on a buttered baking sheet and bake for about 15 minutes. Makes 18-24 little pies.

# Almond/jam tarts

*Formákia*

*2 eggs*

*1 full tablespoon cornstarch*

*1 tablespoon softened butter*

*100 grams (1/2 cup) sugar or less, to taste*

*120 grams (3/4 cup) almonds, blanched and finely chopped (in the food processor) plus several left whole for decoration*

*1 teaspoon vanilla extract*

*1 packet fyllo*

*220 grams (1 cup) melted butter for painting fyllo*

*1/2 jar of your favorite jam, apricot, strawberry, cherry, raspberry*

**Mundanely called formakia after the muffin or cupcake tins they are baked in, these delectable concoctions are terribly rich and terribly good. The crunchiness of the fyllo contrasts blissfully with the creaminess of the crushed almonds and the piquancy of the jam. This may be the ultimate jam tart.**

*From the notebook of Evangelia Dokoumetzidi.*

To make the almond cream beat the eggs with the cornstarch, butter and sugar until light and fluffy. Stir in the almonds and vanilla.

Preheat the oven to 200°C (400°F). Butter 14 muffin tins. One by one paint each fyllo sheet with melted butter and fold it over and over lengthwise and crosswise until it is 10 or 12 layers thick. Place it in a muffin tin, pressing the bottom and sides slightly so that the fyllo adjusts to the shape. Repeat the procedure, lining each tin with a folded, buttered fyllo sheet. Trim the edges, for appearance's sake. Put 1 tablespoon of jam on top of the fyllo and top that with some of the almond cream. The tins should be no more than 3/4 full. Put a whole almond on top of the cream for decoration if you like. Bake for 20 minutes. Serve hot or warm and eat while fresh.

# CRETAN FRUIT

Tropical enough for oranges, lemons and grapefruit to thrive, yet cool enough to bear crunchy apples, Crete is blessed with a range of microclimates worthy of a continent. Most of the citrus groves are concentrated along the northwest coast, just behind the ever-expanding strip of featureless hotels, bars and pizza parlors catering to tourists. Not even a mile from the beaches, the vegetation turns almost jungle-thick, with barely a roof to be seen through glossy leaves and globed fruit. The smells of the blossoms in spring are almost hallucinatory they are so intense.

Aubyn Trevor-Battye, who camped in Crete in 1913, was overcome by the oranges from the groves west of Chania. "Fournes [is] a very pleasant place with orange orchards near it, the oranges lying in great golden heaps waiting for panniered donkeys to carry them away. A kind, nice-mannered woman brought me an apronful and insisted on my acceptance … wonderful oranges they were, too." As for Chania's lemons, in 1566 alone the Turks imported 450,000 liters of their juice to Constantinople, indicating a remarkable thirst combined with a passion for lemon-based sauces.

But the Lassithi plateau in the eastern half of the island is another story. T.A.B. Spratt compared it to the Happy Valley of Samuel Johnson's hero Rasselas, "with a climate more Swiss than Mediterranean… the fruits of Europe, combined with the vine alone, flourish in this happy valley; for neither the olive nor the carob-tree can flourish in it, although indigenous and most productive in all the lower parts of these mountains." In spring, Lassithi too is awash with blossoms; in autumn, the orchard floors are dappled with fallen fruit. One October I saw red rivulets of fiery apples and autumn-blooming poppies streaming into pools beneath the trees. A couple was vainly attempting to sell baskets of apples and pears by the side of the road, but why buy when you can just scoop up what you need from a myriad windfalls? In the villages, garlands of tomatoes and apples hung from window ledges and beams to dry, but no one could give me a recipe for apple pie, baked apples or even apple sauce. There is however an apple spoon sweet, made with *firikia*, a small, sweet variety, and flavored with cinnamon, cloves and lemon juice.

# Cherry pudding

*Poutínga me kerásia*

This recipe comes from an old notebook found in Chania. The baking powder called for was so novel it is referred to as "angliki skoni" or English dust. Though this clafoutis-like pudding could never be considered traditionally Cretan, for the locals cook fruit rarely except to make the preserves known as spoon sweets, I have included it as an indication of how foreign influences creep into the kitchen. The original calling for 400 grams (two whole cups) of sugar, I have altered for modern tastes.

If using fresh cherries, mix them with 2-3 tablespoons of sugar and set them out in the sun, on a sunny windowsill or even in a low oven for a few hours. This will bring out their juices.

Preheat the oven to 190°C (375°F). In a blender jar or large bowl blend or beat the butter, sugar, milk, baking powder and flour into a smooth batter and pour it in a well buttered baking dish (26 cm or 10.5 inches in diameter). Place the cherries and their liquid on top of the batter and bake for about 45 minutes. Serves 6-8.

*1 large can (450 grams or 16 oz) pitted sour cherries and their juice, or*
*2 cups fresh pitted black cherries (about 500 grams or 1 lb)*
*2-3 tablespoons plus 50 grams (1/4 cup) sugar*
*2 tablespoons melted butter*
*360 ml (1 1/2 cup) milk*
*1 teaspoon baking powder*
*140 grams (1 cup) flour*

# Mary's tangerine layer cake

*Toúrta mandaríni*

Crete provides lemons, oranges and tangerines to much of Europe. They are incomparably colorful and juicy. I copied this recipe from a turn of the century notebook. Its owner lived in Neapolis, a small inland town closer to Agios Nikolaos than Heraklio, which before World War II was one of the island's intellectual centers. Her teacher parents used to hold musical soirées in their neoclassical house – there are not many left standing today – for which her aunt would produce an array of "imported" desserts, such as this extravaganza of a cake, which has a custardy filling and a meringue frosting. Before saying goodnight, the guests might go out onto the balcony and look at the stars, for Mary's mother was a passionate amateur astronomer.

To avoid confusion, squeeze your tangerines into two separate containers for the various stages of this recipe.

*With thanks to Mary Panethymetaki for sharing this recipe.*

PAIN D'ESPAGNE
(SPONGE CAKE)

*140 grams (1 cup) flour*
*1 teaspoon baking powder*
*5 eggs, separated*
*200 grams (1 cup) sugar*
*180 ml (2/3 cup) tangerine juice*

FOR THE FILLING

*4 tablespoons cornstarch*
*360 ml (1 1/2 cups) tangerine juice*
*200 grams (1 cup) sugar +*
*6 tablespoons*
*1 tablespoon butter*
*Finely chopped peel of 4 tangerines*
*3 egg yolks, whites saved for the frosting*
*A few shavings of bitter chocolate (optional)*

Sift together the flour and baking powder. Beat the egg yolks in a separate bowl until light. Gradually add the cup of sugar, beating until the mixture becomes thick and creamy. With a wooden spoon stir in 120 ml (1/2 cup) of the tangerine juice alternately with the flour until you have a batter. In a third bowl beat the egg whites until they form peaks and fold them into the batter.

Preheat the oven to 180°C (350°F). Butter a 24 cm (9.5 inch) springform cake pan, pour in the batter and bake for about 50 minutes.

Let cool and set it in the freezer for 30 minutes so that you'll be able to slice it into three equal layers. Sprinkle each layer with the rest of the tangerine juice.

Mix the cornstarch with 120 ml (1/2 cup) of warm water.

Pour the tangerine juice and 240 ml (1 cup) of water into a saucepan and bring to the boil. Remove from the heat and stir in the cornstarch. It will thicken at once. Return the pan to the stove, stir in the sugar, butter and tangerine peel and simmer, stirring constantly, until the sugar dissolves. Remove from the heat, let cool for about 10 minutes. Stir in the egg yolks, one at a time, simmer very gently for two minutes. If you're worried about possible scrambling, set the pan in a double boiler or larger pan of hot water and cook, stirring, for another 5 minutes.

Cool the filling by placing the saucepan in a basin of cold water and let it cool completely. Spread the cream on each layer of the cake, including the top.

FOR THE FROSTING

Chill the egg whites and beat them together with 6 tablespoons of sugar until they form peaks. Spread the meringue on top of the cake and brown quickly under the grill. Sprinkle with grated chocolate, if desired, and serve.

# Danae's tangerine "truffles"

*Troúfes me mandarínia tis Danáes*

**These little balls are not too sweet and are wonderfully elegant and original. Danae Malinaki served them at her daughter's wedding reception in the courtyard of a deserted monastery on Akrotiri. They freeze beautifully so Danae made them in the winter when tangerines are in season to accompany the raki traditionally offered to guests at the start of the party. I wouldn't be surprised if they become established as a Chania tradition.**

*Peel from 30 unblemished tangerines*
*450 grams (1lb) sugar*
*450 grams (1 lb) almonds, blanched and ground in food processor*

Boil the tangerine peels in lots of water to get rid of their bitterness until they are soft. Drain. Leave them to dry overnight wrapped in a big dish towel.

The next day crumble the peel between your fingers until you have a "purée" of tangerine peel. Put the peel and the sugar in a saucepan and boil, stirring with a wooden spoon, until the sugar turns to syrup. Be careful not to let it burn. Remove the pan from the burner and stir in the ground almonds and mix thoroughly. When cool, pinch off bits of the mixture and roll it into little balls and arrange them on a pretty platter. If you are not going to use them within the next day or two, lay them between sheets of wax paper and store them in the freezer. Makes about 60 pieces.

# Mary's prunes with yogurt

*Yaoúrti me damáskina*

**Mary Panethymetaki has elevated lowly ingredients into a quick and easy dessert you can even serve at a dinner party.**

*1/2 kg (1 lb) prunes*
*120 ml (1/2 cup) brandy (optional)*
*2 tablespoons sugar or to taste*
*750 grams (1 1/2 lb) strained yogurt*
*as many walnut halves as you have prunes, plus a few chopped for garnish*

Soak the prunes in the brandy for an hour or more, depending on how alcoholic you wish them to be. Mix the sugar and yogurt together. Split open the prunes, remove the pits and stuff each prune with a walnut half. Close the prunes and stir them into the yogurt. Refrigerate until ready to serve and sprinkle the top with chopped walnuts. Serves 6-8.

# Chestnut and chocolate truffles

*Troúfes me kástana kai sokoláta*

500 grams (1 lb) chestnuts
125 grams (4 oz) bitter chocolate,
    broken into pieces
250 grams (1/2 lb) unsalted butter
125 grams (1 1/4 cup) confectioners'
    sugar
125 grams (3/4 cup) walnuts
2 tablespoons brandy or other
    preferred liqueur
chocolate sprinkles

**This is a modern recipe. Although chestnuts grow prolifically in Crete's White Mountains, the sugar, butter and chocolate would have been hard to come by in the old days. These truffles are an original treat for the holiday season, satisfying both chocoholics and those who are passionate about chestnuts.**

Slice a cross in the flat side of each chestnut, the longer the slices the easier it will be to peel. Cook them in boiling water for 20 to 40 minutes until tender. While they are still warm, peel off both the hard shell and the reddish-brown skin. Purée the chestnuts with a ricer or food processor and place them in a large bowl.

Melt the chocolate and butter together with 4 tablespoons of water over a low flame. Add this mixture and the sugar to the chestnuts and stir until well blended.

Grind the walnuts until only small bits remain. Fold them and the brandy into the chestnut mixture.

Set aside to cool. Form into small balls and roll them in a dish of chocolate sprinkles. Makes 60 truffles.

# Quince paste and jam

*Kydonópasto kai marmeláda*

(ALL CRETE)

**The Greek word for quince, *kydoni*, could not be more closely associated with Crete. Kydonia was the Minoan and ancient settlement at what is now Chania, and the pre-Greek Kydonians who lived there considered themselves the descendants of Kydon, one of the sons of Apollo. The pale yellow fruit is too puckery to be eaten raw but cooked it produces a wonderful deep red jelly the color of a magical sunset and a jam that seems to have been invented as the perfect topping for thick Greek yogurt. With this recipe, you can use**

**the pulp left from the jelly/paste to make the jam. As with the procedure for home-made tomato paste, an unwanted pillowcase or large dishtowel will come in handy if cheesecloth is unavailable.**

*With thanks to Irini Lyritsaki for sharing these recipes.*

Wash and quarter the quinces but do not peel them. Remove the cores and seeds and tie them in a little muslin or cheesecloth. Slice the quinces fairly thinly and place them with the cores and seeds in a large stewpot. Pour in enough water so that it is level with the top layer of fruit. Bring to a boil and cook over moderate heat until the fruit is soft.

Mash it into a purée with a fork or potato masher and put the contents into an old, clean pillowcase or make a bag out of a large piece of cheesecloth, doubled. Tie the top with a piece of string, place it in a bowl or basin and give it several good squeezes, kneading the fruit to make a paste. Hang the bag over the bowl and leave overnight. If you want a clear jelly knead only slightly.

The next day measure the juice and pour it into a nonstick saucepan. For every 240 ml (cup) of juice you will need 200 grams (1 cup) of sugar (or up to 1/3 less if that seems too sweet for you). Bring the juice to a boil and boil vigorously to reduce. The paste is ready when it detaches from the sides of the pan when you stir it with a wooden spoon. Just before you remove it from the heat, stir in the lemon juice.

Pour into a baking tin so that it is about 3 cm (1 inch) thick and leave to set. When the paste has cooled, cut it into bite-sized pieces and store them between layers of greaseproof paper in a tin. Many people like to put 2 or 3 rose geranium leaves in the mixture at the end and others either top them with a blanched almond or boil a handful of slivered blanched almonds with the juice.

To make **quince jam** with the pulp, weigh it and turn it out of the pillowcase/bag into a saucepan along with 2 apples (peeled, cored and grated). For every pound/gram of pulp you will need the equivalent amount of sugar. Bring to the boil and proceed as for quince paste, but don't overboil this time. To judge whether it is ready, submit it to your favorite jam test: put a bit on a plate, run your finger through the middle, and if the two sides do not rejoin, it will set. Or dip a tablespoon into the juice. If the last drop fails to fall, it's ready. Pour into warm jars that you have washed, sterilized in the oven or in a pot of boiling water for 20 minutes, and left to dry. Cover with melted paraffin wax if you want to give it to friends or a little brandy to keep from spoiling in the refrigerator.

*2 kg (4 lbs) ripe, deep yellow quinces*
*sugar*
*juice of 1 lemon*

# Orangeade from bitter oranges
## *Nerantzáda*

*Peel of 4 or 5 Seville oranges*
*400 grams (2 cups) sugar*
*960 ml (4 cups) bitter orange juice*
*960 ml (4 cups) tangerine juice*

**This is a recipe left over from Ottoman days, conjuring up images of genteel ladies sipping refreshments in their jasmine-scented courtyards on a sultry August afternoon. In those fridge-less times, the ice would have been brought down from the White Mountains on donkeyback. One English traveller in 1913 described watching an old man carve out two pillars of ice with his adze. He put each one into a long sack, which he hung on either side of his donkey. On the steeper sections of the path down to Chania, he braked the donkey's descent by holding onto its tail and dug in the heels of his high leather boots. He got 10 pence for his labors.**

Soak the orange peel in 960 ml (4 cups) of water overnight.

The next day combine the sugar, peel and water in a saucepan and boil gently together to make a syrup. Let cool.

Have ready the bitter orange and tangerine juice. Mix them with the syrup and store the liquid in the refrigerator in 1 or 2 water jugs or other suitable container. On hot days pour a tablespoon or two of the syrup into glasses, top up with cold water and ice and you have an excellent, refreshing alternative to soda or iced tea.

# Lemonade
## *Lemonáda*

**This recipe for lemonade is based on the same principle as the bitter orangeade. Both were given to me by Danae Malinaki.**

*800-1000 grams (4-5 cups) sugar*
*1200 ml (5 cups) lemon juice*

Dissolve the sugar in 240 ml (1 cup) of water slowly over a low heat. Let cool. Stir in the lemon juice. Store it in sterilized bottles in the fridge.

Like the English lemon squash, 1 or 2 tablespoons of this topped up with with ice water will make a glass of lemonade. This essence keeps well and comes in very handy in places where lemons cannot be found in summer. Believe it or not, this happens even in some parts of Greece where there is a surfeit of lemons for most of the year.

# Viktoria's herb tea

*Tsái apó vótana tis Viktorías*

**Viktoria Athanasiadou-Tzanidaki has a radio program devoted to Cretan traditions, especially those connected with food. One June I visited her in Chania, where she lives with her brother, the *despoti*s or bishop, in a magnificent neoclassical mansion surrounded by a garden filled with apricot, fig and lemon trees, and unbelievably fragrant frangipani bushes. To greet me she had prepared a wonderful herbal infusion, a mixture of camomile, mountain tea and dittany, which simmered for some time before she added a sprig of verbena. She sweetened it with one spoonful of honey and another of homemade apricot jam. Some herbal teas can taste medicinal, not this one.**

**Then she sat me down in the official dining room at one end of a table spread with white linen where 20 dignitaries would have had ample elbow room. And plied me with sweet breads, garden fruit (strawberries, apricots, baby plums), store-bought cherries, dunking biscuits, dried almonds and country rusks. We talked about her childhood in Spili, a village famous for its lion-head fountains in the hills above Rethymno, where breakfast consisted of left-overs from the night before – boiled greens, bean or lentil soup and sometimes wheat crushed with the handmill with milk poured over it. "We ate till we burst."**

**Though Viktoria believes in tradition – she has never eaten a commercially prepared pastry, for example – she lives quite differently from her mother. "When she got hold of sugar, such a luxury in those days, she'd be wildly extravagant, whereas I sweeten things with honey, which is more natural. We used to preserve pork in its own fat and my mother would sometimes fry the greens in it. I'm sure she wouldn't do that today. In fact, I often simply boil our food, fish soup, let's say, and add the olive oil afterwards. That's healthier." Her 19 year old daughter who has just walked in nods gloomily, "But not as good," she adds.**

Bitter orange trees (Seville oranges to some, *nerantziés* in Greece) line city streets all over the country and Crete is no exception. In early spring the aroma from the blossoms is dizzyingly intense, blocking out all other odors. While marmalade is not a part of the Cretan larder, bitter oranges both green and ripe are used to make spoon sweets, and some cooks put the juice in taramosalata, mayonnaise and chick pea soup instead of lemon juice. Sometimes, too, bitter orange slices are substituted for lemons in fish dishes.

### Kóllyva

This dish cannot properly be considered a dessert for it is usually eaten at the various memorial services held at intervals after a funeral as well as on All Souls Day (November 1). A mixture of hulled wheat (*sitari*), almonds, walnuts, raisins, sesame and pomegranate seeds, sweetened with sugar or honey and cinnamon, its origins are so ancient that it predates Christianity and Islam but has somehow been incorporated into both their rituals. Nicholas Stavroulakis compares it to *assuré*, given to the poor on Asure Gunu, the day commemorating the death of Mohammed's grandsons Hassan and Hussein, and tells us that the Jews of Greece also prepared it for the festival of Tu B' Shevat which marks the beginning of spring. The name kollyva, which is the same in Italian (*coliba*), derives from the coin – *kollyvos* – that was offered along with the fruits and grains to the gods of the underworld when a person died. It also seems to be connected with the idea of offering the first fruits on a tray to the Mother Goddess. The pomegranate seeds are an immediate evocation of Persephone, the daughter of the goddess of the harvest (the Great Mother), who had to remain in the underworld six months of every year because of the six pomegranate seeds she sneaked while Hades' prisoner.

Yiannis Savvakis, a Cretan agronomist with a deep interest in folklore and its origins told me that in his father's day, it was still the custom to hold large feasts called *trapezia* (laden tables) at funerals. They would make pilaf with the broth from boiling a whole ox and serve kollyva, sprinkled with mint and basil, as a sweet, which his father used to devour with gusto.

# ACKNOWLEDGMENTS

How do I begin to thank everyone who played a part in the creation of this book, whether by providing recipes, introductions, literary criticism or help with the testing?

I'll start at the beginning with friends and acquaintances in Athens who pointed me in the right direction by steering me towards some of the most wonderful home cooks and tavernas in Crete: Anne Kokkotou, Susie and Zikos Tassios, Thalia Tsinglaki, Arianna Kyriakou, Carol P. Christ, and Cheli Duran in London. Lila Tsantila did me the great favor of giving me a copy of her mother Evangelia Dokoumetzidi's notebook, and clarifying some of the recipes.

On the island the network expanded as the people they had sent me to sped me on to others. In Heraklio, of the greatest help were Marita Grammatikaki and her mother Kostanza Gavrilaki, the agronomist-Minoan historian Yiannis Savvakis, Despina Rasidaki and her godmother Eftyhia Mavrokosta, Maria Melambianaki, Chrysanna Karelli, Akrivi Mouzouraki, Nada Petrandi, Maro Manolidou, Mary Panethymetaki; Nikos Markakis and Christina Moudataki in Skoteino; and Irini Lyritsaki in Archanes.

In Eastern Crete, Elianna Kokkotou hosted me at Elounda Mare and introduced me to Ypapanti Velivasaki, Maria Pangalou and Georgia Vasilaki, and I also got a tremendous welcome in Zakros from Mary Daskalaki, her son Nikos, and her sister Alexandra Nerolidou. Despina Makrynaki in Myrsini, Maria Petraki in Mochlos, Christine and Vasilis Karyiotakis in Tzermiado, Lassithi, Jane and Yiannis Kafetzakis in Siteia gave me time and insights, recipes and food for thought. Panayiotis Delvenakiotis showed me how a contemporary chef deals with traditional tastes at the Istron Bay Hotel.

Rethymno was a revelation thanks to Dimitris Kalaitzidakis, a Grecotel manager renowned for his love of good food and culinary matters. He sent me to Agapi Hourdaki at Petres, Efthalia and Titos Makridis at Armeni, and Kalliopi Kechayiadaki at Potami, and to many fascinating food artisans in his home town. In Margarites, both Maria Tsiragopoulou and Anna Papadaki gave me wonderful recipes. Grecotel chef Stamatis Moros added imaginative tips to old favorites.

In Chania my list of extraordinary benefactors is even longer with special thanks to Dorothy Andrews who put me up in her Venetian apartment and introduced me to Evrydiki Katsouloudaki. Babis Mastoridis spoiled me at his Nychterida and Anemos restaurants, Effie Manoulaki did the same at Anaplous, Litsa Anagnostaki of Rififi was generous with wonderful recipes, and Petros Apostolakis of the Topanas Cafe provided proverbs and lore. Nikos Stavroulakis, Katerina Farandaki, Antonia Miloyiannaki, Ritsa Hatzidaki, Haris Bounatos, Nikos Payiavlas, Sifis Karkanis, Manousos Daskalogiannis and his mother Marika Daskalogianni, Viktoria Athanasiadou-Tzanidaki, and in Vamos Maria Fragiadaki also filled me with stories and recipes. I am particularly grateful to Danae Malinaki who was unstinting with her hospitality and knowledge.

But I would never have progressed as well as I did in Crete without the assistance and encouragement of two remarkable people, my niece Annoula Louis and my friend and colleague Rianne Buis.

Halfway through my research I was lucky enough to be invited to the symposium commemorating the 50th anniversary of the "discovery" of the Cretan Diet, organized by the Oldways Preservation & Exchange Trust. I cannot thank Dun Gifford and Sara Baer-Sinnott enough for giving me this more scientific view of Cretan traditions and the chance to compare the Cretan with the Ligurian and Puglian versions of the Mediterranean Diet.

Back in Athens, other friends helped with suggestions regarding the manuscript, including the Theseion Writers Circle, Frosso Vassiliades, Ann Thomas, Pat Hamilton, Doolie Sloman, Vicky Smyrli, my son Petros Ladas and Aliki Chapple, while still others helped with the recipes, particularly my dear friends June Marinos, Jane Harborne, Gillian Kyriakou, Pat Boxer and Anne Apgar.

Thanks are also due to the Gennadios and British School of Archaeology libraries where I pored over books written by early travellers to Crete.

And finally all my love and gratitude go to my husband, Harilaos Louis, for doing without my presence in the kitchen (and elsewhere) on my several extended visits to Crete and for being my faithful guinea pig while I tried out dozens of Cretan recipes over the past year.

# BIBLIOGRAPHY

AIKATERINIDIS, GEORGIOS N., *Kriti, Istoria kai Politismos* [Crete, History and Culture] (Syndesmos Topikon Enoseon Dimon kai Kinotiton Kritis, Crete, 1988).

ALLBAUGH, LELAND, *Crete, A Case Study of an Undeveloped Area* (Princeton University Press, Princeton, 1953).

*Anexerevniti Kriti* [Unexplored Crete] (Road Editions, Athens, 1996).

BAUMANN, HELLMUT, *Greek Wild Flowers* (The Herbert Press, London, 1993).

BICKFORD-SMITH, R.A.H., *Cretan Sketches* (Bentley, London, 1898).

BOWMAN, JOHN, *Crete* (Jonathan Cape, London, 1981).

BUONDELMONTI, CRISTOFORO, *Enas Gyros tis Kritis sta 1415* [A Voyage around Crete in 1415] (translated from medieval Latin by Martha Aposkiti) (Society for Cultural Development, Heraklio, 1983).

CLARKE, OZ, *Wine Atlas* (Little, Brown & Co., Boston, New York, Toronto, London, 1995).

DALBY, ANDREW, *Siren Feasts* (Routledge, London, 1996).

DALBY, ANDREW & SALLY GRAINGER, *The Classical Cookbook* (British Museum Press, London, 1996).

DAPPER, G.O., *Description des Isles de l'Archipel*, vol. 1 (Gallet, Amsterdam, 1703).

DAWKINS, R.M., "Folk memory in Crete," *Folklore* (London, March 31, 1930).

DER HAROUTUNIAN, ARTO, *A Turkish Cookbook* (Ebury Press, London, 1987).

DILLON, EMILE-JOSEPH, "Crete and the Cretans," *Fortnightly Review* (London, 1897).

EDWARDES, CHARLES, "Crete and the Sphakiots," *Fortnightly Review* (London, 1890).

EDWARDES, CHARLES, *Letters from Crete* (Richard Bentley & Son, London, 1887).

HERZFELD, MICHAEL, *A Place in History* (Princeton University Press, Princeton, 1991).

HOMER, *The Odyssey*, trans. Robert Fitzgerald (Granada, London, 1971).

JENKINS, NANCY HARMON, *Flavors of Puglia* (Broadway Books, New York, 1997).

KAZANTZAKIS, NIKOS, *Report to Greco* (Simon & Schuster, New York, 1965).

KOCHILAS, DIANE, *The Food and Wine of Greece* (St. Martin's Press, New York, 1990).

KOCHILAS, DIANE, *The Greek Vegetarian* (St. Martin's Press, New York, 1996).

KONTOVOUNISSIOS, FATHER NIKOLAOS, "Olive oil, the link between God and man," *The Official Olive Press*, Athens, 14 Feb. 1997.

KOURAKOU, STAVROULA, "Flavors of Minoans and Mycenaeans," *Kathimerini* (English edition), Dec. 8, 1999.

KREMEZI, AGLAIA, *The Foods of Greece* (Steward, Tabori & Chang, New York, 1993).

LAMBERT-GOCS, MILES, *The Wines of Greece* (Faber & Faber, New York & Boston, 1990).

LAMBRAKI, MIRSINI, *Ta Horta* [Greens] (Trohalia, Athens, 1997).

LAMBRAKI, MIRSINI, *Bakaliaros* [Cod] (Trohalia, Athens, 1997).

LAMBRAKI, MIRSINI, *Ladi* [Olive Oil] (Ellinika Grammata, Athens, 1999).

LEAR, EDWARD, *The Cretan Journal (1864)*, ed. Rowena Fowler (Denise Harvey & Co., Athens-Dedham, 1984).

LEMONICK, MICHAEL D., "Eat your heart out," *TIME*, July 19, 1999.

LITHGOW, WILLIAM, *The Totall Discourse of the Rare Adventures and Painfull Peregrinations of long Nineteene Yeares Travayles from Scotland to the most famous Kingdomes in Europe, Asia and Africa* (James MacLehose & Sons, Glasgow, 1906 [first printed in 1652]).

LOUIS, DIANA FARR & JUNE MARINOS, *Prospero's Kitchen* (M. Evans & Co., New York, 1995).

MAKRIS, LINDA, "Eating, drinking and shirt-tearing signal a real wedding on Crete," *Kathimerini* (English edition), Oct. 1, 1999.

MAMALAKIS, ILIAS, *Elliniko Tyri* [Greek Cheese] (Trohalia, Athens, 1999).

MANESSI, NICO, *The Greek Wine Guide* (Olive Press, Corfu, 1996).

*Mi Xenate tin Paradosi stin Kouzina sas* [Don't Forget Tradition in your Kitchen] (Heraklio Department of Agriculture, Heraklio, 1995).

JOHN MURRAY, *Murray's Handbook for Travellers in Greece* (London, 1872).

MCCONNELL, CAROL & MALCOLM, *The Mediterranean Diet* (Norton, New York & London, 1987).

PASHLEY, ROBERT, *Travels in Crete* (London, 1837). Facsimile reprint Athens 1989.

PERROT, GEORGES, *L'île de Crète* (Hachette, Paris, 1867).

POCOCKE, RICHARD, *A Description of the East and some other Countries*, vol II, part 1 (W. Bowyer, London, 1745).

PSILAKIS, NIKOS & MARIA, *Kritiki Paradosiaki Kouzina* [Traditional Cretan Cooking] 6th ed. (Karmanor, Heraklio, 1998).

PSILAKIS, NIKOS & MARIA - ILIAS KASTANAS, *O politismos tis elias, to elaiolado* [The culture of the olive, the olive tree] (Karmanor, Heraklio, 1999).

RACKHAM, OLIVER & JENNIFER MOODY, *The Making of the Cretan Landscape* (Manchester University Press, London, 1996).

SKINNER, J.E. HILARY, *Roughing it in Crete in 1867* (Richard Bentley, London, 1868).

T.A.B. SPRATT, *Travels and Researches in Crete* (Van Voorst, London, 1865).

STAVROULAKIS, NICHOLAS, *Cookbook of the Jews of Greece* (Lycabettus Press, Athens, 1986).

STAVROULAKIS, NICHOLAS, "Crete" in *Greece* (Berlitz Publishing Co. Inc., New York, 1992).

*To Rethemniotiko paradosiako psomi* [Traditional Bread of Rethymno] (The Rethymnon Museum of History and Folk Tradition, Rethymno, 1983).

TOURNEFORT, M., *A Voyage into the Levant* (London, 1718).

TOUSSAINT-SAMAT, MAGUELONNE, *History of Food* (Blackwell, Cambridge, Mass., 1996).

TREVOR-BATTYE, AUBYN, *Camping in Crete* (Witherby & Co., London, 1913).

USHER, ROD, "The fat of the land," *TIME*, Jan. 8, 2001.

WALKER, MRS., *Eastern Life and Scenery* (Chapman & Hall, London, 1886).

WOLFERT, PAULA, *Mediterranean Grains and Greens* (Kyle Cathie Ltd., London, 1999).

# GUIDE TO GREEK GREENS

The following is a list of some of the greens (*horta*) commonly available at a Greek farmer's market during the season (November-April) plus a few found in summer. I have attempted to give Latin names as well, but in some cases this has been impossible, and even botanical dictionaries are not always consistent. Nevertheless, this should help you identify some greens.

*taraxakos*
dandelion (sharp)
*taraxacum hellenicum or dens-lionis*

*radikia glyka, stamnagathi*
sweet wild chicory
*cichorium*

*radikia pikra*
bitter wild chicory
*cichorium indibus*

*italiko radiki*
Italian chicory (with a red vein, bitter), cultivated

*zohi, tsohi*
sow thistle (sweet)
*sonchus oleraceus*

*anginaraki*
a kind of chicory (pungent, iodine-flavored)

*agriomaroulo*
lit. wild romaine
*in the taraxacum family*

*paparouna, koutsounada*
poppy (sweet)
*papaver rhoeas*

*tsouknidia*
nettles (mellow, sweet)
*urtica*

*kafkalithres*
burr parsley or hartwort (sweet)
*tordylium*

*antidia*
curly endive (cultivated)

*lagopsomo*
"rabbit bread"
*picridium*

*vrouva*
mustard greens (sweet)
*sinapis alba*

*mavri vrouva*
mustard greens (sharp)
*brassica nigra*

*roka*
arugula, rocket (sharp)

*lapatho*
sorrel, dock (sour)
*rumex*

*myroni*
wild chervil (sweet)
*scandix*

*kardamo*
cardamom (pungent, sharp)

*volvi, skordoulaki*
tassle hyacinth bulbs (pungent)
*muscari commosum*

*maratho*
wild fennel
*foeniculum vulgare*

*avronies*
ivy-like, looks like wild asparagus (bitter)
*bryonia dioka*

*molocha*
mallow (sweet)
*lavatera*

*sparangia*
wild asparagus (slightly bitter)

*skolymos*
oyster plant (sweet)
*scolymus hispanicus*

**SUMMER**

*glistrida, andrakla*
purslane (cool, mild)
*portulaca oleracea*

*strychnos, styfnos*
solanum (bitter)
*solanum nigrum*

*kritamon*
samphire (usually pickled)
*crithmum maritimum*

*vlita*
amaranth (sweet)

# GLOSSARY

| Greek | US | UK |
|---|---|---|
| *bámyes* | okra | ladies fingers |
| *melitzána* | eggplant | aubergine |
| *kolokithákia* | zucchini | courgette |
| *revíthia* | garbanzos | chick peas |
| *koukiá* | fava beans | broad beans |
| *fáva* | split yellow peas | |
| *róka* | arugula | rocket |
| *derbiyé* | flour-water-lemon juice binder | |
| *kremmydákia* | scallions | spring onions |
| *séskoulo* | Swiss chard | spinach beet |
| *óspria* | legumes | pulses |
| *ambelófylla* | grape leaves/vine leaves | |
| *máratho* | wild fennel | |
| *trahaná* | cracked wheat pasta | |
| *paximádia* | rusks | |
| *cornflour* | cornstarch | cornflour |
| *loukoúmia* | Turkish delight | |

**Note on flour**

None of the recipes in this book call for self-raising flour. If you do use it, in pie dough especially, I cannot guarantee you'll be pleased with the results. Unless otherwise noted, these recipes are based on all purpose flour. Even if bread (hard or strong) or cake (soft) flour is suggested, all purpose (plain) flour will be adequate. When flour is sifted, 1 cup is equal to approximately 100 grams, as opposed to unsifted which is about 140 grams per cup.

# CONVERSION TABLES

## DRY MEASUREMENTS

### BUT

1 cup unsifted flour = 140 grams
1 cup rice or sugar = 200 grams
1 cup butter = 220 grams (8 oz)
1 cup crumbled cheese = 120 grams
1 cup chopped nuts = 150 grams

### APPROXIMATE EQUIVALENTS BY VOLUME

| | |
|---|---|
| 60 ml | 1/4 cup |
| 80 ml | 1/3 cup |
| 120 ml | 1/2 cup |
| 160 ml | 2/3 cup |
| 240 ml | 1 cup |

| METRIC | US | UK |
|---|---|---|
| 5 grams | 1 teaspoon | |
| 15 grams | 1 tablespoon | |
| 28 grams | 2 tablespoons | 1 ounce |
| 55 grams | 1/4 cup | 2 ounces |
| 100 grams | | 3.5 ounces |
| 112 grams | 1/2 cup | 4 ounces |
| 140 grams | | 5 ounces |
| 228 grams | 1 cup | 8 ounces |
| 280 grams | | 10 ounces |
| 425 grams | | 15 ounces |
| 454 grams | 2 cups | 16 ounces (1 lb) |

## OVEN TEMPERATURES

| HEAT LEVEL | DEGREES CENTIGRADE | DEGREES FARENHEIT | UK GAS MARK |
|---|---|---|---|
| Very cool | 120° | 250° | ½ |
| Cool | 135° | 275° | 1 |
| | 150° | 300° | 2 |
| Warm | 165° | 325° | 3 |
| Moderate | 180° | 350° | 4 |
| Moderately Hot | 190° | 375° | 5 |
| Fairly Hot | 200° | 400° | 6 |
| Hot | 220° | 425° | 7 |
| Very Hot | 230° | 450° | 8 |
| Very Hot | 245° | 475° | 9 |

# INDEX

THE BOOK

# FEASTING & FASTING
# IN CRETE

DELICIOUS MEDITERRANEAN RECIPES

*BY*

DIANA FARR LOUIS

WAS PRINTED IN MAY 2001, IN 2.000
COPIES FOR "KEDROS PUBLICATIONS",
3, G. GENNADIOU STR., ATHENS, TEL.
(01) 38.02.007. COLOR SEPARATIONS -
PRINTING: "PROVOLI PUBLICITY S.A.",
46, TATOIOU & PARNITHOS STR.,
METAMORPHOSI, ATTIKI, TEL. 28.51.432.

DESIGN & ARTISTIC DIRECTION BY
POPPY ALEXIOU